MO FARAH
Twin Ambitions

MO FARAH

Twin Ambitions

My Autobiography

with T. J. Andrews

HODDER

First published in Great Britain in 2013 by Hodder & Stoughton
An Hachette UK company

First published in paperback in 2014

1

A CIP catalogue record for this title is available from the British Library

ISBN 978 1 444 77958 5

Typeset by Palimpsest Book Production Ltd, Falkirk, Stirlingshire

Printed and bound by CPI Group (UK) Ltd, Croydon, CR0 4YY

Hodder & Stoughton policy is to use papers that are natural, renewable and
recyclable products and made from wood grown in sustainable forests.
The logging and manufacturing processes are expected to conform to the
environmental regulations of the country of origin.

Hodder & Stoughton Ltd
338 Euston Road
London NW1 3BH

www.hodder.co.uk

For Rhianna, Aisha and Amani

CONTENTS

ACKNOWLEDGEMENTS

THERE are so many people I wish to thank. My beautiful daughters, Rhianna, Aisha and Amani, and my wife Tania: you mean the world to me. I am forever grateful for the love of my family: my twin brother, Hassan, my mum Aisha and my dad Muktar, my brothers Ahmed, Wahib and Mahad, my aunt Kinsi and my cousin Mahad.

I'd also like to thank Alan Watkinson, my old PE teacher at school and the guy who made it all happen for me. My thanks to my coaches down the years: Alex McGee, Conrad Milton, Alan Storey and Alberto Salazar. Success is never down to any one person. Every coach I've worked with has played their part in everything I've achieved. Without them, I might not have gone as far as I have done.

Thanks must go to my support team: my agent Ricky Simms and Marion Steininger at PACE; Neil Black, my physio; and Barry Fudge, my doctor, for all their support and helping me along the way. My in-laws, Bob and Nadia, who helped out with the girls when my career kept me away from my family.

Thanks also to my publisher, Roddy Bloomfield, editor Kate Miles and the rest of the team at Hodder & Stoughton for helping me to put my story on the page.

Finally, my thanks to Allah, for putting me on this Earth, and for giving me the talent to run.

PHOTOGRAPHIC ACKNOWLEDGEMENTS

The author and publisher would like to thank the following for permission to reproduce photographs:

Sean Dempsey/Press Association, Adrian Dennis/AFP/Getty Images, L'Equipe/Offside, Tony Feder/AP/Press Association, Julian Finney/ Getty Images, Stu Forster/Getty Images, Albert Gea/Reuters/Action Images, Getty Images, Owen Humphreys/Press Association, Scott Hurd, Jacob Keuhn/Reuters/Action Images, Dan Kitwood/Getty Images, Kirby Lee/US Presswire/Action Images, Stuart MacFarlane/ Arsenal FC/Getty Images, Tony Marshall/Empics/Press Association, Clive Mason/Getty Images, Keith Mayhew/People Press, Steve Mitchell/Empics/Press Association, Oliver Morin/AFP/Getty Images, Chuck Myers/MCT/Getty Images, Phil Noble/Reuters/Action Images, Raymond O'Donoghue, PACE Sports Management, Doug Pensinger/Getty Images, Stephen Pond/Empics/Press Association, David Pryce/Arsenal FC/Getty Images, Max Rossi/Reuters/Action Images, Don Ryan/AP/Press Association, Mark Shearman/Athletics Images, Matt Sprake/Mirrorpix, Simon Stacpoole/Offside, Miguel Vidal/Reuters/Action Images, Ian Walton/Getty Images, Alan Watkinson, Lewis Whyld/Press Association.

Other photographs are from private collections.

Every reasonable effort has been made to trace the copyright holders, but if there are any errors or omissions, Hodder & Stoughton will be pleased to insert the appropriate acknowledgement in any subsequent printings or editions.

PROLOGUE
THE LOUDEST NOISE
IN THE WORLD

11 August 2012. 7.41 p.m. Olympic Stadium, London.

THREE laps to go in the final of the 5000 metres, on a warm summer's evening in Stratford, east London, and I am 180 seconds from history.

I've been here before. Seven days ago, in fact, on Super Saturday, when first Jessica Ennis, then Greg Rutherford and then me won three Olympic gold medals in less than an hour, adding to the two golds won earlier in the day by the rowing team at Eton Dorney and the women's pursuit team at the velodrome. The feeling is different now. Going into the 10,000 metres final I had so much pressure on me it felt like I was lugging around two big bags of sugar over my shoulders. People were desperate for me to win that race. When I crossed that white line as the winner, this immediate sense of relief washed over me. Now the pressure is off. I'm running free. I have one gold medal in the bag. Whatever happens out here tonight, I'm an Olympic champion. No one can take that away from me.

Don't get me wrong. I still want to win – more than

anything. But this time I'm able to go out there and race and actually enjoy it: the competition, the stadium, the occasion. And the crowd. The pulsating, deafening roar of the British fans.

I'm in second place. Ahead of me is Dejen Gebremeskel, the Ethiopian runner. At the start of the race I'd figured he was one of my main threats going onto the home straight. But Gebremeskel has kicked on early, moving out to the front and pushing the pace. Big surprise. But for me, that's perfect. He's gone early for a good reason: he thinks that I must still be feeling the effects of the 10,000 metres in my legs. Figures I must be tired. That if he pushes the pace quite early on, he can wear me out on the last couple of laps, taking me out of the equation when it comes down to the sprint finish. If I was in Gebremeskel's shoes, I'd be thinking the same thing. I've done more running than anyone else in the field, with the exception of the Ugandan, Moses Kipsiro, and my training partner, Galen Rupp. But Gebremeskel hasn't taken into account my secret weapon: the crowd.

Everyone is roaring me on. The noise is unbelievable. Like nothing I've ever heard before. The crowd is giving me a massive boost. I think about how many people are crammed inside the stadium – how many millions more are watching on TV at home, cheering me on. Willing me to win. None of the other guys out there on the track are getting this kind of support. Everyone is rooting for me. The noise gets louder and louder. The crowd is lifting me. Pushing me on through the pain, towards the finish line.

Every athlete has five gears. That night, in the cauldron of the Olympic Stadium, I like to think the crowd gave me a sixth gear. They played a huge part in what I went on to achieve.

With two laps to go, I pull clear of Gebremeskel. The crowd goes ballistic. I'm getting closer, closer, closer to the line. The crowd is getting louder, louder, louder. Then I hit the bell. I'm still in the lead. One of the other guys tries to surge ahead of me. I hold him off. As I go round the track on that last lap, the entire crowd rises to its feet, section by section. It's almost like a Mexican wave is chasing me around the stadium. I will never feel something like that again in my entire life. I can't describe how loud it is. Without a doubt, it's the loudest noise I have ever heard in my life. The crowd physically lifts me towards the finish. I remember Cathy Freeman describing the atmosphere at the 400 metres final in Sydney in 2000, the euphoria of the crowd almost carrying her across the line. As I head down that home straight in the lead, I start to understand what she meant.

Two hundred metres to go now. I'm still out in front. Somehow the crowd is growing even louder. Gebremeskel tries it on going into the home straight but I hold him off and cross the finish line in first place.

For a few moments I can't believe what has happened. 'Oh my God,' I think. 'Oh my God, I've done it.' I keep repeating it to myself, over and over: 'I've done it. I've won.' All around me the crowd is going wild. Suddenly it hits me: I am a double Olympic champion. I have gone where no British distance runner has gone before.

I sink to my knees. The roar of the crowd booming in my ears. Getting here has taken a lot of hard work and sacrifices. I've had to come a long, long way and go through so many highs and lows. Looking back, it's been an amazing journey.

1
TWIN BEGINNINGS

PEOPLE often ask me what it's like to have a twin brother. I tell them: there's this special connection that the two of you have. Like an intuition. You instinctively feel what the other person is going through – even if you live thousands of miles apart, like Hassan and me. It's hard to explain to someone who doesn't have a twin, but whenever Hassan is upset, or not feeling well, I'll somehow sense it. The same is true for Hassan when it comes to sensing how I feel. He'll just know when something isn't right with me. Then he'll pick up the phone and call me, ask how I am. Or I'll call him. From the moment we were born, on 23 March 1983, we were best friends.

We come from solid farming stock. My family has always been based in the north of the country, going back generations. My great-greatgrandparents on my dad's side were farmers in a remote village called Gogesa, in the Woqooyi Galbeed region of northwest Somalia, not far from the border with Ethiopia. It's a rural area with fertile land, so farming is the main occupation for the local people, and if you drive through Gogesa, you'll see farms and open countryside full of grazing animals. My great-greatgrandparents owned cows and sheep and camels and farmed the land. After they died, my great-grandfather, Farah, inherited the farm. He was well known locally because part of the farmland he owned contained a natural spring that pumped fresh water to the surface. Water was scarce in the region at the time, and soon many locals were collecting water from the spring. My great-grandfather was the guy with the water.

His daughter, Amina, my *ayeeyo* (grandma) on my dad's side of the family, spent time in Djibouti as a young woman. Djibouti is a tiny country that shares borders with Eritrea, Ethiopia and Somalia. To the north you've got the Red Sea, and on the other side of the water is the Arabian peninsula, with Yemen, Oman and Saudi Arabia. A number of people from places like Gogesa made the same journey across the border as Grandma Amina. As a former French colony, Djibouti offered better prospects than an agricultural village. There were more jobs in Djibouti City, better education, and a higher standard of living. Even as a kid, I remember having this idea of Djibouti as a place where people wore nice clothes and earned good salaries. For much of the year, my grandma lived and worked in Djibouti City. When Djibouti got too hot in the summer, Grandma would travel back to Gogesa for the holidays. The details are a bit sketchy – this is all such a long time ago – but I believe that when my great-grandfather died, the farm was sold up and my grandma moved permanently to Djibouti. They pretty much settled there. Grandma was still living in Djibouti with my grandad, Jama, by the time I was born.

My parents met while my dad was on a trip back to Somalia from the UK, where he was studying and working.

They later settled down to married life and shortly after, me and Hassan were born. Hassan came out first. Twenty-nine years later, my wife Tania also gave birth to twin girls. Hassan even married a twin. You could say that twins are in our blood. My brother was named Hassan Muktar Jama Farah. I took on the name Mohamed Muktar Jama Farah.

I should explain something about our names. Everyone in Somalia belongs to a clan. Our clan was the Isaaq, the biggest clan in the north of the country. Your family name and your clan are linked together as a way of identifying not only who you are, but where you come from and what clan you belong to. Take my name. Mohamed is my given name. After your first name comes your father's first name (Muktar). Third is your grandfather's first name (Jama). The fourth part of your name is your great-grandfather's name (Farah). If someone stopped me in the street and asked, 'What's your name?' I would tell them, 'Mohamed Muktar Jama Farah, nice to meet you.' And then they would say, 'Ah, I used to know your grandad, Jama! I remember your dad, Muktar, as a little boy!' Usually it was the oldest guy in the village asking the questions. They could trace my ancestry that far back, they'd know what clan I belonged to and the names of distant relatives.

It's been written that I was born and raised in Somalia. Strictly speaking, this isn't true. While I was born in Mogadishu, the capital in the south of the country, I spent the early part of my childhood growing up in Somaliland, the area to the north of the country and although it's not recognized by the UN, to all intents and purposes, Somaliland is an independent country and claims ownership of land roughly the size of England. Somaliland has its own currency – the Somaliland shilling – its own police force, and its own capital, Hargeisa. It even has its own flag (horizontal green, white and red stripes with Arabic script across the top bar). It also has its own national anthem, 'Samo ku waar', which translates as 'Long life with peace'.

Historically, people from Somaliland and those from the south of the country have struggled to get along. The tensions were inflamed by Siad Barre, the former military dictator who ruled Somalia. When he was deposed in 1991, the government in Somaliland declared independence, although it escaped much of the violence and chaos that engulfed the south of the country in the years that followed. I remember my childhood as a mostly happy time. For the first four years of my life we lived in Gebilay, a small town about an hour's drive west from Hargeisa and forty minutes from the border with Ethiopia. The land in that region is mostly desert scrub, though there are some hilly green areas and the occasional forest. In the distance you can see vast mountain ranges lined up along the horizon. The scenery is beautiful. The people are warm and welcoming.

Two years after I was born, my mum gave birth to another baby boy, Wahib. A fourth son, Ahmed, followed when I'd reached the grand old age of four and Wahib was two. Looking after four children was a full-time job for my mum, but she was only doing what Somali culture expected of her. Somalis are a strong, resilient people, and very conservative. The culture is big on tradition. The values haven't changed much in hundreds of years. The men work, the women cook and clean. I'm not saying this is the way things should be. It's just that people in Somaliland grow up in a conservative environment and this is all they know.

People have described my childhood as poverty-stricken and surrounded by bullets and bombs. That's not really true. In the memories I have of Gebilay, there were no soldiers in the streets, no bombs going off. Whatever violence was going on at the time, as children we weren't exposed to it. Most of the problems were taking place far to the south. Around the time I was living in Gebilay, the government in Mogadishu was about to collapse. But we lived far from trouble. Although as it turned out, we had a lucky escape.

One day my mum sat Hassan and me down and told us both that the five of us, including Wahib and Ahmed, would shortly be leaving Gebilay to go and live with our grandma, Amina, and our grandad, Jama, in Djibouti. Our dad wouldn't be following us, however. He had to return to England – for his studies and his work, I believe. I accepted this decision without protest. Of course, every young kid wants their dad around. But I had seen very little of him while growing up in Gebilay. He always seemed to be away working and we didn't have a chance to build that bond. Besides, Hassan, my best friend as well as my twin, would be coming with me. That reassured me. Plus, I couldn't wait to see Grandma and Grandad. Living with them would be fun, I thought. I was sad about having to leave Gebilay. But mostly I was just excited about spending time with my grandparents, exploring a new country and getting up to no good with Hassan.

I wasn't aware of it at the time, but a year after we moved out of Gebilay, Somali forces under Siad Barre bombed Hargeisa and Berbera. The cities were flattened. Water wells were blown up. Grazing grounds were burned. Tens of thousands of people died in the bombings. Many more fled to Kenya and Ethiopia. It hadn't been the reason for our move, but we had a lucky escape all the same. If we hadn't moved out of Gebilay, we might have been caught up in the violence that followed. If you visit Hargeisa today, there's a war memorial in the middle of the city: a Russian fighter jet, like the ones that bombed Somaliland.

Grandma Amina and Grandad Jama had already been living in Djibouti for a number of years when we moved in with them. My grandparents had done okay for themselves in Djibouti City. My grandfather had a decent job working in a local bank. They had a good standard of living compared to Gebilay. Grandma looked after the family at home. Life wasn't a walk in the park, but it wasn't the struggle that some people have tried to make out. I guess by Western standards my grandparents might have appeared poor, but to us kids, we looked at Djibouti as a big step up from life in rural Somaliland.

Almost everyone in Djibouti lives in the capital. As soon as you get there, you can see why. It's this huge, frenetic place, with traffic and noise everywhere. Men pushing wagons through the streets selling fresh loaves of bread and honking their bicycle horns. There are goats and camels everywhere. In the distance you can hear the *athan*, the call to prayer sung by the muezzin: 'Allah Akbar! God is great!'

Our grandparents lived in a stone house on the outskirts. Each part of the city is named using a number scale: Quarante-Deux-Trois (40–2–3), Quarante-Deux-Quatre (40–2–4), and so on – a legacy of French colonialism, which continued until 1977. When I was a kid, our house seemed huge. I remember arriving at the house and thinking that Grandma and Grandad lived in a mansion. When I returned to Djibouti many years later, I revisited my old home. I couldn't believe it when I found the right address. I was like, 'Seriously, we lived here?!?' The house seemed so much smaller than I'd remembered it.

In Djibouti we had access to all kinds of things that we didn't have in Gebilay. There was a local cinema, basically a dark room with a TV at one end wired up to an old-school VHS recorder. Whenever Hassan and me had a few coins, we'd be straight off to the 'cinema' with our friends to watch a movie. Sometimes the cinema owner would show one of those old black-and-white Westerns with cowboys and Indians. Other times it was a Disney cartoon or a Hollywood action movie – whatever they happened to have on tape at the time. We didn't care. Most of the time we didn't under-stand what was being said by the actors anyway (there was no dubbing, and we couldn't read or write in English). We just liked watching the films, seeing all these exotic locations, people doing crazy things. Sometimes I'd get bored and make animal noises over the film. We were just kids having fun.

Dad occasionally visited, flying back to Djibouti from London for a week here or a few days there. I was probably too young to appreciate the difficulties of travelling back to Djibouti from London at the same time as working and studying, not to mention the cost. Looking back, I can understand the reasons why my dad wasn't able to visit more often. But that didn't make it any easier to accept as a young boy. We never had that normal father-son relationship. For me, there was my grandma and my mum, and my brothers, and that was it.

A few people in our neighbourhood had TVs, and we watched programmes whenever we could. My favourite was *Esteban, le Fils du Soleil*, which translates as 'Esteban, Son of the Sun'. It was a French cartoon series from the early 1980s about a Spanish kid called Esteban who goes on this great adventure to the Americas to find a lost city of gold. (In English it's known as *The Mysterious Cities of Gold*.) His friends accompany him on his epic quest, including an Incan girl called Zia, and Tao, the last survivor of an ancient civilization. But although Esteban is on the hunt for the cities of gold, that isn't his real mission. Actually, he's searching for his dad. Esteban also wears this cool medallion around his neck that allows him to control the sun. As a kid, I thought this show was the best thing ever on TV. Every day at 6.30 p.m. on the dot, I'd find a TV to watch it. I never missed an episode. I was totally addicted.

But following the adventures of Esteban and his crew was a bit of a challenge for a kid living in Djibouti. The city suffered almost daily power cuts, and more than once I'd sit down to watch the latest episode and then – phhtt! – the power would cut out. The TV screen went blank. No way was that going to stop me. I simply had to know what happened next, so I'd sprint out of the house, racing across the streets and running towards the lights of a friend's house several streets away, where I knew the power would still be working. In a matter of minutes I'd get to my friend's house, catch my breath and tune in to *Esteban*. A few minutes later, same thing. Power cut. I'd dart off again in search of the next house where I could watch the programme. Sometimes I'd have to rush between three or four houses across the city just to catch a single episode of *Esteban*. But it was worth it. I was totally mad about that cartoon show.

Looking back on it, I guess it was pretty good training for a career in distance running.

2
THE MECHANIC

I GOT my first experience of school in Djibouti when I was five. There was no formal primary school system as such. Kids like Hassan and me were required to attend the local madrasah each morning from eight o'clock through to midday. The madrasah was basically a long, narrow room built next to the local mosque, with rickety chairs for the kids and a massive blackboard at the front of the classroom. Our teacher was an old man with a shaven head and a stern look in his eyes. If he spotted you misbehaving in class, he'd march you to the front of the classroom and start whipping you on the backside with a cane in front of the other kids. Sounds pretty shocking now, but this was the norm in Djibouti. The cane had the desired effect. None of us dared step out of line.

Our studies at the madrasah focused on the Koran, but we also studied French and local history. Some mornings at the madrasah we'd take turns to read out passages in front of the class. This was hard for me because I couldn't read or write and I suffer from dyslexia. When it came to my turn, I'd spend the evening before class learning the passage until I had it committed to memory. The next morning I'd head to the madrasah with Hassan and 'read' in front of the teacher and kids, with my eyes glued to the page to

15

make it look as if I was reading rather than reciting. Most of the time I got away with it.

Part of my problem was that I never had anyone sit me down and help me with my studies. Half an hour, forty-five minutes a day outside of school, with one of my relatives patiently teaching me how to read and write – I never had any of that. It's not the Somali way. I was just expected to go to school and get on with it.

Typically, Somali mums and dads want their children to become doctors or lawyers when they grow up. They want their kids to have the kind of opportunities they didn't have themselves, to have the things they didn't have, to be able to afford a good house and provide for a family. From my perspective I can't understand that way of thinking, given that, in that environment, it's very, very hard to obtain the qualifications necessary to become a professional. It seems naïve to expect children to do well whilst at the same time not providing them with the educational tools they need.

In those days, I wanted to be a car mechanic. I loved the idea of handling bits of machinery and fixing things up. To this day, I'm forever taking things apart and fiddling with stuff. If I see a button on a wall, I have to press it. Fire alarms, intercoms, whatever. I can't keep my hands by my sides. Being a mechanic, I thought, was a great way to put my fidgety nature to good use. And I loved cars. It was the perfect match.

There were always bits of scrap metal and rusted parts lying at the sides of the road in Djibouti. People often dumped their rubbish out on the street, so you could find all sorts of stuff piled up by the road. One day I was walking home from the madrasah with Hassan when I stumbled upon a few pieces of scrap metal that looked like the kind of things used to assemble cars: spark plugs, exhaust pipes, that sort of thing. My eyes instantly lit up. I grabbed as many of the parts as I could carry and raced home. I must have been six or seven years old at the time, and I didn't really have a clue what I was doing. I remember being really excited as I laid out all the parts on the ground in front of the house and began playing around with them whistling to myself, when suddenly this stern voice barked out behind me: 'What have you got there?'

I spun around.

Uncle Mahamoud, the strictest man in the family, towered over me. Whenever me or Hassan stepped out of line and needed to be taught a lesson, it was our uncle who sorted us out. Once I took a pee in the bowl at the back of the family refrigerator. When Uncle Mahamoud found out, he punished me. So I must have looked a sight to him, standing there with my grubby hands, my T-shirt and shorts smeared with grease and dirt from handling the car parts. Uncle Mahamoud just stood there and waited for an answer.

'I'm putting something together,' I replied.

Uncle Mahamoud peered over my shoulder and saw all the car parts spread out.

'You shouldn't pick up things from the street,' he said. 'What are you doing with all this junk, anyway?'

I grinned. 'It's not junk, Uncle! These are car parts. I'm learning what they do. I want to be a mechanic when I grow up.'

Uncle Mahamoud's face went dark. 'A mechanic?' he spluttered. 'Tell me something, then,' he demanded, rolling his eyes in the direction of the madrasah. 'Why am I paying all that money for you to go to the school and get an education if you want to waste your life fixing cars?'

That was the end of my brief experiment with building my own car. But I didn't give up on my dream of being a car mechanic – at least, not for a few more years.

Unlike me, Hassan had a natural talent for learning. He did well at the madrasah; he had a sharp mind. This is one of the few ways in which we were different. When it came to learning something new, Hassan had this ability to pick it up like *that*. My dyslexia held me back and hindered my ability to learn. I would continue to struggle with it throughout my years at school.

In the mornings we went to the madrasah. In the afternoons, we stayed at home. Djibouti has a hot, humid climate and for several months a year the temperature can hit over a hundred degrees. It was too hot to walk around the streets, let alone study. By around one or two o'clock the sun would be scalding the ground under your feet. It's impossible to do anything in that sort of heat. Everyone disappears indoors to keep cool.

That's the thing I remember most about living in Djibouti: the heat. It was relentless. On the really bad days the soles of our feet would get blistered from the baking earth. Even having a wee was hard. We'd drink loads of water, but because the heat was so dry, we'd still be badly dehydrated and unable to squeeze out so much as a drop. In the evenings the temperature would drop a bit, but it was still hot. There was no escaping it.

Hassan and me did everything together in Djibouti. We were twin brothers and best friends. We went through the same things at the same time. I was close to the rest of my family, especially Grandma and Mum. In Somali families everyone tends to sleep in the same room – it's not unusual for eight people or more to sleep in a single room. Me, Hassan, Wahib, Ahmed, our aunts and uncles and grandparents: we'd all sleep next to each other in one big room in the house. You're that close, you end up seeing your relatives more as friends. In Somali culture there's no real concept of privacy. It took a bit of getting used to when I moved to Britain, where people tend to sleep in separate rooms. I never quite got used to it. I like having people around. It reminds me of my family in Somaliland. When I went to university at St Mary's in Twickenham, I treated my bedroom as more of a place to hang out with all my friends. It wasn't a bedroom for me. Any day of the week, you'd have to step over somebody sleeping on the floor in order to get from one end of the room to the other. To me, that was normal. I like it that way.

Among all my relatives, Hassan and I were definitely the closest, although he was the real troublemaker. Whenever I did something mischievous, he'd have to do something twice as bad. There was no limit to what Hassan was prepared to do for a laugh. He was daring and totally unafraid. He was like the extra-crazy version of me as a kid. Hassan was forever pushing it just that little bit further than me. And then sometimes he'd go and totally overstep the mark.

One sweltering hot afternoon we were throwing stones across this open field not far from our house. We often had a competition to see who could throw a stone the furthest. Hassan had a pretty good throw on him, and he wound up his arm and launched this stone a huge distance, clearing the field – and smacking against the head of a middle-aged woman who happened to be walking along the road on the other side of the field. The woman let out a shriek. It wasn't a big rock, but it struck her in such a way that it opened up a cut on her head. From where we were standing I could see the blood. The woman clamped a hand to the side of her head and screamed at other passers-by to catch the person who'd thrown the rock. Hassan and me both froze on the spot.

'Shit!' Hassan cried. 'I hit her, *walaal* [brother]! This isn't good. Let's go now, before anyone catches us. Hurry!'

Before I could answer, Hassan seized me by the arm and dragged me away from the field. People shouted after us. We sprinted through the streets, running as fast as we could, but I was convinced we were going to get caught. Hassan, being the quick-thinking one, hit upon an idea and tore off his T-shirt, telling me to do the same. He was wearing a distinctive red shirt that you could spot from a mile off. 'So no one will recognize us,' Hassan explained. It seemed to do the trick. We got home without anyone stopping us; everyone was out looking for a kid in a bright red shirt. We both thought Hassan had got away with it until a neighbour recognized him from the field and told Grandma. Uncle Mahamoud dished out the punishment that day.

That stone-throwing incident was typical Hassan. He'd do crazy stuff I wouldn't even dream of doing. But we were always there for each other. Sometimes we'd get into fights with other kids in our neighbourhood. Nothing serious – just the usual scrapes that young boys get in from time to time. If someone tried it on with Hassan, I'd be right there at his side. Likewise, Hassan would stand up for me in a fight.

One of my best memories of childhood in Djibouti is the food. At dinner we'd usually eat a traditional meal of pasta (*baasto*) and chicken (*digaag*), usually with some spices mixed in for flavour. In between meals we'd snack on samosas, or have a treat such as black beans mixed with butter and sugar. For breakfast, Grandma cooked a type of thin, sweet pancake called *malawah*. Every morning I'd wake up to that smell. Grandma made the best pancakes. She liked to drench them in honey and serve them with cooked liver or heart. To this day, I'll order pancakes for breakfast if they're on the menu – although they never quite taste as good as Grandma's.

I remember hurrying home to eat dinner one evening while Hassan was still playing outside with some friends of his, kicking a ball around.

'Save me some food,' he called.

The fact that Hassan and me looked identical gave us plenty of opportunities to cause all kinds of trouble and confusion. One of our favourite games was to play tricks on people by pretending to be each other. I saw a golden opportunity to play a joke on Grandma.

'Where's your brother?' Grandma asked as I arrived home. 'Dinner's ready.'

'He's out, *Ayeeyo*,' I replied, licking my lips at the smell of the feast Grandma was serving up. 'He says he'll be in soon and to save him some.'

No sooner had we sat down than I'd finished off my plateful. I had a voracious appetite in those days. Still do. Once I was finished, I stood up, made my excuses and ducked out of the room. Hassan, meanwhile, was still busy playing outside. Making sure no one was looking, I snuck out of the back door, scurried around the side of the house and waited a couple of minutes. Then I sauntered through the front door again pretending to be Hassan. In those days we often wore each other's clothes, had the same haircuts and the same tall-but-skinny build. Even for someone who knew us as well as our grandparents, it was almost impossible to tell us apart.

'Hi, *Ayeeyo*, I'm home!' I announced. 'Where's my dinner? I'm starving!'

Thinking I was Hassan, Grandma handed me my twin brother's plate of food. I scoffed his portion down. Hassan returned home a while later, belly growling with hunger and asking Grandma for his dinner.

'Don't be so greedy,' Grandma snapped at him. 'You've already eaten!'

There is one way you can tell my brother and me apart. I have a large scar on my right arm around the elbow joint. I got it one day when I was mucking around in the kitchen during Ramadan. I must have been five or six years old at the time. Grandma was making samosas in preparation for the feast to celebrate the end of the fast. The air was filled with the smell of fried pastry and coriander. While my grandma was cooking, I started spinning around in a circle on the spot.

'Stop it, Mo!' Grandma warned. 'You're going to cause an accident!'

All of a sudden I lost my balance and stumbled backwards. There was this deafening clang as I crashed against the oven and a bunch of pots and pans went flying and clattered to the floor. Grandma shrieked. I shook my head, wondering what the fuss was about. Then I felt this searing pain on my right arm. I lifted up my arm to get a better look at it. The skin was all blistered and scalded. Suddenly I realized what had happened. My arm had slammed against the frying pan as I'd crashed into the stove, tipping the pan over and spilling the hot cooking oil down my arm. I don't remember the pain, but I do remember having to stay in the nearby hospital for three months while the doctors treated my wounds. The burn marks ran along the back of my arm past my elbow and up towards the underside of my biceps. I was told that although I'd be scarred for life, I should consider myself extremely lucky. If the cooking oil had scalded me one or two centimetres further up my arm, the nerves would have been irreparably damaged and I wouldn't have been able to move my arm properly for the rest of my life. I came within two centimetres of never being able to run at all.

Despite the occasional freak accident, Hassan and me couldn't resist joking around. It almost became a competition to see who could draw the biggest laugh. When we weren't hanging out at the local cinema, we'd be chucking stones at people's doors or throwing balls around the streets. We never deliberately set out to hurt or upset anyone – we were just regular kids. And if we ever stepped out of line, we could be sure that word would get back to our grand-parents or our mum. We lived in a close-knit neighbourhood where everyone knew each other. Being identical twins makes you instantly recognizable to passers-by. We were forever annoying the neighbours. 'I know who you are!' one of them would shout at us. 'I've seen you two around. I'm going to tell your grandparents what you've been up to, mark my words!'

'Please don't!' we'd beg. 'We won't do it again. Just please don't tell on us.'

Usually our pleading did the trick. We'd be let off with a few stern words and a warning that if we dared step out of line again, they'd be straight round to our house to tell Grandma and Grandad. We'd agree to behave, of course. Then the next day we'd be out causing yet more mayhem.

We were restless. We needed an outlet for all the energy we had. Playing football was pretty much the only thing that kept us out of trouble. When we weren't at the madrasah or escaping the heat, Hassan and me would join the other kids playing in the streets. (Wahib and Ahmed were too young to join in.) Football was my passion. I fell in love with the game as a young kid when I saw my first-ever football match on TV. It was the World Cup in Italy in 1990. Brazil were playing Argentina, wearing their famous yellow shirts. I knew next to nothing about the game or the players. But there was something about the way the Brazil players moved, playing with incredible skill despite the fact they were running at such a fast pace, the huge crowd inside the stadium, the immaculate green pitch – the sheer scale of it all. I was hooked. Hassan too. From that moment on, we both played football whenever the unforgiving Djibouti weather allowed. Street football was our thing. There were no pitches. We lived for those street games. We didn't have a proper football, so we'd make our own by gathering up a load of old socks and tying them together, just like the kids do in Brazil.

I never had much skill with the ball at my feet. My ability was in my 'engine': I was full of energy, and I'd chase that ball around all day if I had to. I had a bit of pace on the turn too. But I was football mad. I wasn't interested in anything else. We'd play for hours on end: me, Hassan and the other kids from our neighbourhood. We'd arrive home covered in cuts and bruises from diving and sliding around the streets. Grandma would inevitably get angry with us both for getting our clothes dirty.

Life wasn't easy in Djibouti, but it wasn't desperately hard either. We experienced the same ups and downs as anyone else. Perhaps we didn't have some of the things that children in other countries take for granted, but for us this was never a big deal. In some ways, it was an advantage. In Djibouti everybody had to work hard for what they had. No one got given anything on a plate, but you wouldn't find people sitting around feeling sorry for themselves. Everyone rolled up their sleeves and got on with it. We learnt to appreciate what we had. We learnt that you didn't get anywhere in life without putting in the work. In that sense, Djibouti made me tough. I saw a lot while growing up there. Had to deal with a lot too: moving from country to country, being separated from my dad, having to adapt to a different culture. My mum used to repeatedly tell me, 'In life, make sure that you adapt to whatever you do.'

I managed to adapt. Some people aren't so lucky. They grow up with too much, too soon, so when they really need to work hard towards a goal, the motivation isn't there. They can't live without certain comforts. They can't adapt. Me, I never had that problem.

Some time after our arrival in Djibouti, Grandma Amina's daughter, our aunt Nimco (pronounced 'nee-mo' – the 'c' is silent) won a scholarship to study at university in Almelo, a city in the Netherlands. She used to send Grandma letters and pictures of her new life in Europe. I couldn't believe how different everything looked – the neatly paved streets and grey skies and old church buildings. I started thinking to myself, 'Wow! There's this whole other world out there.'

After our grandfather passed away, Grandma decided that she wanted to move to the Netherlands to live with Aunt Nimco and build a new life for herself. I suppose she felt there was nothing left for her in Djibouti after Grandad died. There was Hassan and me, of course, and her other relatives, but Aunt Nimco was her daughter. I was upset. I loved my mum, but Grandma had been the one who'd looked after Hassan and me for most of the time we'd been in Djibouti. I was closer to her than anybody except Hassan.

After she left I told myself, 'I have to find a way of getting to Holland to live with *Ayeeyo*.' I just couldn't imagine a life without Grandma. My mind was made up: I wanted to move to Almelo. I would build a new life there. And Hassan would come with me.

My wish seemed to come true when Mum took me aside one evening after Grandma had moved to Almelo, looked me hard in the eye and explained that we would soon be leaving Djibouti as well. Like Grandma, we were moving to Europe to begin a new life. I wasn't upset to leave Djibouti. I was just excited. As I understood it, we'd all be going to live with Grandma in the Netherlands. Mum added that first we had to go and visit my dad in London. I thought she meant we'd be staying with our dad for just a few days. I didn't really give any thought to the implications of moving to Europe – having to learn a new language, making new friends. I was too young to understand all that. I simply wanted to be close to Grandma. Whatever it took to be by her side again, I was willing to do it. I couldn't wait.

Much has been written about the circumstances which led to me and Hassan being separated for the best part of twelve years. The truth is this: the original plan was for all of us to travel to England as a family. But shortly before we were due to fly, Hassan fell ill which meant he wasn't able to fly. We couldn't cancel or change our flights because there were five of us booked on that plane and that would have meant losing an awful lot of money. As a short-term solution it was decided that me, my mum, Ahmed and Wahib would fly to London as originally planned, with Hassan remaining with our extended family in Djibouti. The plan was always to go back and get Hassan a couple of months down the line, after the rest of us had settled down. Of course, I didn't like the idea of being separated from Hassan even for a short period of time. We'd been inseparable from the day we were born. Everything we experienced, we had experienced together. I was consoled by the fact that we wouldn't be away from each other for very long – a couple of months perhaps. Then we'd be back together. Had I known how many years would pass before I'd see him again, I would have been heartbroken. But as far as I knew, Hassan falling ill was a temporary hitch; eventually we'd all be living together as a happy family. My parents, my grandma, me, Hassan and my other brothers.

At least, that's what I thought.

Actually getting to Europe from Djibouti was quite an undertaking. We had to take a train from the city to the Ethiopian capital, Addis Ababa – a journey of 800 kilometres. We arrived at a crumbling old railway terminal which looked as if it was falling apart, and from there made our way to Bole International Airport, where we boarded an Ethiopian Airlines flight direct to Heathrow.

We almost didn't make it to London. Two hours into the flight, the warning lights flashed on, the alarm began squawking and buzzing and the plane started dropping speed all at once. I remember being stunned by the intense painful popping in my ears. Then the oxygen masks dropped down. That's when the panic really set in. Everyone on board started shouting and screaming. Some people were crying for help, others grabbing the oxygen masks and hurriedly fitting them over their faces. People were holding hands, like they believed they were going to die. One guy actually bolted out of his seat and started wrestling with the airlock on the emergency exit, shouting that he was going to jump before the plane crashed and killed us all. A bunch of people tackled him to the ground. I saw all this happening, my heart absolutely pounding with terror. Somehow I managed to put on my oxygen mask. I gripped onto my seat and the surreal thought entered my head that this was the first time I'd flown on a plane, and it might well be my last.

That moment was the most scared I have ever been. I've never known a fear like it.

Somehow the pilot managed to regain control of the plane and made an emergency landing. Amazingly, no one had been seriously injured. There was this strange silence when the plane finally touched down, the doors opened and everyone breathed a massive sigh of relief. We stepped off the plane one by one. My ears were still aching. Mum was shaking. Wahib was trembling. Ahmed screamed with the pain in his ears. Some of the passengers had to be treated for shock. An official from the airline told us that the plane's cargo door had suddenly sprung open in mid-flight, resulting in a massive drop in cabin pressure. He then explained that our flight would be delayed for at least twenty-four hours. In the meantime they offered to put us up in a hotel close to the airport. We ended up spending four days in this cramped room before the company told us our rescheduled flight was ready to board.

Five days after leaving Djibouti, we finally arrived in England. I remember my first sight of London. It was late at night when the plane began its final descent towards Heathrow. I had a window seat. As we broke through the clouds I looked out and saw this incredible sea of lights, red and yellow and blue, blinking and shimmering across the land. I'd never seen anything like it. I wondered how they could have so many lights switched on at the same time. In Djibouti the power would have cut out after about five seconds. The size of the city was unbelievable – it seemed to stretch on for ever.

I had no idea then that I was looking at the city I would soon be calling home.

3
HOLLAND, ENGLAND

THERE were a lot of things that surprised me about England – but one of the biggest shocks was finding out that Holland wasn't part of it. When we arrived in Britain, I had this idea in my head that Holland and England were part of the same country. A bit like Wales, I guess. That all I'd need to do to visit Grandma in Almelo was to hop on a train in London and buy a ticket. Before I'd left Djibouti I'd always thought of Europe as tiny. I imagined that everything must be really close together.

To begin with, we stayed with Aunt Kinsi, my dad's sister, in Hanworth. This was a tough corner of southwest London in the borough of Hounslow. We lived there for a few days while we got settled in. Aunt Kinsi had lived in Britain for a long time and knew the ins and outs of how things worked. She spent those early days showing my mum the ropes. After three or four days, we moved to a rented flat in Shepherd's Bush directly overlooking the Green. We stayed there for a week or two. I remember my dad coming to visit us after work. He'd take me, Wahib and Ahmed down to the playground on the Green, where there were swings and roundabouts and slides.

I'd never used a swing before. I'd never seen anything

remotely like it. Growing up in modest surroundings in Somaliland and Djibouti, there were no such things as playgrounds with swings and roundabouts and slides. Playing on that swing in Shepherd's Bush was a big deal for me. Dad showed me how to use it: how to thrust out my legs on the rise, then quickly bend them on the way back to build up some decent momentum. It took me a few tries to properly get the hang of it. Then I was flying! Like a lot of things in my first weeks in the UK, it was an alien experience, but also an amazing one.

Those first few days in Shepherd's Bush were a real eye-opener for me. It was like nothing I'd ever seen in Djibouti. The buildings were bigger. The cars were bigger. Everything just seemed huge. People talked in strange accents. I didn't understand a word of English and had no idea what they were saying. I tasted chocolate for the first time. A Snickers bar. I remember taking a bite and thinking that it was the most amazing taste in the world. And the toys . . . wow! Back home, I owned one toy: a push-wheel thing with a stick attached to the front and lights fitted to the wheel spokes so that whenever you pushed it, the wheel would light up and flash all kinds of bright colours. Here there were computers and gadgets and action toys and all kinds of stuff. People dressed differently from back home, too. It was rare to see women wearing short skirts and high heels in Djibouti. I'd known that things would be different in Britain. I just hadn't known how different.

I counted down the days until we'd leave for Holland to see Grandma Amina. A week or so after we had moved to the flat in Shepherd's Bush, my dad came round one evening. Instead of taking us out to play on the Green like he usually did, he sat the family down and explained to me that I'd be starting school in a few days.

'In Almelo?' I asked.

My father cleared his throat and glanced at my mum. '*Walad* – my son – you're going to go to school here. In Hounslow. You can begin there immediately.'

I was confused. '*Maan fahmin* – I don't understand. What about Grandma?'

'You can't go there now, to Almelo,' Dad said. 'It's not possible. You will stay here, with me, and go to school in London. You always wanted to go to a proper school, didn't you?'

Then it hit me: I wouldn't be living with Grandma. My parents explained that the Netherlands was this whole other country on the other side of the North Sea, and to visit there I'd need a passport, but the visas that me, Mum, Wahib and Ahmed had entered the country with didn't permit overseas travel. It sounds crazy, but this was all news to me. I have this tendency to see things in simple terms. I try not to focus on the small print. For whatever reason, I'd automatically assumed that moving to Europe meant being reunited with Grandma Amina. I would live with her, and Hassan would join us and everything would be great. Now I was starting to see that things were a little more complicated. Once I got over the disappointment that I wouldn't be seeing *Ayeeyo* for a while at least, Dad explained that there was a school not far from Aunt Kinsi's house

– Chatsworth Primary School on Heath Road. He'd already made enquiries and I could begin there immediately.

To be honest, I had mixed feelings about staying in London. On the one hand, I really wanted to go to school, mixing with all the other kids. Up to that point, I'd only studied at the madrasah in Djibouti, and for me, schools were all about making new friends. Going to a British school, that would be fun. On the other hand, I had my heart set on living with Grandma. She was a big part of my life and suddenly she wasn't there. Hassan too. I kept believing it wouldn't be long before I saw them both again. In the meantime, we moved out of the rented flat in Shepherd's Bush and into a house in Hounslow, close to Aunt Kinsi's home in Hanworth.

I joined the Year Five intake at Chatsworth. Although I was only at the school for a few months, I remember it being quite small. All the other kids had been going there for years and knew each other, and I couldn't speak any English. I struggled to make friends at the school. Mostly, I just kept to myself. In the summer I left Chatsworth, and that autumn I started at Oriel Primary School. My little brother Mahad was born the same year at West Middlesex University Hospital.

In the meantime Dad had returned to Djibouti to bring back Hassan and reunite the family. But after a fortnight he returned home empty handed. I was devastated. This also put a big strain on my parents' marriage. I was only eight years old at the time but even then I noticed my mum and dad growing apart and becoming more distant from one another. At the time I didn't know why Dad had come back without Hassan. He wouldn't say much about it. Many years later, I discovered that when Dad had arrived in Djibouti, Hassan was nowhere to be found. The extended family he'd been staying with had left the city. Dad tried his hardest to look for Hassan but just wasn't able to locate him. Two weeks passed. Still no sign of Hassan. Dad couldn't put off coming back to the UK any longer. He had a job and a family to support. So he reluctantly gave up the search and flew back to London without Hassan. As a young kid, and not understanding the situation fully, I blamed my dad for not bringing Hassan back with him. In my mind, he was responsible for why I wasn't reunited with my brother. Added to the fact that we never had a strong bond to begin with, those deep-rooted feelings grew stronger and I began to resent my dad. I missed Hassan daily.

I tried to focus on school. Oriel was a much better environment for me than Chatsworth. I was joining at the start of the year, so I'd have a better chance of making friends. And I had a cousin at Oriel – my wingman. His name was also Mahad, and he was our Aunt Kinsi's son. Mahad was my age and we enjoyed the same things, shared a lot of the same interests and spent a lot of time hanging out together.

Hanworth has a reputation for being a bit rough. Most of that reputation is because of the Young Offenders Institution in neighbouring Feltham. On a Friday or Saturday night, there's usually a fight kicking off somewhere in town, with the police getting involved. It's also fair to say that, generally speaking, there's an element of troubled youth in the area. There were a few kids at Oriel who liked to go around picking on others. Anyway, thanks to Mahad, I had memorized a few phrases in English ahead of my first day at school. Simple things, really, to help me get by: 'Excuse me', 'Where's the toilet, please?' and 'Thank you'. I also picked up another phrase: 'C'mon then!'

When the bell rang for break-time, all of us kids charged outside to the playground. A group of kids started playing football, kicking a ball around. My eyes lit up. Of course, I immediately joined in and began tearing up and down the field, chasing after the ball. Halfway through the game, this huge kid marched over and kicked our ball away. I recognized him because Mahad had pointed him out as the hardest kid in school. He was literally twice my size. I didn't like the fact that he'd interrupted our game, so I marched up to him and said, 'C'mon, then!'

The kid just stood there for a moment, looking at me funny. Then he threw a punch and clocked me clean on the face. I saw red. I hit him back. Now all the other kids in the playground gathered round in a circle, cheering and yelling as we traded punches. Even though my opponent was way bigger than me, I gave him as good as I got. Eventually, the teachers pulled us apart and dragged us both to the head teacher's office. I got a black eye and a suspension for my troubles. When I returned from my suspension, no one ever tried to intimidate me. Everyone knew about the crazy Somali kid who'd picked a fight with the hardest kid on his first day of school. That gave me a certain respect with my classmates. They knew I wasn't weak.

Mahad showed me the ropes around the school. He was good like that. We sat next to each other in class. We might have been cousins, but we'd grown up in very different worlds. Mahad had been born in Britain, he spoke fluent English and he had dreams of becoming a singer when he was older. He was more British than Somali. Having him around made it easier for me to settle at Oriel, for sure. More than anything, I just wanted to have friends.

One of my earliest memories of my days at school in England is when I invited a classmate over to my house after school. I didn't know this kid very well; I just desperately wanted to introduce my parents to my 'new white friend'. My mum liked to be told about guests coming over and didn't like strangers randomly showing up unannounced. She wasn't exactly thrilled when I showed up one day after school proudly showing off my new friend. While this other kid sat in the front room, Mum pulled me to one side.

'What do you think you're doing?' she hissed. 'You can't just bring strangers around here! Tell him to leave at once!'

'But *Hooyo* [Mum]!' I protested, 'he's my friend!'

There was still so much I had to get used to when it came to life in Britain. Like the weather, for example. I'd never seen snow before. That first winter it snowed so heavily I couldn't believe what I was seeing. The whole town was blanketed in thick white. Then there was the cold. Djibouti stayed hot all year round. In December and January the temperature might drop to around 29°C. That's about as cold as it ever got. My first winter in England, I remember my fingers and toes turning numb from the freezing cold. I wore gloves but I could never warm up my hands. I'm fine with the rain, but I can't be dealing with the cold. I'll probably never get used to it.

My time at Oriel came to an end in the summer. I'd finished Year Six and would now be going to secondary school. At home, my parents decided to separate.

My dad coming home from Djibouti without Hassan had a big influence on the breakdown of their marriage, I think. It cast a shadow over the family. Eventually, Mum and Dad decided to get divorced. As kids, we all had a choice with regards to whom we wanted to live with. My three brothers chose to move to Brighton with my dad. For me, things were different. I had already grown close to my cousin, Mahad. I still missed Hassan every day – he was a big void in my life – and in a way Mahad was the closest thing I had to Hassan. It was Hassan all over again. We did everything together and I looked up to him. I'd been so used to having a wingman to do everything with, and having grown close to Mahad, I didn't want to go through that trauma again of being separated from someone I'd bonded closely with. I wanted to stay with Aunt Kinsi so I could be close to Mahad. Out of sympathy for my situation, and knowing what I had already been through with Hassan, my parents agreed. Aunt Kinsi had been good to me. This was also good for me because my mum remained local – she lived just up the road from my auntie, which meant I was able to see her regularly. I shared a bedroom with Mahad at Aunt Kinsi's. We had a bunk bed. I got the top bunk; Mahad slept at the bottom.

Several years later – I'm not sure of the exact date – Mum flew back to Djibouti to search for Hassan. She'd missed him as much as me and was desperate to find out what had happened to her son. She flew back with a view to spending as much time as possible looking for Hassan, doing whatever it took to find him. Mum went round all the villages, asking everybody – family, friends, neighbours – if they knew Hassan's whereabouts. Finding someone isn't easy in that part of the world. You can't just pick up the phone and ring around or look someone up in the telephone directory. You have to physically travel from village to village, knocking on door after door, asking this person and that person. Mum walked miles upon miles in the sweltering heat. She had to ask scores of people before she finally got an answer and discovered what had happened to Hassan. It turned out that the extended family he'd been living with in Djibouti while he'd been ill had returned to Somaliland before my dad returned. Mum was reunited with Hassan not long after. But it would take another nine years before I saw my brother again.

In September 1994 I started secondary school at Feltham Community College. The school was based on Browells Lane, a leafy street just off the busy Uxbridge Road, and only a short walk from my aunt's place. However, I ended up starting two weeks later than the other kids. Towards the end of my time at Oriel the Year Six kids were invited to the college for an open day – a chance to have a look around the classrooms and meet the teachers in preparation for the autumn. After being dragged around the school grounds all day long, me and a few mates decided to play a game of football on the school fields. During the game I jumped for a header and landed awkwardly on my side. Instantly I felt this sharp pain ringing in my shoulder joint. I could hardly stand up. The shoulder began to swell up. I remember someone from the school calling an ambulance. I was taken to the West Middlesex A&E department, where the doctors did some scans and told me I'd broken my collarbone. They wrapped my arm in a protective sling and ordered me to rest for three weeks. I missed the start of term because of that injury.

As a young kid in Africa, fear gets beaten out of you pretty quickly. Some of the scrapes and trouble I got into at Feltham were purely down to the fact that I don't have any fear. I remember heading down to the local swimming pool with Mahad and another friend one day. I was a bit naïve at the time and I didn't realize that you actually needed lessons in order to be able to swim. So while Mahad did the sensible thing and got into the baby pool, I jumped into the deep end of the adult pool after our other friend, who was a confident swimmer – and promptly sank to the bottom like a stone. Then I started panicking. I thought I was drowning. My arms and legs were flailing as I frantically tried to reach the surface. In my sheer panic I began scratching my friend's arms and legs. Half the people in the pool emptied out.

I suppose the school might have been a little nervous about me starting there. I didn't know it at the time, but apparently there had been another Somali kid at the school a couple of years before I enrolled there. He was also called Mohamed Farah. Apparently he was a handful – even more so than me! After six weeks, this other Mohamed Farah left the school. No doubt a few of the teachers saw the name 'Farah, Mo' on the register, heard that I'd missed the start of term with a busted collarbone and probably thought, 'Oh, no – here comes another one.'

My biggest struggle in those days was with my English. I could speak a few words but I couldn't read or write, and sometimes I had to communicate with people using hand gestures because I didn't know the word for certain things. To help improve my English, the school placed me in an English as an Additional Language (EAL) group. I still struggled. In a way, I wished I'd had a year or two of just studying English. I would've been better prepared for life at Feltham then. Instead, I found myself sitting in this EAL class and finding it difficult to concentrate. There was a Ukrainian kid in the group called Sergiy. We used to fight all the time. It was like Frazier–Ali between Sergiy and me. I learnt more about fighting than I did about English in that class.

I got into a fair few fights in my early days at Feltham. It was never anything serious, just the odd scrap here and there. Because I usually have a smile on my face and try to be nice to people, my kindness often gets mistaken for weakness. I suppose I stood out at school. I was slightly different from the rest of the kids. I came from another continent, I was a Muslim, I spoke another language. Some kids probably looked at me and thought, 'Yeah, here's someone we can push around.' They didn't know me. I've never been afraid to stick up for myself. I'd had a tough childhood – tougher than a lot of kids. From a young age I had to learn to be a fighter. I never backed down from a fight.

There were isolated incidents of racism. Feltham, as a school and a general area, was predominantly white, and black kids were in a minority. I remember one time, me and Mahad were heading down to the local youth club in Hanworth. The club was 300 metres up the street from our house and backed onto Hanworth Park, where travellers would regularly camp throughout the year. We'd head down there after school to play football and muck about. On this one afternoon, a load of kids from the travellers' camp decided to make their way down to the club. Me and Mahad saw them hanging about there. Suddenly, for no reason at all, one of the traveller kids reached out and grabbed hold of me. He was much bigger than me and the other kids at the club looked on in silence.

'You wouldn't mind if I hit this one, would ya?' said the kid who'd grabbed me, nodding to the others.

No one said a word. The kid punched me in the face. His mates were there too. I tried fighting back. But there was loads of them.

'Leave him alone!' Mahad shouted. 'He hasn't done anything.'

In a flash several of the other travellers rounded on Mahad. They began laying into him too. It was two of us against about ten of the travellers. We were helpless to fight back.

We couldn't do anything. We couldn't even leg it home because we didn't want the traveller kids finding out where we lived, given that we were just up the road. To this day I'm convinced they picked on Mahad and me because of the colour of our skin. There were plenty of other white kids around the club that afternoon but the traveller kids didn't start on any of them. Mahad and me were the only ones they targeted.

I recall another incident which happened later on, when I was fifteen years of age. I was hanging around the local arcade with Mahad when another kid from school began dishing out racist remarks at me. We squared up and for a brief moment it looked as if it was going to get physical. Sensing that trouble was brewing, I pulled a pool cue from the nearby table and cracked this kid over the head with it. Me and Mahad quickly legged it out of the arcade. Sometimes I couldn't avoid getting into trouble, just because of the colour of my skin. But I wasn't afraid. I could handle myself.

In the classroom I was disruptive. My poor English meant that often I couldn't understand what the teachers were saying and I couldn't read from the textbooks. I quickly grew bored in class. To pass the time I'd make noises at the teachers when their backs were turned. I did a good lion impression. My deer noises were scarily realistic. The other kids in class would be in hysterics. Then the teacher would spin around and demand to know who was making the noises. No one could prove a thing, but I'm sure the teachers knew who was responsible.

Part of the problem for me was that I was dyslexic. But I was also restless and had a lot of energy, and I needed some kind of outlet. Put simply, I couldn't keep my hands still. I'd take apart anything that was to hand. To this day, I'm forever fiddling with things, unable to sit quietly. Tania says that she dreads it when I'm out of competition, those rare weeks when I have no training. I'm not the type who likes to sit around, and for pretty much the entire week I'll be fidgeting, searching for something to do. Often I'll try to get reactions out of people. I'll do this thing where I'll flick the tip of my wife or oldest daughter's ears, just because. Or I'll tease them. Practical jokes are a way of burning off all this energy that I've got. By the end of my break from training, I'll have gotten on Tania's nerves so much with my continual silliness that she'll be counting down the minutes until I'm due to tie up my laces and get back on the running track.

My lack of English led to more problems in the classroom. One day I received a letter from my geography teacher at the end of class. The letter was addressed to Aunt Kinsi. My teacher told me not to read the letter, but to take it home. Even if I'd wanted to, I couldn't have read it. I raced home after school, beaming from ear to ear, convinced that the teacher had given me some sort of certificate. I bolted through the front door, proudly waving my 'certificate' in front of my aunt. I handed her the letter. As she read it, her face changed. Her expression suddenly went severe.

'This isn't a certificate. This is a letter warning about your behaviour.'

It wasn't the last such letter Aunt Kinsi received. Sometimes it was my fault. Other times, my friends were just as culpable. They'd teach me swear words, pretending they meant something else, something innocuous. The next class, I'd try out my new words on the teacher. They'd look at me in horror and, as if on cue, the other kids would fall about laughing. Only then would I realize what I'd done. Result, another trip to the head teacher's office. Other times, I'd bunk off school. Things continued like this for a while. The fights, the animal noises, the detentions. Being dragged into the head teacher's office to be given yet another warning. It's fair to say I was a bit of a wild child. It's also fair to say that if I had continued on that same path right through school, I wouldn't have ended up in a good place.

A lot of the time I was frustrated because I couldn't properly express myself. I didn't have the ability or confidence when it came to speaking English. In Djibouti I'd picked up a bit of French, the national language, from lessons at the madrasah and from talking to people in the streets. English I found much more difficult to master. I think this is because I was trying to learn it at an older age. At four, learning a new language is easy. At ten or eleven, it's much trickier. Unfortunately, I couldn't get extra support from the school because technically I had a linguistic problem, not a learning one. My learning skills – my ability to understand things – were fine. I just couldn't understand the question to begin with. That's what caused me problems. In fact, the only two subjects I enjoyed at Feltham were maths and PE. And if it hadn't been for PE, then I might well have ended up being permanently excluded from Feltham.

PE class was twice a week, in the afternoons. I was forced to sit out the first few classes because of the sling I was wearing to help heal my broken collarbone. Once my injury healed, I was able to join in with the other kids. The athletics season was in full swing. The first lesson I took part in, Alan Watkinson, the PE teacher, gathered us around in two separate groups to teach us how to correctly handle and throw a javelin. As he spoke to the other group, I spotted a football goal on the field next to where we were sat with orders to be on our best behaviour, for obvious safety reasons. Great, I thought. I used to love swinging from the goalposts. Whenever I saw a football goal, I just had to swing from it. Couldn't resist it. So off I went. While Alan lectured the other group, I started swinging back and forth from this crossbar.

Suddenly Alan looked up and spotted me. A look of horror crossed his face.

Alan Watkinson was a young teacher at Feltham. He was outgoing, friendly and bursting at the seams with enthusiasm. He even had hair in those days. At the time I joined Feltham, Alan and the head of PE for the school, Graham Potter, were in the process of creating something special. The school was building a reputation as one of the best in the area for athletics and had won several borough athletic championships. A lot of that came down to the hard work put in by Alan and Graham. I was fortunate to be at a school where the PE department was continually on the lookout for young athletic talent, and where the teachers wanted to nurture that talent. For me, it was definitely a case of right time, right place.

Football was my passion. Athletics was fun, but for me, football was where it was at. My life was football, football, football. As soon as my collarbone had healed up I was back out in the fields every lunch-break, kicking a ball and running around with the other kids. I thought about nothing else. Football was more than just a sport: it was a way of making friends at school without having to deal with the whole language thing. But it also got me noticed. Alan later revealed that he used to watch me play football during lunch. According to him, even at that age, I had incredible stamina. Wherever the ball was, that's where I'd be too. I was relentless. The ball would be down one end of the pitch, one of the kids would hoof it all the way to the other end, and I'd chase it down as hard as I could. Then someone else would collect the ball and launch it back in the opposite direction. Without pausing for breath, I'd turn around and sprint back the way I'd come. I must have bombed up and down that pitch a hundred times a day.

Our school athletics season was divided into winter and summer. During the summer months and early autumn, when the weather was sunny, we did track and field sports. In the winter and spring, we switched to cross country. That first year we did a month or so of track work. Then Alan had us doing cross country races. It was on the cross country course, rather than the cinder track, where I first started to come into my own as a runner. I quickly realized that I was faster than everyone else. Not just in my class, but in the school. I won the races easily. However, being the fastest kid in school could be a problem. At the start of each race Alan would explain the route for us to follow. I remember one occasion early on at Feltham when Alan pointed out the course we'd be running.

'Right, then. To make the course longer,' Alan explained, pointing to the school field, 'you'll cut across to the middle of the field, race back around the outside, go down and round some crooked ferns, and then head out onto that path you can see in the distance. That's the course.'

All the kids nodded. I did too, although I didn't have a clue what Alan had just said. 'No problem,' I thought. 'I'll just follow the other kids.' The race began. I got off to a good start and swiftly broke away from the chasing pack. With no one to follow, I ran along what I thought was the route. A short distance further along, I glanced over my shoulder. Then I saw that every other runner had gone in completely the opposite direction.

I'd gone the wrong way.

From the corner of my eye I spotted Alan shouting at me, frantically gesturing for me to turn around and chase after the other kids. There were a few talented athletes at Feltham. One or two kids were bigger and physically more developed than me. I looked ahead, to the front of the pack. This much bigger kid was in the lead. I took a deep breath and charged back down the field, running as fast as my legs could carry me in a desperate attempt to catch up with the lead group. I managed to overtake most of the kids. But the lead runner kicked away from me as we drew near to the finish line. I wasn't slow, I never lacked for speed, but back then my leg muscles weren't strong enough to maintain my speed for a long stretch. I suffered a rare defeat. After that race, whenever I was running a course for the first time, I'd constantly look back across my shoulder to see where all the other runners were, just in case I ended up taking a wrong turn. No more playing catch-up.

Without a doubt, PE was my favourite lesson. It still lost out to football, but I enjoyed running in a competitive environment. Sport was my chance to shine. My English ability was never really an issue, even if I occasionally misunderstood some of Alan's instructions. On the track, on the grass, all that truly mattered was how I performed. This was my chance to get involved. It made me feel that I was part of school life. I won almost every event at the annual school sports day.

Alan started to see potential in me as a runner. He was convinced that I needed further training, and asked me if I'd like to go along to the local athletics club.

'Borough of Hounslow, it's a great club,' Alan said. 'They've coached guys who've run for Great Britain. Why don't you give it a try, Mo? If you don't like it, you don't have to go back. But you're too good to be coached here. There are specialist running coaches at the club. They can give you the training you need to get better.'

I shrugged. 'I don't know. I like football.'

Alan persisted. He was good at that. 'Look, Mo. You're the best runner in the school – by a country mile. There's nothing more for you to learn here. If you want to get better, you owe it to yourself to check out the local club.'

I nodded. 'Okay, I'll go.'

'Great!' Alan said. 'Next Tuesday, that's the next training session. See you then?'

Honestly, I wasn't sure about going along to the club. I didn't know what to expect. But I understood what Alan was saying. I was a decent runner. Training at an athletics club was the logical next step up from competing against the other kids at school. Looking at it from another point of view, Alan, Graham and the school stood to benefit from me training at Borough of Hounslow, since I'd be representing Feltham in the regional athletics championships, which in turn would benefit the profile of the school. I figured going along couldn't do any harm.

The following Tuesday, Alan introduced me to the world of the athletics club.

4

AN EDUCATION, PART I

Feltham Arena was pretty run-down by the time I joined Borough of Hounslow Athletics Club. The track was badly in need of repairs. There was no grandstand; spectators watched from a grassy bank running along the side of the track, and the officials sat in a glorified Portakabin. In the middle of the track was a muddied football pitch. It wasn't exactly a glamorous introduction to athletics.

At that first training session when I was eleven Alan introduced me to Alex McGee, the coach in charge of the junior runners. I had a look around the place, did a few runs around the track with Alex looking on. I exchanged a few words with some of the other runners I recognized from school, though they were not all in the same year as me. Everyone at the club seemed genuinely friendly and welcoming, but I was in two minds as to whether I wanted to go back for another session.

'How did you find it, Mo?' Alan asked as he drove me home after training.

I shrugged. 'It was okay.'

In truth, I still preferred football.

I knew I was good at running. The fact I was winning every race going at school told me that I had something in my legs, for sure. But I didn't know how good I was. In fact, I wasn't even sure I wanted to pursue running, and certainly not as a career. I was more interested in playing football. At the weekends I played Sunday League, turning out at right-back for Bedfont Town in the Surrey Counties Intermediate League against the likes of Cranleigh, Chiddingfold and Farnborough North End. I could sprint up and down that pitch all day. My thing was to reach the by-line, put in a bad cross that some creaking old centre-back would inevitably head clear. Then I'd have to thunder all the way back up the field towards my goal before the opposition could launch a counter-attack. When I wasn't playing football, I was watching it or thinking about it. Honestly, I never gave a career in athletics a moment's thought. And if it came down to a choice between playing Sunday League or competing for Borough of Hounslow, there was going to be only one winner.

The following Tuesday Alan asked me the same question: did I want to go along to the athletics club? This time I hesitated to reply. I was due to play football with some mates on the same night. Instead of telling him the truth, I made up an excuse and muttered something about my family not wanting me to train at the club. 'My aunt needs me to help out around the house, I can't get out of it,' something along those lines. I felt bad about lying to Alan, but my heart was in football.

Next week, Alan asked me the same question: 'How about a run at the club, then, Mo?' I came up with the same excuse about family pressures and went off to play football. For sure, there were times when I went along to train at Feltham

Arena, mostly when I wasn't playing football and didn't have anything better to do. But my attendance was sporadic at best. Sometimes I went, other times I didn't. Still, Alan kept on at me. Did I mention that he can be persistent? For weeks on end he tried to convince me that it was worth my time giving athletics a proper chance, that I should commit to regular sessions at the club.

Everything changed one Tuesday afternoon when I showed up at Alan's office an hour before training was due to begin at the club. On the days that I trained with Hounslow, I'd leave school at 3.30 p.m., hurry home, grab some food, change into my running gear and head back to the school grounds for around 5–5.15 p.m. and wait to get a lift from Alan to the track. Alan was busy with paperwork and I was kicking my heels sitting on the bench outside his office, looking for something to do – when Alan suddenly chucked me a football and nodded at the hall.

'I've got some more work to finish before we can leave,' he said. 'Why don't you have a kick-around in the gym until I'm done, and then I'll drive you to the club?'

Brilliant! I took the ball and raced into the gym. For the next thirty minutes I practised keep-uppys, one-twos against the wall, dribbling up and down the flanks. When the half-hour was up, Alan drove me to the club. And, hey, I did a good session on the track.

'Here's the deal,' Alan told me on the drive home. 'How about you show up early at my office before training each week at the club? While you're waiting, you can play football. You can turn up half an hour early, or even an hour if you like. I'll be doing work, so it's no problem for me. Bring Mahad along too. What d'you say, Mo?'

I nodded. It sounded like a good idea. Winter was drawing near and the weather was turning cold and wet. It was getting dark earlier and earlier, we were running out of places to play football in the evenings, and there was nowhere around where I lived. Playing in a nice, warm gym was just the ticket.

'But,' Alan warned, 'I'll only let you and your mates play on one condition: when your time is up, you'll promise to come with me to the athletics club for a running session. No ifs or buts.'

Of all the decisions I've had to make in my life, this was an easy one. I'd get to play football *and* go running at the club. It took me about a second to make up my mind.

'Deal!' I said.

Thanks to Alan, I settled into a good routine after that. Each week I'd show up at his office before training to kick a ball around the gym for half an hour or so, often with cousin Mahad and sometimes a few friends in tow. Sometimes Alan would join in too. Mahad loved football, although it's fair to say he had his limits when it came to the unforgiving English winter. Once, we were playing football during PE in the freezing cold, participating in these little three-a-side games, the idea being that we'd keep moving and keep warm. Much as Mahad loved football, he hated having to run around in the cold, so when the whistle blew, he lashed the ball into the corner of the goal with almost his first kick of the game and promptly wheeled away to celebrate, running all the way back to the changing room to escape the cold. If it had been me, I would've kept on playing. Nothing stopped me from a game of footy. But the two of us enjoyed those kick-abouts in the gym.

At 6 p.m. Alan would call time and drive me across town to Feltham Arena, where I'd join in training with the other kids at Hounslow.

Training at the club was twice weekly, on Tuesday and Thursday evenings after school. Borough of Hounslow AC had a good reputation for distance running, and by the time I joined, there was a solid core of international competitors based at the club. I was soon making friends. One of the first guys I got to know at Hounslow was Abdi Ali. He also came from Somalia. We'd hang out away from the track too. The two of us would go into town, jump on the buses and ride around Hanworth and Hounslow, not doing anything, just chilling really, the way kids do. Abdi had potential on the track, but he proved that little bit elusive. From time to time he'd suddenly stop coming to the club. No reason. He just wouldn't feel like running any more. I wouldn't see him at the track for ages, then one evening he'd appear out of the blue, grinning at me and taking the mick, like he'd never been away. He once asked Alan Watkinson, 'Why am I not as fast as Mo? We're both from the same country!'

Another early friend at Hounslow was Mohamed Osman. Mohamed was such a talented athlete it was almost ridiculous. He had enormous raw potential. Sadly, he fell in with a bad crowd and never fulfilled his early promise on the track. This is a story I've heard more than once – kids I knew growing up who got involved with the wrong type of people. At Feltham there were kids from my year who ended up in gangs, taking drugs, that sort of thing. I wasn't close to these guys personally, but living in the area, you'd hear the stories from time to time. So-and-so's in trouble. This person is in prison. I'd hear these stories and think, that could've been me slipping between the cracks. Easily. If it hadn't been for running, who knows where I would've ended up? Not somewhere good, I can tell you. Life is tough in Hounslow. Things happen.

Later on, I'd get to know the senior runners more – the guys who were running for their country, who were being talked about as future hopes on the big stage. But to begin with, I hung out with the likes of Mohamed and Abdi and the other juniors being coached by Alex McGee.

Alan Watkinson has sometimes mistakenly been referred to as my coach; that's not true. Alan has been many things to me – mentor, friend, best man at my wedding – but he would be the first to admit that he never actually coached me. My first coach was Alex McGee. He was good to me during my early years at the club – he really looked out for me. I remember meeting him for the first time. He spoke in this slight Scottish accent that I'd never heard before. 'Where is that accent from?' I asked myself.

As a junior coach, Alex took a longer-term view of training. Rather than trying to push us too hard to get the wins and recognition at national level, Alex was more interested in developing us into athletes capable of competing in the senior ranks. Training as a junior is a delicate balancing act. You're young, you're still developing physically, and if you put too much pressure on your body too soon, you run the risk of over-training and potentially giving yourself problems when you try to make the step up from the juniors to the senior ranks. If you look at junior athletics records, there's plenty of kids who've won English Schools titles at Under-15 level and then failed to make the grade in the professional ranks. Equally, there are a number of kids whose development is slower and who don't shine at junior level. Paula Radcliffe, for example, placed 299th when she competed in her first English Schools cross country race. Physically, I was a lot smaller than many of the runners in my age category, and in Alex I was fortunate to have a coach who resisted the temptation to overcook my training programme. He recognized my talent from day one and knew that I needed to be nurtured. Again, it was a case of right time, right place.

Training was hard but fun. Alex always found a way to keep it interesting. We'd start off with fairly simple stuff, doing repetitions across short distances that are ideal for juniors. Alex also introduced me to the concept of *fartlek*, a Swedish term meaning literally 'speed play', and perhaps better known as interval training. This is where you mix up intense sprint bursts with slower recovery periods so that over time you begin to build up your strength and stamina. On a *fartlek* session Alex would get us to choose how much effort we were going to put in on the sprints, the idea being that whatever effort we put in would be halved for the recovery period. So, say I did six minutes of intense running, I'd have to do a recovery interval of three minutes at a slower pace.

I started to get pretty good at running. By the end of a track session, I'd have lapped some of the other athletes a few times. It wasn't long before I started competing in races.

My first runs for the club were in cross country because I'd begun training at the club at the end of the track season. I loved running cross country – back then I enjoyed it more than track. The course was usually held in some new and interesting place, and the courses themselves had lots of variations in the hills and dips. I have special memories of some of the courses. Twice a year I competed in the cross-country competition at Parliament Hill, on the fringes of Hampstead Heath. Britain has plenty of good cross country courses but Parliament Hill is right up there as one of my favourites. It's hosted several English Schools races. It's a tough, hilly, muddy course, and to win it I had to be at my best.

Running cross country was a lot less fun when it was cold. In the winter it used to be so chilly that I couldn't feel my fingers or toes. No matter how fast or hard I ran, how high my pulse rate was, I couldn't warm up my hands and feet. I tried everything. Hats, gloves, extra pairs of socks. During one race, the cold was brutal. A sharp wind was whipping across the hill, my hands were frozen to the bone and my ears were stinging. It got so bad that I ran the second half of the race with my hands tucked under my armpits in a desperate effort to warm them up.

Running for the club had an unexpected benefit: it helped me at school. Word got around that I was a star at running. Suddenly the other kids in class had this respect for me. I'd always been a popular kid at Feltham because I was warm-hearted and made people laugh, and I wasn't afraid of having a go. But doing well at athletics made me something of a local hero at Feltham. Alan likes to tell this story of how, a couple of years after I'd joined the school, our class was taking part in an endurance lesson: two laps of the field, with a few twists and turns to make it interesting. The best kids could finish the course in around nine minutes. I sailed around the course, did it in maybe six or seven minutes. Graham Potter, the head of PE, happened to be observing the class. When the last kid had completed the second lap, Graham called everyone together in a big group.

'Right, you lot,' he said to the other kids. 'Get your diaries out. Not you, Mo.'

Everyone did as they were told. I stood there scratching the back of my head, no idea what was going on. Then Graham pointed to me and said to the others, 'Mo is going to sign all your diaries. Keep them safe because they'll be worth something in the future. Mo is going to be a star.'

Having to sign my classmates' diaries was slightly weird. There are some people who'd let that kind of stuff go to their heads, but I didn't think too much of it. That was one of the reasons I had so much love at Feltham. I didn't go around acting like I was better than anyone else. That's never been my style. Whatever I've done, I've always tried to follow the example of my family and be kind and humble. I mean, how hard is that?

On Tuesdays and Thursdays I trained. At the weekends I raced.

The way it works in athletics is this: first you win your school races; then you represent your school in the district competitions, racing against other schools from the same borough. When you win those, you get to race for your school in borough events. Win the boroughs and you get the chance to run in the county schools competitions. If you finish in the top eight in the county event, you're selected to race in English Schools for your county, competing against all the other counties from across England.

When I was a kid, English Schools was like a mini-Olympics. You had all the best runners from across the country competing in the same race. The field of runners at English Schools was usually strong, and one or two were marked out as the Next Big Thing in British athletics. You'd hear people talking about the times some of these guys were posting at races around the country and you'd think, 'That guy is looking good. I'm gonna have to watch out for him at the Schools.'

Having breezed through the school cross country trials, I was entered into the Hounslow Borough Championships, competing for Feltham. Sadly, my English still wasn't up to scratch and I had great difficulty understanding the course route. Early on in the race I moved to the front of the lead group and took a wrong turn. By the time I looked over my shoulder and saw the rest of the pack heading in a completely different direction, I'd lost a lot of time on the leaders. I frantically spun around and gave chase to the other kids, clawing back on them metre by metre, fighting my way to the front of the group as we bulleted towards the finish line. A hundred metres to go, I'd managed to push my way to the front of the pack. All of a sudden, this huge kid sprinted away from me to leave me trailing in his wake in second place. I was pretty beat up about it at the time, although Alan told me I'd done brilliantly just to catch up with the others after going the wrong way. For me, I felt I should have done better.

I told myself, 'No way am I gonna lose to that kid again.'

In the classroom I continued to struggle, but when it came to running, I was proving to be a quick learner. I've got what they call a good athletics brain. Simply by observing other people in training sessions at the club and trying out different things, I began to build up an idea of how to run a race, which tactics to use in which situations. I had this compulsive desire to improve – this determination to win. There are some extremely talented people who fall into a trap of believing that because they have talent, they don't have to work hard. I was never fooled by that. I took the toughness and the work ethic that I'd learnt as a child in Gebilay and Djibouti and carried it with me into competitive running. The pain was no big deal. I could handle the pain. If it hurt, it didn't really matter to me. I would keep on running, no matter what.

Alan likes to say that I never won a big race the first time I competed in it. He's got a point. Competing in the borough races was very different from running against twenty-odd kids in my class at Feltham. Not all junior athletics coaches shared Alex McGee's philosophy of putting long-term development over short-term gain. There were some big kids in the same age category as me and at first I found it hard to win races.

Losing a race was hard to stomach. I hated losing more than anything. In my first year at Feltham I took part in the school relay, running the last leg of the race. I started in lane six. With three legs of the relay done, the race was on a knife-edge. The kid handed me the baton. I snatched it and sprinted away to win the race by a huge margin. Graham and Alan had been watching from the side of the track. I noticed them swapping a look after the race. Alan approached me, shaking his head.

'I'm afraid we're going to have to disqualify you,' he said.

I frowned. 'What for?'

Alan pointed at my feet. I looked down and realized my mistake. I wasn't in lane six any more. Somewhere along my mad dash to the finish line I'd accidentally moved out of my lane.

'You're in the wrong lane, Mo,' Alan went on. 'Sorry, but it's the rules.'

In the heat of the moment I flipped and launched the baton through the air with this huge throw, furious with myself for making such a simple mistake. The baton landed somewhere on the other side of the track. Losing my temper that day was a mistake. I rarely lose my cool these days, but I hated that feeling of being beaten. When I crossed the finish line in a counties race in second or third place, I might not show it, but I'd be hurting inside for a few days. I'd go away and mull over my defeat, asking myself why I'd lost the race, what I could have done differently, how I could improve. By the time the next race would come around, I'd be even more determined to beat the kids who'd finished ahead of me. You'd find me at Feltham Arena in the evenings doing extra training sessions. Pushing myself harder. Wanting to win.

The second time I ran a race, I usually won.

After a few months I began competing in the county championships for Middlesex Schools. My first race at that level, I got revenge over the kid who'd beaten me near the finish line in the borough race, easily placing ahead of him. I only finished fourth, though. At the start of the race everyone took off in a flurry of colour and excitement, when I felt this blow land on the small of my back, like someone had struck at me with a hammer. The force of the blow knocked me off my feet. In the rush to take the lead, one of the other kids had pushed me over. Whether it was deliberate or not was impossible to tell. Accidents happen in races; there are lots of you running in close proximity and sometimes an arm or a leg catches someone. It was a foul day. The ground was thick with mud, the wind biting and fierce, and I was wearing flat trainers because I didn't own a pair of spikes. Under the circumstances, I could have been forgiven for throwing in the towel, but I was determined to win that race. I scraped myself off the ground and imme-diately set about chasing down the lead pack, running through the course as fast as I could. I came close, but not close enough. At the end of the race Alan threw an arm around me.

'That was a remarkable achievement,' he told me. 'To claw your way back to fourth like that. Well done, Mo.'

I smiled. But all I could think was, 'I didn't win . . .'

Alan was a constant source of encouragement. He never gave up on me. He drove me to training. He took time off from his weekends whenever his teaching commitments allowed him to come and watch me compete, travelling up and down the country, cheering me on from the sidelines in the borough and county championships. He'd make sure I stuck to the training programme Alex McGee set for me at the club. Whenever I needed help, Alan was there for me. I remember one time I climbed aboard the club coach on a Saturday morning. We were off to race somewhere in another county. I had no money for lunch and didn't know what I was going to do for food. Alan must have seen the look of concern on my face because he stopped beside my seat on the coach and asked if I had any money for lunch. I shook my head. Just like that, Alan dug out his wallet and handed me a crisp £5 note. I was touched. Five pounds was a lot of money to me back then. Alan didn't have to do that. It came out of his own pocket, not the school. But he genuinely believed in my talent. He wanted to see all his students from Feltham succeed to the best of our abilities. And if that meant helping me out with things like lunch money, he was willing to do it. Without Alan, I would never have been able to take those first few steps towards my Olympic dream.

You might wonder why my mum, or my Aunt Kinsi, didn't watch me race. The truth is, in Somali culture people don't really view running in the same light as we do here. If you go out for a run in Somalia, people think there's something wrong with you. To them, running is a crazy man's sport. You should only be running if there's a good reason – fetching water, perhaps, or escaping danger. In their eyes, the idea of someone running in a pure race format is puzzling. I think Mum viewed my running in this way. As a sort of hobby – something I did in my spare time to burn off energy. She didn't attend my races because it never occurred to her that running was something to be taken seriously. The same was true for Aunt Kinsi. As it would be for most Somalis.

One Thursday after training at the club Alan reminded me that I had an event at St Albans on the Sunday. He wanted to know how I intended to get there. 'Are you going to go on the coach with the other runners, Mo?'

'Coach?' I repeated, nodding. 'Yeah. Cool.'

In those days, although I'd been in England a couple of years, my English was still rough around the edges. I could have a conversation, but there were gaps in my vocabulary and sometimes I didn't understand what people were saying. Instead of admitting that I was confused, I'd simply smile and nod and pretend that I understood. If that drew a puzzled response from the other person, I figured I'd given them the wrong answer, so I'd change my 'yes' to a 'no', quickly shaking my head. In my mind, it was preferable to owning up that I didn't know what the other person was saying.

On the Sunday morning I got up and waited for the coach to arrive. No sign of it. An hour passed. Still nothing. It was getting dangerously close to the start of the race and I was starting to think that the driver had forgotten to pick me up and gone without me. Just then I gazed out of the window and saw a car pull up outside our house. Alan bolted out of the car.

'Mo, what's happened?' he exclaimed breathlessly. 'Why didn't you get on the coach?'

Alan had gone to watch the race, arrived at St Albans and waited for me to get off the coach. When I had failed to emerge, he'd driven to my house to come looking for me. As he explained all this, I scratched my head.

'I thought you meant the coach was going to pick me up from my house,' I said.

There was no time to lose. I grabbed my stuff and hurried into the car with Alan. We raced north to St Albans on the M25 and made it to the course in the nick of time. I won easily, having almost missed the race.

My cousin Mahad used to come with us on the trips. I'd ride up front with Alan, while Mahad sat in the back seat singing or making jokes. It was nice to have him tag along. He was the more vocal of the two of us. When we weren't taking the mick, I'd take the opportunity to brush up on my English, pointing to things in the fields at the side of the road and saying the English words to Alan. 'Cow.' 'Sheep.'

'Tree.' Alan just nodded. I don't think he realized how poor my English was back then.

We had some great fun at the club. One night, close to Christmas, we went out for a run along a regular route through Feltham. As we set off, someone decided we should go carol singing instead. We went from house to house and knocked on each front door. I'd never sung Christmas carols before. As soon as the owners answered, everyone began singing. In return, they gave us sweets. It was the weirdest thing I'd ever seen.

I soon progressed from the county championships to English Schools, representing Middlesex. At the same time, I was competing for the Borough of Hounslow in the athletics league. But there were still times when I was reluctant to go training or wanted to hang out with my friends and play football. As any athletics coach will tell you, football and training don't go well together. The kicks to the legs take the speed out of you; the general wear and tear of running up and down on the pitch, striking a ball – it impacts on your running ability. But I can be stubborn, and at that age I just wanted to play. As I progressed through the junior ranks, from school races to borough, then county and finally English Schools, it soon became obvious that I couldn't keep up both running and football. One or the other had to go.

By the age of twelve, I'd reached English Schools level and was close to achieving something special. The top eight runners in English Schools events got to wear an England vest and had the chance to compete against Scotland, Wales and Northern Ireland in the National Championships. Whoever won those races was then selected to represent Great Britain in the junior European Championships. The thought of representing my country in athletics was a huge motivation for me. Britain was my home now. It's the place where I first went to school, where I made friends and learnt to become a runner.

For me, competing for my country was the ultimate goal.

5
AN ARSENAL KIT

In 1996, when I was twelve years old, I was selected to run in the annual English Schools Cross Country Championships in Weymouth, Dorset as a reward for finishing second in the counties race. It was my first race at national level.

Weymouth was a 4.5 kilometre race. I'd started out running 3 kilometre races and worked my way up to the longer distance from there, with the length of the races increasing year by year. But this was my first race at 4.5 kilometres, and on top of that, the race was open to both Year Eight and Year Nine students. I was competing against 300 kids, about half of whom were older than me, some as old as fourteen, and I was smaller than most of the other Year Eights. Before the start of the race, Alan had given me a pep talk.

'Look, Mo,' he said. 'You've done really well just to get here. If you come in the top fifty, you'll have done an amazing job. Even top hundred would be a good result.'

Alan was careful to manage my expectations. For sure, there's a danger in telling someone they can win a race because if it doesn't happen for whatever reason, they're crushed with disappointment. Psychologically, losing when you expect to win is harder to process than winning when you don't expect to place that high. No doubt Alan saw the size of the field, realized that many of the other runners were physically more developed than me, and wanted to make sure I didn't feel under any pressure to win as easily as I'd done at the borough and school competitions. But I saw things differently. This was my first English Schools run. I wanted to win.

The race started. The pace was ridiculous. I focused on my own race and didn't worry too much about what the guys in front were doing. I tore round the first bend in the middle of this huge pack of runners, most of whom were twice the size of me. At that point I was down in a hundredth place and quite a way back from the front. As we started making our way round the various loops of the track, the thought suddenly hit me: 'I'm faster than most of these guys.' Slowly but surely, I began overtaking kids in the chasing pack. After 1 kilometre I was somewhere in the top fifty. After 2 kilometres I'd made it into the top thirty. By the time we clocked up 3 kilometres, with 1.5 left, I had managed to catch up with the lead group of nine runners, with the top eight automatically selected to represent England in the Nationals. The chance to represent my country was in my grasp.

As we scudded round the final bend I nudged ahead of the eighth-placed runner. Now I was top eight. I sprinted towards the finish line with a couple of hundred metres to go. But as I closed in, the kid immediately behind me, the one I'd overtaken, kicked on and caught up with me. We were neck and neck. I was so close to that England top. I kicked again, pushing fiercely, giving it everything as I fought to cling on to eighth place and the England spot. I couldn't do it. I didn't have the strength in my legs. With less than 50 metres to go, my rival surged ahead of me. I crossed the finish line in ninth place.

I was bitterly disappointed. I remembered what Alan had said about top fifty being a great result, but to come so close to a qualification place only to lose it at the very last moment was gut-wrenching. Alan was waiting for me at the finish line. He came over, put an arm round my shoulder and said, 'You did really well, Mo. Don't forget that. Ninth place is a fantastic result, you know.'

I forced a smile. Alan was right. I had no right to expect to be anywhere near the front of the pack, considering my disadvantage in age and size. But I couldn't stop thinking about the end of the race. I'd given it everything and come up short.

'Run like that again and I reckon you'll come back next year and win it,' Alan added. 'Tell you what. If you win the next English Schools Cross Country, I'll buy you a football kit. Can't say fairer than that, can I?'

My eyes went wide. 'For real?'

Alan nodded. 'Any kit you want.'

'Arsenal,' I replied instantly.

Arsenal were my team. As a young kid, I sort of followed Manchester United. When I first moved to Britain, lots of the kids at school supported the Gunners, and after a while I started looking out for their results. They had top-class players like Tony Adams, Ray Parlour, Ian Wright, Dennis

Bergkamp, and they had just appointed Arsène Wenger as manager. He was in the process of revolutionizing football in England. Suddenly, they were my team. Now I had the chance to wear their shirt. That was all the motivation I needed to win.

I trained all-out for the next English Schools Cross Country Championships. The 1997 championships were going to be held in Newark and I had my eye on that Arsenal kit. First up, though, I had the English Schools Track & Field Championships, due to take place in Sheffield in July (the Cross Country Championships take place early in the year, with the Track & Field Championships held in the summer). In order to qualify for the finals, I had to post a top-eight finish for Feltham in the Middlesex Schools Athletics Championship. Ordinarily, this wouldn't have been a problem. Then, one week before the regionals, disaster struck. I was playing football in the field with Mahad before athletics training. It was a warm afternoon, the sun was out and we thought we'd kick the ball around outside rather than play inside the stuffy sports hall. I booted the ball really hard. It soared through the air and landed on top of the sports hall roof.

I'd kicked the ball over, so it was my job to fetch it. Grabbing hold of the gutter, I boosted myself onto the roof, scooped up the ball and threw it back down to Mahad. As I lowered myself from the roof, however, I slipped and felt this intense burning pain as something sharp scraped against my right leg. I stacked it, hit the ground and looked down at my leg. There was blood everywhere. The sharp edge of the gutter had ripped a gash from the top of my thigh all the way down to the back of my knee. I clamped my hand over the wound to stop the blood gushing out.

My immediate thought was, 'I can't let Alan find out.' I wasn't even thinking about the county championships at that moment. All I cared about was not getting Alan in trouble. He'd been kind enough to let Mahad and me kick the ball and I worried that he might get the blame for letting us play unsupervised. A few moments later he came rushing out of his office. He must have heard the noise from me falling off the roof. Alan asked me what was going on. I mumbled something about falling over whilst going for the ball. After he helped me clean up the wound, Alan drove me to A&E at West Middlesex Hospital, where I had several stitches in my leg. Once I got the all-clear from the doctor, Alan took me to the athletics club for a meeting with Alex McGee. The look on Alex's face told me it wasn't good news.

'No Middlesex Schools for you this weekend,' he said. 'You can't run carrying an injury like that. Out of the question.'

I was gutted. Missing the Middlesex county championship meant that I wouldn't make the cut for the English Schools Track & Field that summer in Sheffield. I was doubly determined to win the next English Schools Cross Country race the following March at the County Showground in Newark, a few days before my fourteenth birthday. I gave maximum effort in the build-up and didn't miss a training session that season. I ran well all year and felt in great shape going into the competition.

Then I got off to the worst possible start. Someone clipped

my heel at the beginning of the race. I tripped, lost my footing, stumbled to the ground. The leading pack took off ahead of me while I scraped myself off the ground. No big deal. I just had to run even faster. There was no way I wasn't going to win that race. Not after having put so much effort into training.

At the 1 kilometre mark I was down in twentieth place. I steadily worked my way up the group, picking off the other runners one by one. Winding it up. With less than 1 kilometre left of the course, I caught up with the ten guys leading the race. This time I had learnt my lesson from Weymouth the year before. Instead of kicking on early and wearing myself out, I just kept pace with them. Pushing and pushing, burning off my opponents. I had to fight hard to keep the pace. It was really windy that day and I was running into a hard breeze. But, with 500 metres to go I drew level with the race leader. At 400 metres to go I left him in my shadow and broke clear of the chasing pack. First place was up for grabs. I dug deep, concentrated on holding my position and maintaining my pace. All I had to do now was hold it for another 200 metres, kick on for the last 100, and then the English Schools title was mine.

All of a sudden, this kid flew past me, going crazy fast. He was wearing the Durham colours. I recognized him immediately. He was a friend of mine, Malcolm Hassan. A Sunderland kid, born and bred. Talked in a northern accent so thick you could almost stir it. There was still 300 metres to the finish line. My first instinct was to kick on and match Malcolm before he won the race, but then I thought, 'There's no way he can sustain this all the way to the finish. Don't panic. Just keep your stride. He'll burn out.' I held back, kept my stride and stuck to my race strategy. Two hundred metres to go, and sure enough, Malcolm started losing speed. He'd made the same mistake I did in Weymouth and gone too early. Finally, with less than 100 metres to go, I pulled clear of Malcolm and swept ahead to cross the line. I'd done it. I'd won. I had the English Schools Cross Country title. Then it sank in: I'd be competing for England in the Schools International. I was on a high after that race, absolutely buzzing. This was what it was all about. Alan came over to congratulate me.

'You owe me an Arsenal kit,' I said.

That race was the start of a big rivalry between Malcolm and me. He was a phenomenal runner, and a great rival. Sometimes I'd beat him; sometimes he'd beat me. Despite this, we were really good mates and often competed against each other in the English Schools Championships. We'd go on to represent England together. Malcolm's dad used to come along to the races. He'd drive Malcolm around in this comedy van. Whenever we raced, I'd take the mick out of Malcolm's Geordie accent. He gave as good as he got, did Malcolm, calling us southern softies for wearing gloves in the winter and so on.

In 1997, the year I won the cross country at Newark, I also competed at Chepstow for England and won the Home Countries International Cross Country title. Wearing that England kit was a special moment for me. I was filled with pride. I was starting to assert my ability on bigger stages now. Things were starting to happen for me. The following summer Alan drove me up to Sheffield for the English Schools Track & Field Championships held at the Don Valley Stadium – the championships I'd been forced to miss the previous year because of injury. I was scheduled to run in the 1500 metres. Alan felt that I lacked a bit of speed, and before the race he told me I'd do well to get a medal.

'If the pace is silly, don't go with it,' he said. 'It'll be too quick. You know how to run a good 1500 race, Mo. Don't worry about what anyone else is doing out there. Run your own race.'

I don't know why, but I had this feeling that I could hold my own out there against the other kids. As a runner, you have to believe in yourself. Sure, there's a fine line between self-belief and arrogance, but no one who didn't believe in themself ever won a gold medal in athletics. You see it time and again on the circuit: someone posting crazy fast times in training, but when it comes to a big competition, for whatever reason, they fail to make the podium. I had this absolute belief in what I was capable of. The way I saw it, I already had the English Schools Cross Country title and the Home Countries title in the bag. I had nothing to lose at the Track & Field Championships. I went out there ready to give it my best shot.

Malcolm was competing in the same race. As ever, we were both desperate to finish above the other. At the start, Malcolm took off like a bullet. BOOM! In next to no time he'd established a huge lead over me – 50 metres, easily. Maybe more. He was going for it, big time. With 500 metres to go, Malcolm was pushing hard and still out in front. In the corner of my eye I saw Alan screaming at me from the sidelines, yelling for me to pick up the pace. All right, then. I started winding up. With just over a hundred metres left, I pulled level with Malcolm. Now we both went for the sprint finish. It was a question of who had more strength left in their legs, who could kick on harder. Who could dig deeper. We were both going flat out, giving it absolutely everything. I could feel the muscles in my legs burning.

Suddenly, Malcolm was out of sight. I risked a quick glance over my shoulder and saw him trailing behind me. I had that little bit more in the tank than he did on the home straight. I made it across the line for a time of 4.06.41. Malcolm had run me very, very close, but I felt sheer joy at winning a third title in a row. That year, I was the only athlete from Middlesex to win a gold medal at the English Schools Track & Field Championships.

I first met Tania in 1997 when she was eleven and I was four-teen. New kids from school who had athletic talent were always coming along to Feltham Arena, and Tania was one of the faces I started seeing regularly both in school and at the club. I already knew her well by the time she started running for Hounslow, since we'd hung out at school and we both knew lots of the same people. By this time I was training with the distance runners; Tania was more into the sprint and hurdles events. We'd get chatting by the side of the tracks between events. She was smart, funny, warm. We just clicked from the beginning and soon became really good friends, hanging out socially. Tania lived just round the corner from my house.

Occasionally I'd go round to her place for a cup of tea with her mum, Nadia, her dad, Bob, and her older brother, Colin Nell. Nadia had an interesting background. She'd been born in Saudi Arabia, was half-Yemeni and half-Palestinian and had mixed Arab heritage. Nadia spoke Arabic; she could even recognize one or two Somali words since the languages were somewhat close. Sometimes Tania would plait my hair, back in the days when I actually had some. On one occasion she happened to be riding her bicycle up and down the street, recognized my front door and randomly decided to pop in and say hello. I answered the door. We didn't talk for long. Five or ten minutes tops. As soon as I closed the door, Aunt Kinsi was on my case.

'Why is that girl knocking for you?' she demanded.

'We're just good friends,' I said to my highly sceptical auntie. 'It's the truth. She goes to the same running club as me, that's all.'

I'm not sure my aunt believed me. But back then, Tania and me *were* just good friends. It took a while for things to develop between us.

I thought about Hassan all the time. Although he lived thousands of miles away, I felt very strongly that he was a part of me, and I was a part of him. It was a powerful thing, that connection. Sometimes I would find myself wishing that we all lived in one house, one big happy family, but life isn't always like that. And for me, there was no point dwelling on it. The situation was what it was. I knew that Hassan would always be there for me, and I'd always be there for him, and that one day soon we'd see each other again. That was good enough for me. It had to be.

Mum had gone back to Somalia by this point and located Hassan. They were living near Hargeisa and I would talk to them from time to time. Mum would go to the shop in a neighbouring village to wait for my call. On one occasion I told her I'd ring a few days later, but something came up and I wasn't able to contact her. I later found out that Mum had arrived at the shop early that morning and stayed there all day waiting for my call. She's like that, my mum. If someone tells her something, she expects it to happen. If someone tells her they're going to meet her at such-and-such a place at such-and-such a time and they don't show for three days, she'll still be waiting for them three days later. She doesn't have time for people who don't stick to their word. Once she decides on something, that's it. There's no going back. I was only able to speak to Mum by phone over the next several years until I was finally reunited with my family in 2003. I'd tell her to bring Hassan so I could talk to him. But it was hard.

I threw all my energy into training, going extra hard in the runs. In sessions at the club I'd be on the case with Alex, asking him for news on the next race, what events I'd be competing in, what club we were up against.

'I want you to do 3000 metres in the next young athletes' league meeting,' Alex would tell me. 'Judging by the standards that we've seen, you should win it quite easily.'

My next question was, 'What's the record?'

Before long I was way ahead of the other kids in Alex's group, beating them far too easily. I was ready for the next step. I can't recall exactly when it happened, but after one session I asked Alex if, whilst maintaining our regular

Thursday sessions together, I could start training on Tuesdays with the older age group of runners coached by Conrad Milton.

'Sure,' Alex said. 'Why not?'

Conrad had run for Great Britain as a junior. After his running career was ended early by knee troubles, he turned to coaching. He was smartly dressed, well-spoken – a thinker. Conrad coached Hayley Yelling, the British runner who was a three-time champion at 5000 and 10,000 metres in the Nationals. In addition to Hayley, he also coached a steeple-chase athlete called Benedict Whitby. Benedict was a few years older than me, although I can't talk about him too much – these days he's a policeman with City of London! Benedict was that extra level above me at the time. He had a kit contract with Nike and everything.

We used to go on *fartlek* runs together, Benedict and me. We'd meet up with ten or twelve other guys from the club and do a route through Feltham, the twelve of us running at a fast pace along the slip road leading to Heathrow Airport's Terminal Four. We'd be pushing hard, with the constant roar of planes overhead. Then, at the big roundabout in front of the terminal building, we'd hook a left and head back towards Feltham.

But for me, the runner I looked up to the most was Sam Haughian.

Sam was three years older than me. He was a class apart, pure and simple. He had a reputation as one of the brightest prospects in British endurance running at the time. In 1997 Sam had won the Inter Counties Championship. The following year he added the English Schools Cross Country senior title.

One time Sam had competed in an Italian 5 kilometre race packed with Kenyans – the Rome Golden Gala, I think it was. He finished in 13:25.56, his previous best being 13:38.52, which was a huge improvement in one fell swoop. With two laps to go, Sam was out of it. His legs were gone. In a tough race like that he could easily have drifted out of it. However he regrouped and with a 2:04 last 800m was able to improve his PB by 13 seconds. That was Sam. He was a really tough runner. He had records coming out of his ears, including the biggest winning margin in English Schools, and he ran in five World Cross Countries. He got salmonella poisoning the day before the 1998 World Cross Country Championships in Morocco. The doctors told him not to run, but Sam went against their wishes. He was in fourteenth position going into the last 400 metres, the highest-placed European in the field, when he blacked out. The smallest winning margin Sam had in any big domestic race was usually over a minute.

Without a doubt, Sam was one of the best cross country runners in Britain.

While I was with the juniors, I'd watch Conrad training Hayley, Benedict and Sam at the club. I took a special interest in them because all three were running for Great Britain. They were talented athletes who were clearly going places. I'd look at them and think, 'That's where I want to be.' Sometimes I would race against these guys in the league. Sam always beat me. Benedict too, although I did beat him once as a junior.

Training with the guys in Conrad's group gave me an instant

lift. All of a sudden, instead of breezing through races, I was having to chase older, more developed runners like Benedict and Sam, having to push very hard to keep up with them. I really had to up my game. Conrad would point out aspects of my running that I needed to work on, such as my bad habit of reaching (leaning forward) when I drew near the finish line. A lot of athletes do this. You see it on TV all the time, especially in the sprint events. But if you lean too early, you change your running gait and start losing pace.

If there was one runner at the club that I wanted to be like, it was Sam Haughian. I already knew his younger brother, Tim. He was a couple of years younger than me but we immediately hit it off and became good mates. I guess athletics must run in the Haughian family genes because Tim was also an outstanding running prospect. Tim and Sam were similar runners. They even shared the same running style. I had a few things in common with Sam too. Neither of us was exactly star students. We both liked to push ourselves on the track. Now we were training together, I made rapid progress, learning a lot not just from Sam, but from Benedict and Hayley too. I was getting faster, stronger, leaner. I wanted to do more. After several months of splitting the sessions, I told Alex, 'I want to move over to Conrad's group completely.'

There were no hard feelings on Alex's part. He was more than happy for me to make the move. It's the job of junior coaches to train their athletes until they're ready for the next step, and it was obvious to both of us that I was too good for my age group, and I stood to gain a lot more by training with the older guys being coached by Conrad.

One day after training Benedict mentioned that he knew the sports marketing manager at Nike, a guy called Dave Scott. Benedict offered to put in a good word with Dave Scott on my behalf, see if he could sort out a deal for me. 'Great,' I thought. 'Free kit!' Two weeks later I arrived at the arena and Benedict presented me with this big bag of training kit from Nike: T-shirts, shorts, tracksuits, socks. Tucked away in the bag was a signed letter from Dave Scott, congratulating me on my success so far and wishing me all the best for the future. At the end of training I lugged the bag onto the bus. A few stops down the line, the bus pulled over next to a police car.

I wondered what was going on. Then I saw a police officer thumping his fist on the automatic doors and ordering the driver to open them. As the officer climbed aboard the bus he turned to me and nodded at the bag.

'Have you got a receipt for all that?' he asked.

I felt every pair of eyes on the bus swing towards me. The skinny black kid with the giant bag of Nike kit. The police officer explained that they'd received a call from someone reporting a theft. Someone must have seen me lugging this enormous bag of Nike kit on the bus, figured I was handling stolen goods and dialled for the police.

I looked up at the police officer and shook my head. Of course I had no receipt. I told him that I was a distance runner for Hounslow Athletics Club, that the clothes were a special gift from Nike. This was all true, but Hounslow had a reputation. Kids used to nick stuff from the shops all the time. It was easier to believe I'd nicked this stuff than been given it by Nike. For a brief while I feared I might get dragged off the bus and hauled down to the local police station. Then I remembered the signed letter from Dave Scott. I'd stashed it somewhere in the bottom of the bag. In a flash I dug out the letter and showed it to the police officer. He read it through once. Then a second time. At last he handed the letter back to me. I was off the hook. Close call.

All my hard work in training paid off in early 1998 when, on the back of winning the English Schools Cross Country in Newark, I got a letter in the post informing me that I'd been selected to compete for England Schools in the International School Sports Federation (ISF) World Schools Championship Cross Country in Latvia in early May. I was only fourteen years old when I was informed that I'd been selected, and it was an early recognition of my talent. I hurried to school the next day, over the moon with the prospect of travelling abroad to compete. I found Alan in his office and breathlessly showed him the letter. As he read it, straight away I could tell that something was wrong.

'This is all well and good,' he said. 'But what travel documents have you got?'

'Travel documents?' I repeated.

Since moving to England, I had never needed to travel abroad. I had the right to remain in the UK, to work and study here. But I didn't have a passport or any other travel documents authorizing me to travel. The truth was that unless I could get my paperwork sorted and fast, I wouldn't be going anywhere. Alan agreed to help me fix it.

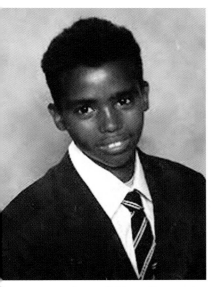

As a young student at Feltham Community College – I started two weeks late after breaking my collarbone playing football.

In 1998 I suffered a rare defeat and finished second at Cheltenham behind Lee McCash (337). Lee was a tough competitor, one of the few runners who seriously pushed me.

Running in the English Schools Cross Country Championships in 1997, when I beat Malcolm Hassan to win my first English Schools title.

Beating Malcolm Hassan on the way to the under-17s at Crystal Palace. There was a big rivalry between me and Malcolm, a phenomenal runner.

Me as a junior athlete with Dave Moorcroft. Many years later I broke his British record at 5000 metres.

Competing for Great Britain in the European Junior Championships in December 1999 in Slovenia. I helped the team to win gold.

I reached the finals of the 5000 metres at the World Junior Athletics Championships in Chile. Here with Chris Thompson, one of my fierce rivals at junior cross country.

Sam Haughian had a reputation as one of the brightest prospects in British athletics – and the runner I looked up to the most as a junior.

I benefited a lot from training alongside guys like Benedict Whitby, the steeplechaser.

With the two Alans – Alan Storey (*left*), my coach at St Mary's and beyond, and Alan Watkinson. In the background is my old sixth-form school, Isleworth and Syon.

Above: Before I shaved my head, I had plaits! Tania would often plait my hair for me after school.

Right: Happy days working at the Sweatshop branch in Teddington.

Below: Bushy Park – where I'd often go for training runs with the Kenyans.

Back to winning ways at the European Cross Country Championships in San Giorgio, Italy. I crushed Sergiy Lebid, the hot favourite.

Running the Great North Mile in 2006 – competing on the Saturday before the Great North Run is something of a tradition for me.

Jesús España nudges ahead of me to win the 5000 metres in Gothenburg. There was one hundredth of a second between us.

I badly overcooked it in the lead-up to Beijing and failed to qualify from the heats. I was devastated.

With my beautiful daughter Rhianna. From the moment we first met, the two of us hit it off immediately and developed an immense bond. The rest is history.

High up in the mountains at Iten – I was the first British athlete to get out there and train with the Kenyans.

Me and Hassan wore the same clothes when I returned to Hargeisa; it was like reliving our childhood all over again. Hassan even shaved his head in honour of me, so we now had the same bald head!

Getting married in April 2010. It was a beautiful day: everyone was there to see us tie the knot.

Above: My old friend Chris Thompson won silver to make it a one-two for Great Britain.

Left: My first major title at Barcelona in 2010. I became the first Briton to land 10,000 metres gold at the European Championships.

Me, Tania, Rhianna and Colin Nell, Tania's brother, celebrating after the European Championships, enjoying a bit of down time in Barcelona.

Early the next morning, before school, we drove up to the Home Office public enquiry building in Croydon. Alan thought if we made my case in person, we'd stand a better chance of getting my travel documents in time for the trip. Latvia was only three weeks away. I had just turned fifteen.

The response of the staff at the Home Office was pretty short and sharp. They basically told Alan, 'There's no way you're going to get this young man's application processed in three weeks.' I thought that was the end of it. I wouldn't be going to Latvia after all. I was disappointed, although I try not to let things like this get to me too much. 'There'll be other opportunities to race abroad,' I told myself. 'Don't worry.' People who know me well often say that I don't show much reaction to things. For sure, I don't celebrate too wildly and I don't beat myself up too badly when I lose. There's a day or two of pain or joy after a race, and then it's back to work. Before we left, Alan told the staff at the Home Office that he at least wanted to begin the process so that I wouldn't have to miss out on events like Latvia in the future.

'How long will this take to process?' Alan asked them.

'Don't know,' came the reply. 'Could be a couple of months. Could be much longer.'

I'd picked a bad time to apply. They explained to us that the Home Office systems were being computerized and the staff were having to work their way through a huge backlog of applications. Any new applications, they said, were going to take a lot longer to process than normal. We filled out the paperwork anyway so that the trip wasn't a complete waste. Then we jumped into the car and headed back to Hounslow in time for the start of school. I wouldn't be going to Latvia. I tried to put the disappointment of missing out on the World Schools Cross Country Championships behind me and concentrate on my running.

Then, in mid-January of 1999 I got another letter in the post.

I opened it up. Read it. Went piling into Alan's office as soon as I got to school.

'I'm going to Florida!' I shouted.

Alan gave me a funny look. 'Pardon?'

Bubbling with excitement, I showed him the letter I'd received in the post. 'It says right here, look!' I replied, excitedly tapping a finger against the letter. My English had steadily improved, partly thanks to the time I had spent around the athletics club, talking to people there, picking things up through conversation. 'I've been picked for the British Olympic Futures camp in Florida!'

The letter said that I'd been identified as an athlete of great potential. Thanks to National Lottery funding, I (and a group of other young British athletes) had been awarded a place on a two-week, all-expenses-paid training camp at Disney's Wide World of Sports Complex in Florida. The date of departure was set for 22 March 1999, the day before I turned sixteen. This was an incredible birthday present. But before I got too carried away, Alan raised a hand.

'Hang on a minute, Mo. You still haven't got your documents sorted,' he reminded me. My application at the Home Office had been dragging on and on. Then Alan pointed to the bottom paragraph of the letter. 'It says here that you need a ten-year passport in order to go on this trip. You don't have that. Even if we get your documents in order, I'm not sure it's possible for you to fly out there.'

I tried to hide it, but I'm sure Alan saw right through me. I badly wanted to make this trip. Latvia was one thing. I'd never dreamed of going to Latvia as a kid. But this was Walt Disney. Florida. The USA. I'd never been anywhere on holiday in my life, and I really wanted to go.

Alan said, 'We'll give it our best shot, Mo. Just don't be disappointed if it doesn't happen. This is a big ask. But I doubt very much whether we'll be able to get everything sorted in time.'

We had two months until the trip. To his credit, Alan worked round the clock to get me on that plane. He really stepped up, big time. He got on the phone to the Home Office and begged them to speed up my application. He wrote to our local MP. He drove me up to the Home Office in Croydon again. This time my Aunt Kinsi came along for the ride. Some official turned us both away without giving an explanation. Both my aunt and me were left totally confused. Alan had momentarily disappeared to buy a bottle of water. When he came back, he saw us trudging out of the building and asked me what had happened. I told him about being turned away. Alan marched us back inside and went up to the nearest member of staff and demanded an answer. Finally, we got an appointment. Alan explained to the member of staff that I was a talented young athlete who'd been picked for this once-in-a-lifetime opportunity and we had only a few weeks to get my papers in order, and was there any way in the world that things could be speeded up? We got the same non-committal response as before: 'We'll see what we can do.'

Not to be outdone, Alan then spoke to Alan Keen, the local MP for Feltham and Heston, to try and get my application fast-tracked. Even Tony Banks, the sports minister at the time, got involved. But the Home Office weren't sympathetic. They said to Alan, 'Why should we process this young man's application ahead of someone who wants to go home and visit a sick or dying relative?'

I didn't know what else we could do. I was starting to think that maybe Florida wouldn't happen. And then one day at the end of February, I got a letter through the post. It was my indefinite leave to remain. Now I could apply for the documents permitting me to travel, which I duly received.

There was still one more hurdle to overcome. I couldn't fly anywhere without a visa for the country I was visiting. We had only two weeks left before the flight to Orlando and I needed to get a US tourist visa in order to have permission to fly. There was no time to lose. Alan wrote to the American Embassy in London and told them about my exceptional circumstances, asking if there was anything they could do. I think someone must have called in a favour because my application was automatically bumped to the top of the queue. I had my appointment at the embassy on the Thursday, just over a week before I was due to travel. A week later they issued me with the tourist visa. I flew out of Gatwick the following Monday.

I was going to Florida.

6
DREAMLAND

FOR the second time in my life, I flew on a plane. This time there were no alarms going off. No cargo holds opening in the middle of the flight. Just a planeload of teenage athletes bubbling with excitement. I couldn't wait to arrive in Florida. I was going on the trip of a lifetime.

I can't emphasize enough how important this trip was in my decision to become an athlete. Florida was my first chance to spend time away from home, to live and train in a pure athletics environment. More than a hundred of us travelled to the camp: runners, cyclists, swimmers, gymnasts, badminton and basketball players, the best emerging talent in Britain. Among the other runners at the camp was Tim Benjamin, who went on to win the European Junior and World Youth titles, place 5th in the 2005 World Championships and compete in the 2004 Olympic Games. Also there was the sprinter, Mark Lewis-Francis. He was the top 100 metres talent in the world at the time. He won everything as a junior – World Youths, World Juniors and European Juniors. He went on to win gold in the 4 x 100 metres in the 2004 Olympic Games and took silver in the 100 metres in both the European Championships and Commonwealth Games in 2010. Borough of Hounslow AC was well represented with Nicola Sanders, who won silver in the 400 metres in the World Championships in 2007 in Osaka and gold in the 4 x 400 metres relay in the World Indoor Championships in Istanbul in 2012. There was also Goldie Sayers (a javelin thrower who won a string of national titles), Aaron Evans, who was doing great things at 400 metres – not to mention Nathan Palmer, a Welsh kid who specialized in the 110 metres hurdles and was posting faster times than Colin Jackson (a three times world champion and world record holder) at the same age. There was an awful lot of young British talent at that camp. Malcolm Hassan, my 'partner-in-crime', was in the group too.

Some of the national newspapers sent journalists to cover the trip. They asked me about growing up in Somalia, how I had found life in England to begin with. One reporter asked me who my hero was. 'Haile Gebrselassie,' I replied without hesitation. 'I like the way he runs. I'd like to do the same. It would mean a great deal for me to run for Great Britain.'

My jaw hit the floor when we arrived in Orlando. I'd been amazed at how big everything was when I'd first arrived in Britain. But compared to the US, everything back home looked tiny. Cars, buildings, food portions: they were all double the size in America. Actually, I didn't know how big the US was until one of the other kids pointed it out to me at the camp. They were like, 'Can you name all fifty states?' and I was like, 'For real, there are *fifty* states?' I'd figured that the US and the UK were about the same size. It's safe to say that geography was never one of my favourite subjects at school.

The idea behind UK Athletics (UKA) sending a large group

of kids to a warm-weather camp in Orlando was to bring together the best young athletes in the country and allow us to train in the same environment as the likes of the senior USA team. Nowadays training camps for promising athletes are standard, but back then none of us had ever worked in such an environment. I've already described how Feltham Arena, where I trained, was badly in need of repairs. Some of the swimmers at the camp told me that back home they had to get up at the crack of dawn and train in 25-metre pools, half the size of the Olympic standard. Similarly, gymnasts talked about practising in knackered old sports halls. For many of us, Florida was the first time we had access to state-of-the-art training facilities. There was a brand-new athletics track where several of the Team USA sprinters trained. There was a state-of-the-art gym with weights rooms and exercise machines, a sports stadium with seating for 9,000 people, an Olympic-standard swimming pool, specialist medical facilities, playing fields, clay tennis courts, baseball fields and football pitches. There was even a cross country course designed to the specifications of the International Amateur Athletic Federation (IAAF). The list was endless.

The camp had everything we wanted. The weather was beautiful: warm, clear skies, hot in the day but cool and breezy in the evenings. Everything was paid for. We were put up in a luxury hotel and offered as much food as we could eat. Pancakes, just like Grandma did them back in Djibouti, were served for breakfast in the hotel restaurant. There was a big swimming pool where we'd chill out after training. It was just like being on a real holiday.

Each morning we took a bus from the hotel to the training complex. There was this intense focus on athletics at the camp. Everyone took their sport seriously. Everyone trained to a high standard. It was an eye-opening experience. At Hounslow I trained twice a week. In Orlando I trained every day. There was a real professionalism about the camp. We did workshops on nutrition and sports psychology, even on how to deal with the media. I'd never seen anything like it. I got to meet some of the US track stars who were training at the camp at the time, including Gail Devers, the American sprinter and hurdler who had won Olympic gold three times: in the 100 metres in Barcelona, and in the 100 metres and 4 x 100 metres relay at Atlanta in 1996. Gail was famous for having these really long nails, and I couldn't take my eyes off her hands. Her nails really were as long as they looked on TV.

When we weren't training on the track, we went to Disney World and got to go on all the famous rides: Space Mountain, the Haunted Mansion and the Frontierland Shootin' Arcade. I loved every minute of it. Towards the end of our stay at the camp Brian Hall, the team manager, gave a speech to all the athletes. He told us that we'd trained well and shown great potential – that we were the future of British elite running. I took what he said to heart. As we checked out of the hotel and left on the coach for the ride back to the airport and the long trip home, something clicked inside my head. Being good at distance running had given me the opportunity to train in the US. I'd had a preview of what it meant to be a top-class athlete. Doors opened for you.

Things happened. If it wasn't for running, I would never have made that trip. Suddenly it was obvious: I'd achieved all this without being truly dedicated to athletics. So imagine what I could do if I put everything into running – to being the best I could be.

On the flight home I asked myself a simple question: 'What is it that I need to do in order to come back here again?' The answer was staring me in the face: 'I've got to train more. I must train harder, longer. I've got to put in more effort in sessions. That's what I've got to do.' When I returned to London, Alan asked how my trip had gone.

'Good,' I told him. 'I want to be a professional athlete.'

Florida changed everything for me. On the back of that trip, my attitude completely altered. Now I approached training with the right mentality. I'd say to myself, 'This is what I'm going to do this year. I want to win X, Y and Z races, and compete for Great Britain. What do I need to do in order to get there?' I trained with more discipline, pushed myself to go that extra mile. Before Florida, I had this habit of missing runs that Conrad had included as part of my training programme. He'd say to me, 'Make sure you go for a run this weekend, Mo.' And I'd nod and be like, 'Yeah, sure.' Then I'd play football instead. All that changed after Florida. I never missed a run or a training session again. I still loved football, but at the same time I knew I had to devote myself to athletics if I was going to fulfil my potential.

Alan noticed a big difference in my attitude when I came back. I stopped having kick-abouts in the sports hall before training. Athletics became my whole life. Before Florida I was restless. Now I channelled all my energy into athletics. I wanted to make it as an athlete and nothing was going to stop me. I had Alan to thank for getting me on that plane, for opening up my horizons and showing me what was waiting out there if I was willing to reach out and seize it. As a thank you, I brought him back a gift – a mug with 'WORLD'S BEST TEACHER' written on the side.

One of the good things about athletics is that there's no downtime, no off-season. There's always a race coming up to focus on. For a restless guy like me, that's perfect. I don't think I'd handle a close-season, with loads of time off, very well. When the cross country season was over, it was straight on to the track for the athletics season. There were races sponsored by Reebok, English Schools races, trials for the European and World Junior Championship. In July 1999 I won the 1500 metres at the English Schools Track & Field Championships in Bury St Edmunds. I started travelling more. Up to that point, I'd competed mainly across England, Wales, Scotland and Northern Ireland. After Florida and my victories in the English Schools races, I had more and more opportunities to compete abroad. Unfortunately, I needed a visa for every country I wanted to travel to. Alan stepped up again. Over several months he took me to all the major embassies in London: Poland, Italy, Belgium, Germany, Switzerland. We got to know West London pretty well.

But there were times when even having the visa wasn't enough. Like the time I had a race meeting in Belgium. Because of bad weather our ferry was rerouted from Ostend to Calais in France. I had my Belgian visa stamped and ready but I didn't have a French visa, so they wouldn't let me through. I was gutted. All I wanted to do was get into the country, catch a train across the border and head across to the race meeting. Alan argued my case, but the border guys wouldn't budge. Eventually we gave up and returned home. I didn't understand why it had been such a problem. For me, all I wanted to do was race.

I put that episode behind me and in mid-July I competed in the 3000 metres event at the World Youth Championships in Poland. This was my first taste of running against the Kenyans and Ethiopians. I finished fifth. Pius Muli of Kenya won it; a promising young Ethiopian runner called Kenenisa Bekele finished second. (Bekele went on to dominate world distance running, winning three Olympic golds, five World Championships golds, 11 World Cross Country titles and setting world records at both 5000 metres and 10,000 metres.) I was nearly 13 seconds behind Muli. In domestic and European meets, with no East Africans to compete against, I continued to win easily. At the Under-19s European meet in Neubrandenburg in Germany I won the 3000 metres in a four-way race against Germany, France and Poland. I was starting to achieve recognition on the athletics circuit, making a name for myself.

That summer, at the age of sixteen, I finished at Feltham Community College. Alan Watkinson also left and took up a new post as head of year at Isleworth & Syon School, which was up the road from Feltham. This was great timing. I was looking for a way to continue running, and switching to the sixth-form college at Isleworth was perfect. My grades weren't up to scratch, but Alan promised to have a word with the head teacher at Isleworth to see about bringing me over with him. At the time, Isleworth were Feltham's great rivals in school athletics in the borough, and, as it turned out, the school was only too happy to welcome me. I still had to work on my grades, so I divided my time between going to Isleworth, studying to resit my English Language and Maths GCSEs at a college in Richmond, and training at the athletics club. At the weekends I went out for runs and competed in events. The only downside was that I didn't see as much of Alan at Isleworth. He was teaching history for a year instead of PE, and I was spending more and more time training at the club under the guidance of Conrad Milton.

A year or so after I started at Isleworth, our athletics club merged with another club: Windsor Slough & Eton. This wasn't a major surprise. The writing had been on the wall for a while for Borough of Hounslow. Feltham Arena had that worn-out look about it. The council didn't have the funds to lay down a new track. Eventually the club couldn't even get insured to host competitions. Conrad, Alex and the other coaches didn't feel very confident working there. There had been talk of the club moving from Feltham Arena and the local council laying down a brand-new track at my old school, Feltham Community College. Everyone was in favour of it – the school, the club, the coaches. They mentioned my name as someone who'd benefited from the club and could inspire other kids to get into athletics. Sadly, nothing ever came of the talks. The track never got built. Feltham

Arena fell into neglect. Borough of Hounslow had no choice but to merge with their Berkshire neighbours. The new club was named Windsor Slough Eton & Hounslow Athletic Club.

The big positive from the merger was that Hounslow got the benefit of sharing top-class training facilities. The club was based at the brand-new Thames Valley Athletics Centre in the grounds of Eton College. Still, leaving Feltham was a bit of a blow for athletics in Hounslow, and for me personally. Instead of a short drive north up the A312 to Feltham Arena, going to training sessions now involved a 25-mile round trip beyond Heathrow. It doesn't sound far, but for a schoolkid, that's quite a trek. If the club had been based at Eton when I started running at the age of eleven, I doubt I'd have made it over there.

I began making more friends both inside and beyond the club. Scott Overall was a good mate of mine. He was a member at Windsor Slough Eton & Hounslow and later competed in the marathon at London 2012. Scott was never a troublemaker. He was the complete opposite of me. I'd be taking the mick with Abdi Ali, but Scott never went in for any of that stuff. He was always that little bit more serious. That didn't stop us from getting on really well. We had that same competitive drive. Often we'd meet up outside the club to go for runs around Bushy Park in nearby Teddington. We'd arrange a meeting place, usually the McDonald's on Twickenham Road, and then head down to the park for a few laps.

I also got to know Carlton Cole, a sprinter who later became a professional footballer and played for Chelsea, Aston Villa and West Ham. We met through a mutual friend, another sprinter by the name of Darren Chin. Darren is still one of my best mates. He used to teach me about sprinting techniques. He was on the verge of qualifying for the 2005 60 metres final at the European Indoor Championships in Madrid when he pulled up with a hamstring injury. If it hadn't been for that injury, Darren would've made the final, and who knows what he might have gone on to achieve?

Outside the club, I made good friends on the athletics circuit. There was Malcolm Hassan, of course. There was also Chris Thompson, who was based over at Loughborough. He ran for Aldershot, Farnham & District Athletics Club. I'd come up against him a few times and we were considered fierce rivals at junior cross country. Chris had been the top guy in Britain at junior cross country before I showed up; he'd won a string of UK Trial, English and Southern titles, and finished third in the English Schools race in the year I won it at Newark Showground. We'd both competed in the European Junior Championships in December 1999 in Slovenia (I finished fifth). We also helped the junior GB team to win gold. Chris was a couple of years older than me and that little bit further along with his development, winning silver in the 2000 European Junior Championship in Malmö. I finished the same race down in seventh place.

At that time Chris was studying at Loughborough on a sports scholarship. Loughborough was famous for having world-class sports facilities, sports scientists and coaches, so to be accepted there on a scholarship was a big deal and marked Chris out as being a hot prospect in UK athletics. He used to invite me up to the uni to hang out. He lived in hall on the campus and there was always a spare room available for me to crash. I was still living with Aunt Kinsi, and getting away for a full weekend was tricky. My aunt was very protective of me. I was only permitted to stay out for the whole weekend if I had to race somewhere in Europe. Otherwise, I was supposed to be back by the end of the night. I wanted to go up and visit Chris, so I told Aunt Kinsi that my European races went on for longer than a day or two at a time. Then I secretly planned my trek up to Loughborough to visit Chris.

'Aunt,' I'd say. 'I'm going to go off for a race this weekend. It's in Poland.'

Aunt Kinsi would ask, 'When are you back?'

'Next week,' I'd say. 'We're training for a few days after the race.'

A blatant lie. My return flight would be on the Monday, but instead of travelling straight back home from the airport, I'd catch the train to Loughborough with Chris. Then we'd spend the week on campus. We had some great fun, playing monster sessions of Pro Evolution Soccer on the PlayStation 2, checking out the student union bar in the evenings before going into town. The following Friday I'd catch a train back to Hounslow and arrive home in the early evening. My auntie would be at home waiting for me, asking me about my trip to Poland.

'Yeah, it was good,' I'd reply casually. Then I'd head upstairs and crash.

I travelled up to Loughborough as often as I could – which was about as often as the race calendar allowed. If there was an event being held near Loughborough – say, a cross-country race in Nottingham – I'd pop over to the campus after I'd finished my run. Along with Chris, I got to hang out with a few of the other athletes based at Loughborough, including Steve Vernon. Steve came from Manchester. He'd won the English Schools senior title in 1999, the year after Sam Haughian had won it, and the same year that I won the Intermediate race. Out of the two, Steve was the more sensible guy. Chris was more like me, a bit of a joker. Spending time with them both was really great. I got my first taste of university life. I remember thinking, 'This definitely looks cool.' I wanted more of the same.

I met loads of people on the athletics circuit. The circuit is unique. There's nothing else like it. You'll meet a lot of genuinely warm and friendly people, and make friends, even if you're competing against some of them the next day. As everyone travels to the same meetings, you see the same faces, stay in the same hotels, compete in the same events. The circuit becomes sort of like an extended family. As well as making friends with the likes of Malcolm, Chris and Steve, I got the chance to meet some of the great names in British athletics too, including Paula Radcliffe. Meeting Paula was a special moment for me. She had been one of my role models, and the first time I met her I was a little star-struck.

Over the years, Paula has helped me out in various ways.

She set up a scheme with her sponsors, Nike, to provide grants to promising young athletes to help fund their development. I was among the lucky ones to be awarded a grant of £1,000. I spent the money on driving lessons because I felt I should be less reliant on getting lifts from Alan or club members to get to Eton for training. Learning to drive made it easier for me to get to the track and make my way to race meets. Getting the money to do this was such a wonderful gesture. Paula didn't have to do that. I was just some young up-and-coming kid. I'll never forget how she helped me out.

When I look back on it, my life has been full of these little kindnesses. Conrad Milton helped me set up a bank account. He had a background in banking and we agreed for him to be a joint signatory so that I'd learn how to manage my money properly. I wasn't making much in those days – mostly grants through SportsAid, and the odd bit here and there for winning some race, £100 or so. (I had a contract with Nike that covered my basic running kit.) Sir Eddie Kulukundis, a Greek ship-owner and benefactor of British athletics, stepped in to help with my passport situation. He got his solicitors on the case to help sort out my UK naturalization. Eventually, I was given a full British passport, which meant I was able to travel to meetings without having to apply for a new visa every time I visited a new country. Without these kindnesses, I would've found it much more of a struggle making my breakthrough in athletics.

I also took on an agent. Conrad soon recognized that I

was at a level where I needed professional management and he introduced me to an agent by the name of Kim McDonald. Kim had founded his management company in the 1980s and was famous for representing some of the leading athletes at that time, including Sonia O'Sullivan, Daniel Komen, Moses Kiptanui and Noah Ngeny. Over coffee in Teddington, Kim and I discussed my future in athletics. He explained that he recognized that I had immense talent and told me that he'd be more than happy to take me on and help nurture my career – to help me fulfil my potential. I was over the moon. Now that I had an agent, I felt I was on my way to becoming a professional athlete.

Year by year I was getting faster. I was constantly striving to improve my times at each distance – on reps of 400, 600 and 800 metres, on the road relays and the cross country races. My fastest laps were consistently getting faster, but it wasn't always a smooth progression. There were hiccups along the way. I suffered a disappointment at the World Cross Country Championships in Portugal in early 2000, when I finished way down the field in twenty-fifth – the lowest I'd ever placed in a race up to that point. People congratulated me for being the highest-placed European to finish behind a supremely talented pack of Kenyans and Ethiopians. I didn't see it that way. All I could think was, 'I lost.'

Alan had come to watch me compete in Portugal. As I walked away from the track and made my way over to him, this older man I didn't recognize came over to me and patted me on the back.

'Well done, Mo,' this guy said. 'That was really good.'

I smiled politely and nodded, although I didn't know who this guy was. 'Yeah, thanks,' I said, not wanting to stop and talk, just wanting to go away and process my defeat. 'Wish I'd won, though.'

After the man had left, Alan turned to me and lowered his voice.

'Do you know who that was, Mo?' he asked.

I shrugged. 'Not a clue.'

'That was Steve Cram!'

I frowned. 'Who?'

Alan quickly set me straight. As soon as I got home from Portugal, I borrowed a bunch of videos of Steve's old races and watched them all. After that, I found myself bumping into him all the time and we'd get chatting about this or that. I sought out his opinion on various things. I've got a lot of time for Steve. He's one of the most honest guys on the circuit. You need that, as an athlete. Someone who isn't afraid to tell you how it is. Otherwise, how else are you supposed to improve?

In August 2000 I finished second in the junior 5000 metres in Mannheim, Germany. Two months later I made the finals of the same event at the World Junior Athletics Championships in Chile. Of course, there were the usual injury spells and learning curves, but I was pleased with my progress and confident I could get even better.

In July 2001 I competed in the European Athletics Junior Championships in Grosetto, Italy. My form was good going into the race and I was expected to win the 5000 metres.

Because the officials read out the lap times in Italian, Conrad arranged to stand at the side of the track, calling out my lap times in English so I knew how fast I was going. It was a close race. This guy from Portugal, Bruno Saramago, gave me a good run for my money. He had a good engine and, as Conrad called out the lap times, I realized that I had to change tack and go for a kick finish rather than trying to burn the guy off, because no matter how much I pushed the pace I couldn't drop him. BOOM! I kicked on and pulled clear of Saramago on the last lap to win the race. I wasn't simply winning now; I was also learning about the tactical side of running, learning to adapt to racing in major championships.

Throughout this period of training and competing I found time to spend with Tania. We used to hang out with Abdi Ali and one of Tania's girlfriends. The four of us would meet up at the corner of our road, hop on a bus and head to the high street, where we'd do a whole lot of nothing. Just talking, having fun, joking around. Over time, Tania and me became very close friends. She was really sweet and, as well as being beautiful, she was a good person. I felt that I could talk to her about anything. Tania seemed to understand me in a way that no one else truly did.

I spent time around her family, got to know Bob and Nadia and her brother Colin. I'd go round the house and Tania would plait my hair. (I had hair in those days, believe it or not.) On one occasion Tania was plaiting my hair in the back garden and her grandmother on her mum's side of the family was over from Singapore to see the family. I'd been abroad shortly before, competing at a meet – I can't remember which one – and I had brought back a gift for Tania. It wasn't just some random key chain or tacky souvenir. It was something quite special, although neither of us can recall exactly what it was. At that point Tania didn't know how I felt about her, but her grandmother is sharp-eyed. She saw the chemistry between us and picked up on it immediately. Tania later discovered that, after I left the house, her grandmother pulled her mum to one side and said, 'That kid has a thing for my granddaughter. He likes her.'

After a while I finally plucked up the courage and told Tania that I had feelings for her. I wasn't too pushy about it. I simply had to tell her how I felt. Tania was really good about it. She explained that she didn't see us in quite the same way as me, but she wanted us to stay as good friends. I was like, 'Okay. That's cool.' I took it on the chin. These things happen for a reason and looking back, I think if we had hooked up for real at that point, things might not have turned out as well as they have done. We were both young and immature – especially me. I was still very much a kid at heart. I didn't have that sense of responsibility. Had we got together then, with me being the way I was, it would probably have fizzled out. It's better that we skipped those years and revisited that scenario in later life. How I felt didn't change our friendship. We still talked a lot and continued spending time together. That's just how it was.

At the age of eighteen I was at a crossroads. I was itching to move out of the cramped bedroom I shared with my cousin Mahad and explore more of the world. I was running in different countries and meeting new people. I was ready to move on and live my own life. My time at Isleworth was coming to an end. I wanted to continue training, but at the same time I had to find some way of supporting myself. This is the toughest part of a young athlete's career. Figuring out a way to juggle your training commitments with the need to earn a living. At the back of my head I thought, 'Unless something really big happens, I'm going to have to get a full-time job.'

As luck would have it, something really big did happen. For a few months I'd been seriously considering joining the army. An officer from the local regiment had given a talk to sixth-formers at Isleworth about the benefits of life in the military. To me, it sounded like a good idea. Some of my friends had relatives in the army, and they couldn't speak highly enough of it. Importantly, they claimed that if I joined up, I'd be given time off to compete in athletics competitions. Apparently, the army was generous when it came to stuff like that. I didn't consider the implications of military service. I just thought, if I enlist with the army, I'll be able to train and compete, *and* get paid and have somewhere to live at the same time. It seemed like a good way of solving the problem of how to balance my training and the need to make money. I thought about it some more, and by the spring of 2001, I had pretty much made up my mind that I was going to enlist once I left Isleworth.

That same year the World Cross Country Championships were being held in Belgium. I was determined to do better than my performance in Portugal, but I finished even lower down the rankings. Fifty-ninth. I wasn't even the highest-placed European this time. Guys from Belgium, Spain and Italy – they had all beaten me. That young Ethiopian, Bekele, won again. A clear gap was starting to emerge between the Kenyans and Ethiopians and the rest of the field, a gap I wanted to close. After the race I got chatting to one of the coaches attached to the senior GB endurance team. His name was Alan Storey. I'd heard of him on the circuit and seen him a few times at different competitions when I was competing for Great Britain as a junior. Alan was the Head of Endurance for UK Athletics. He said a few words to me, then the conversation turned to my plans for the future.

'What are you doing next, when you leave Isleworth?' Alan asked.

'I'm going to join the army,' I said.

Alan looked shocked. 'No, no, don't do that!'

'Well, then, what am I gonna do?' I asked. 'I just want to run.'

Alan said, 'You won't believe this, but we've just opened a high-performance sports centre down the road from you. It's at St Mary's University [in Twickenham]. It's a training base for gifted young athletes such as yourself, who have the potential to win medals. I'm in charge of the set-up there. We run a scholarship scheme. What would you say if I had a word, see about getting you on the scheme?'

As Alan told me more about this Endurance Performance and Coaching Centre (EPACC), I started to get excited. This was exactly the opportunity I'd been looking for. The scholarship Alan Storey had mentioned was a joint venture between UKA and London Marathon to produce endurance athletes. Since the glory days of Dave Bedford, Seb Coe, Steve Ovett and Steve Cram, British distance running had been in a terrible state. As part of the deal, London Marathon would pay my board and fees and I'd live on campus, literally on the doorstep of the training centre. Even better, Alan Storey would become my new coach. I told Alan I'd love to go there. He went away and made a few calls. There were still one or two hurdles to overcome. My grades weren't good enough for St Mary's. We reached an agreement where I had to continue studying at college in Richmond in order to keep my scholarship at the university.

A couple of months later it was official: I had a place at St Mary's, and a scholarship thanks to London Marathon. I was one of the first athletes to train at the centre. And if it hadn't been for that chat with Alan Storey, I would've joined the army.

7
AN EDUCATION, PART II

L IVING on campus at St Mary's was amazing. And for a while, at least, I went a little nuts. I suddenly had this sense of freedom. Now I could go out whenever I wanted – do whatever I liked. In my mind, as long as I was making it to training with Alan Storey and running in competitions, I didn't see any problem with staying out late or going to fancy-dress parties (I dressed up as Tarzan). In the end, I would have a serious decision to make. But at the start, I just wanted to have fun.

At the time I was one of only two athletes on the elite endurance programme at St Mary's. The other was James McIlroy. James was a couple of years older than me. Although he began competing for Ireland, James switched nationality to run for Great Britain, and by the time he joined St Mary's, he had a reputation as one of the rising stars of middle-distance running. We both trained under Alan Storey, and from what I saw of James, he had un-believable talent. He had that extra element of commitment that I was lacking; James took training seriously, he paid attention to his diet, sticking to vegetables and salads and high-protein foods, while I scoffed down jacket potatoes and beans on toast in the campus refectory, or grabbed frozen ready meals from the Tesco up the road.

We lived in a plain brown-brick building on the campus. Typical student digs, lots of posters up on the walls reminding people to clean up after themselves. Our dorm was directly opposite the athletics field, although we didn't do much in the way of training at St Mary's: the athletics track had been laid upside down. (In fairness the problem was later fixed and the track is perfect now.) Running on that meant you might as well be running on concrete. To get around that problem I did the majority of my training over at the Thames Valley track with Windsor Slough Eton & Hounslow. I'd roll out of bed, get into my battered old Ford Fiesta and drive up to the club, training with Benedict Whitby and Sam Haughian and the rest.

As the endurance specialist for UK Athletics, Alan oversaw my training. He was a fairly short, stocky man with thin-rimmed glasses and a reputation as one of the world's best distance running coaches. He was something of a guru. His background was different from the likes of Alex McGee and Conrad Milton. Alan had worked at Durham University, looking after several established distance runners before taking over as the National Marathon Coach and training two runners to victory in the London Marathon. After that, he had spent time in Asia and worked as an adviser to women's athletics in China. His star athlete at the time was Sonia O'Sullivan, the Irish distance runner who'd won gold in the 5000 metres at the World Championships in Gothenburg in 1995. She'd won silver in the same event at the Sydney Olympics in 2000. Alan had been a major factor in what Sonia achieved.

Neil Black was also part of the set-up at St Mary's. Neil, nicknamed Blackie, was my physio back then. Blackie is my physio to this day, although he now combines sorting out my body with his day job as the performance director for UKA. I'm not sure which is more demanding! Like Alan Storey, Blackie is world-class at his job. He treated several top athletes, including Christian Malcolm, Marlon Devonish and Kelly Holmes, and we were lucky to have him at St Mary's. From day one, Blackie has been very good to me. He knows my body better than anyone; he's one of those guys who will stop at nothing to get to the root of a problem. Quite simply, he's the best physio an athlete could ask for.

Zara Hyde Peters also worked for the endurance team at St Mary's. Zara was the Technical Director for Endurance, and she worked in the office that Alan had on campus. From the very moment that I met Zara I knew she had Somali heritage. Somalis have this ability to recognize each other from a mile off. In the same way, I suppose, that a Jamaican can spot a native of Kingston at first glance, Somalis can instantly tell when they meet someone else from their home-land. In fact, I can spot the difference between someone from Somalia, Ethiopia, Eritrea or Djibouti. It turned out that Zara had been born in Ireland but her dad came from Somalia. She was the hands-on member of the team. I'd see Zara whenever I popped into the office to pick up my mail. She liked to call me, Chris Thompson and Sam Haughian her three musketeers. If that was true, then I was a musketeer driving without a proper licence.

One day I remember driving back to St Mary's campus after a hard training session over at Thames Valley and seeing Neil Black standing at the side of the field, watching me steer my knackered Fiesta into the car park, windows rolled down, Tupac pounding out of the tinny speakers. I killed the engine, unfolded myself from the driver's seat and nodded at Blackie.

'What's up?'

'Don't take this the wrong way, Mo. But have you got a driving licence?'

'Yeah, yeah, course,' I replied.

Without saying another word I showed him my provisional licence. Neil's eyes went wide with disbelief. '*This* is your driving licence?'

'What's the problem?'

It didn't take long for Blackie to set me straight. I only had a provisional because I'd never taken my driving test. And I'd never taken my test because I thought the provisional covered me to drive just as long as I had the 'L' plate fastened to the rear bumper.

'What about insurance?' Neil asked. 'Do you have that, at least?'

The answer was no. It was pretty clear that I'd had a narrow escape, driving between the club and the campus like that. There were all kinds of things like this that I just didn't know – stuff no one had explained to me, that everyone assumes you know. A lot of my life I've been learning on my feet, having to pick things up as I go along. I booked myself in for my driving test, took it and passed, glad that

Neil had pointed out to me the deal with provisional licences before I'd got into serious trouble.

Later on, I was almost banned after overtaking an old-age pensioner who was driving up a hill too slowly for my liking. I hadn't realized the vehicle behind me was a police car. Another close call. My driving is much better these days.

Kim McDonald, my agent, tragically passed away in November 2001, when I was eighteen. Kim's death came as a real shock. He died of a heart attack in Brisbane, just forty-five years old. Tributes flowed in from around the athletics community and the many athletes he'd taken under his wing. Following Kim's death, an Irish former middle-distance runner called Ricky Simms took over the business. Like Kim, Ricky also really knew his stuff. They had guys like John Mayock, Mark-Lewis Francis and Tim Benjamin on the books, as well as Sam Haughian, and I decided to stay with the company, now called PACE.

Slowly, more athletes arrived on scholarships at St Mary's or to train in the Teddington area. There was Andrew Walker, an Irish runner who trained with PACE. Andrew was a twin, the same as me. I used to wind Andrew up about his taste in music. He was an absolutely massive Bob Dylan fan and he'd always try and get me to listen to some of his songs.

'Mo, Mo, sit down!' Andrew used to say. 'Listen to this *tune*, man.'

I could never get into any of that type of music. Too slow. I like a good beat. I'd listen for a minute, get bored and throw on some Tupac. One of the old classics like 'How Do U Want It' or 'I Ain't Mad at Cha'.

'Now, *this* is the real deal,' I'd say. 'This is what I'm talking about.'

Andrew would just make this face and switch the music back to Dylan.

Then there was Big Frank.

I already knew Yasin Nasser, aka Big Frank, from the athletics club. He lived by himself in a nice flat and sometimes a few of us would head over to his place, play Pro Evo or watch a few DVDs. We loved all the crime movies – *Goodfellas*, *Casino*, *Training Day*. Yasin was half-Somali and half-Arab, and I could never resist taking the mick out of him. He had this down-to-earth, reasonable manner, but I just had the knack of being able to push his buttons and get him properly irate. One time we were watching *Goodfellas* when one of the characters came out with the line, 'Call me Frank.'

I turned to Yasin. He was tall. The Mafia guy on the screen was also tall. And for some reason I thought Frank suited Yasin better than his given name. I grinned at him and said, 'That's your name from now on – Big Frank!'

'What?' Yasin screwed up his face. 'No way, man. My name ain't Big Frank.'

'Now it is . . . Big Frank.'

'Stop calling me that!'

From that day on, whenever we were heading out to a party or to meet up with mates, I'd introduce Yasin as Big Frank. He'd be spitting mad, protesting that his name wasn't Big Frank. But no one listened to him. The name stuck. Everyone around St Mary's knew him as Big Frank. People would pass him in the street: 'Morning, Big Frank.' 'What's

up, Big Frank?' 'Hey, Big Frank, you coming out tonight?'
Every time someone addressed him as Big Frank, Yasin went
through the roof. I cracked up any time I heard someone
call him by his new name. Many people still know Yasin as
Big Frank. He lives in Canada these days. They probably
call him Big Frank out there too. We've become great friends,
so I think he's got over his initial anger about his new name.

I'd find other ways to wind up Big Frank. Sometimes I'd
ring his phone while he was sleeping in the middle of the
night and leave prank messages on his voicemail. Or I'd call
him up on my mobile and say, 'Pal, what's up? I'm just in
Germany for a race. What're you doing?' I'd be saying this
as I stood outside Big Frank's front door. He'd be like, 'Yeah,
cool, how's Germany?' And then I'd knock on his door.
'Wait a second. Someone's knocking.' Then Big Frank would
crack open the door and I'd spring into view, and he would
jump back in surprise.

My main partner-in-crime was Tom Bedford, Dave
Bedford's son. Dave had been a brilliant distance runner in
the 1970s. In 1973 he broke the world record in the 10,000
metres, running 27:30.08. You'd know him if you saw
him – he always sported these bright red socks and a bushy
moustache, a bit like those guys in the 118 118 ads. After
retiring, Dave became the race director for the London
Marathon, so ultimately I had him to thank for being able
to enrol on the scholarship at St Mary's in the first place.
His son Tom became a great friend of mine. Neither of us
could resist playing a joke or doing something nuts. I got
to know Dave better through Tom.

Of all of us at St Mary's at that time, Lee McCash was undoubtedly the craziest. A distance runner from Manchester, Lee was one of the very few runners who seriously pushed me in the English Schools cross country races, even beating me on occasion. Lee had won the English Schools Intermediate title in 1998, running for Lancashire. I came second in the same race. Lee was a talented and tough competitor. We were in the same boat in that neither of us had the qualifications you strictly needed to study at St Mary's. He went to the same college as me, over in Richmond.

Lee also loved a good fight. He used to tell me about all the scraps he'd got into while growing up in Burnley. About how he'd go out to the clubs in town with his mates and as it got towards the end of the night, he'd go up to some lad and ask if he wanted a fight outside. There was no beef with the guy. He just wanted someone to have a scrap with in the street. Usually this other lad would take one look at Lee, who had the slight build of a distance runner, and readily agree to the fight – not realizing how tough Lee was. Then they'd go outside and fight. No weapons, just fists. Lee usually won. When the fight was over they'd shake hands and go their separate ways, as if nothing had happened. According to Lee, this sort of thing went on all the time up north. I couldn't get my head round it. Fighting with someone who's trying to attack you or has done something to hurt you, that's one thing. But just going round a club, asking who wants a fight? It didn't make any sense to me. Lee had put all this behind him by the time he joined the high-performance centre. But still. It was totally random.

Lee was awesome at cross country. Put him on a muddy, hilly course through a park on a cold winter's morning and he'd wipe the floor with the competition. On the track, however, it was a different story and he'd struggle to finish in the top eight. Generally, every runner has a preference for a particular surface, but for Lee the difference between track and grass was like night and day. I'm not sure why. Some people find track runs boring; they like the variation in the scenery on cross country runs, the fact they're actually getting somewhere rather than just running around the same stretch of track over and over. Maybe Lee had the same problem. I can't say for sure. It's something that a few athletes have to deal with, though. I was happy to run on both track and grass. In that way I guess I was lucky.

Take Haile Gebrselassie. This is a guy who won Olympic gold in the Atlanta and Sydney 10,000 metres, who dominated the World Championships between 1993 and 1999, who took gold in the World Indoors four times, and broke twenty-seven world records during his career. Without question, he is one of the greatest athletes of all time. He's a hero of mine, for sure. But it's a known fact that Gebrselassie wasn't as good doing cross country as he was on the track. He twice finished behind his great rival Paul Tergat in the World Cross Country Championships; his best achievement was bronze in the Worlds at Budapest. There are a few other guys who've struggled on either the track or the field. By and large, though, 90 per cent of athletes are good on both surfaces.

In the evenings I hung out with Tom, Lee, Big Frank,

Andrew and a few other lads. During the day, I trained under Alan Storey.

I remember coming away from my first session with Alan and feeling so shattered that I could hardly move. Every muscle in my body was aching. Alan believed in training Hard, with a capital 'H'. You'd have to put in some serious mileage over the course of a week. Alan's theory was that you had to build up a lot of miles in your muscles before you could start to think about running fast. First comes the distance, then comes the speed.

I quickly discovered that training under Alan was very different from anything I'd done at the athletics club. A typical session with Conrad would involve short, fast reps. It was rare for us to do anything very long in terms of distance. There was a good reason for this. Under Conrad, I was still a young athlete. You can't go from doing 400 metres to 1 kilometre overnight, otherwise you're going to get injured. The idea is to train that little bit more each time, then rein it in on the recovery session. That's how you add more power and stamina: bit by bit. Now that I was preparing to race in major international competitions, I had to step it up.

Under Alan, the distances were much longer. Sometimes I'd be out there on the track doing much longer reps. On top of the sheer intensity of our sessions, Alan had me running twice a day. That was a real shock. Before then I'd trained once a day, max. Even recovery sessions under Alan were gruelling. He was always looking to push you that little bit further, which was good. I'd complete my training session, turn away to get changed and leave and Alan would say, 'Not yet, Mo! I want you to do one more set.' I'd be hurting all over. I'd literally have to scrape myself off the track to go around again.

Alan varied my training. Some coaches give you a set programme for four weeks, and that's it. You stick to the plan, done. With Alan, you never knew what was coming next. He'd tell me what I'd be doing for the next session – say, 1 kilometre reps. Then I'd arrive, begin my warm-up, and he might suddenly say, 'Right, Mo. You'll be doing 2 kilometre reps today.' And I'd be like, 'But you said 1 kilometre!' It was all part of his plan to keep me on my toes. To his credit, training was never boring under Alan.

I responded brilliantly to Alan's coaching at first. I've never been one to shy away from hard work, and I had no problem with putting in the extra effort Alan demanded. Anything he told me to do, I'd do it. If Alan told me to jump, I'd jump. I was ready to do anything to become a better athlete. I think that's one of the things that helped us to bond. We were both big believers in the value of a good work ethic. Once I adapted to the training, I started to feel stronger and fitter than ever before.

Running is all about pushing your body that little bit further. That extra inch. Your body can do certain things comfortably, but to win, you need to go beyond that. And it's not easy. That last sprint? Take it from me – it's a lot harder than it looks. Some people think that all I do is flick a switch in my brain that says 'Run' and up my pace. It's not like that. It comes down to effort. As I'm piling down that home straight, I have to dig really deep. At that point, the pain is nearly overwhelming. My legs? Completely gone. All I can think about is holding my stride. Keep going. Don't stop. Hold it for a few seconds more. Then the pain is over. You work in training so that when you're out there on the track, you're prepared for the big hurt.

This is my theory: when I first started to race, if I sat at the back and gradually picked my way through the group and comfortably finished in first place, but felt only a small amount of pain, I wouldn't be happy. Someone would come over and say, 'You won! Great result!' And I'd shrug and think, 'This isn't right. It should have hurt more.' I would feel like I hadn't put in the proper effort. Forget the result, I hadn't tried hard enough. That's why I developed this habit during races of heading to the front of the group and going crazy fast, pushing myself hard all the way to the end. As long as I felt that intense, almost overwhelming pain, then I was happy with my performance. It didn't matter if I placed first, second, third, wherever. That pain told me I'd worked hard. That I'd put in the effort. The result was meaningless. Nowadays I tend to run a more gradual race, but I'll still look to put in a hard shift and really go hard on that final lap. When I run now, I always have the sense that I can go 2 or 3 per cent harder. I can always push more. In training, I'd make it a mission to race my last repetition faster than the previous ones.

Like I said, I've never shied away from hard work.

I developed a very strong bond with Alan. He could be crazy at times, but in a good way. A bit like me, I suppose. Alan was a true curry fiend; he loved the stuff. We often went out to the local curry house in Teddington after putting in a hard session on the track. One time Alan decided that he was going to eat curry for dinner for the next two months. Just like that. He stuck to his plan too. I've no idea why he decided to do it, but that was Alan.

He also went through periods where he'd run every day, no matter what. He would set himself a target – running, say, 7, 8 or 9 miles a day, every day of the week, for a number of months. Even when his legs were sore from the daily pounding, he'd still go out for his run. His weight went down from 15 stone to around 9. To an outsider, this kind of behaviour might seem extreme, but to me it was all part of Alan's built-in determination and steely resolve, and as an athlete I responded to it. Alan had an incredible athlete's brain, an unbelievable depth of knowledge when it came to running. I could ask him about almost anyone on the athletics circuit, and straight away he'd tell me everything there was to know about them: their records, tactics and training regime.

Our relationship was less coach–athlete, more father–son. Some coaches don't like to be questioned, but Alan was never like that. We had a real dialogue. Alan appreciated the fact that I had quite strong opinions on my training needs, and if I didn't feel something was right, I'd question it rather than simply carrying on doing the same thing and letting my frustrations simmer. For a while this relationship worked perfectly. We'd often sit down and discuss sessions. Alan might want me to do longer ones, explaining why he thought that was best for me. Then I'd tell Alan that I felt

I needed to be doing shorter reps. We'd listen to each other's arguments, talk it over for a while and meet in the middle.

Alan was more than just an athletics coach. He was someone who genuinely cared about me as a human being. I always felt I could be open with Alan, that I could tell him about anything going on in my life. I was lucky – privileged – to have him as my coach.

Off the track, the lads and me had a good laugh. There was a real family spirit in our dorm. After training, a few of us would head into town for a curry. Maybe later we'd head out to the Oceana club in Kingston, dancing away until closing time, even though I had two left feet. Afterwards we'd head back to the dorm, listen to some tunes, chill out, play some video games before crashing out at two or three in the morning. Then we'd wake up at ten or eleven, earliest. Train, eat, go out again. Life for me was one big adventure. Simply having my own room was a brand-new experience. There were parties on campus. In the daytime we'd gather round the big TV in the lounge and play mammoth sessions on Pro Evo. The windows were wide open, we'd be effing and blinding at the screen and the warden who lived opposite our dorm would be shouting at us to keep the noise down.

I saw nothing wrong with this at the time. I figured it was perfectly normal for an athlete to eat junk food, go out until past midnight, come back and play video games into the small hours instead of getting the proper rest and recovery my body needed. It sounds crazy, but I was convinced that

I was training hard, putting the effort in, when in reality I wasn't giving it 100 per cent. It's funny how your brain can play tricks on you like that. It didn't matter what time I posted on a lap or what I got up to between training sessions. For me, the only thing that mattered was that I didn't miss a run.

To save up some money and fund my social life I got a job in a local sports shop – a branch of Sweatshop in Teddington. A lot of other young athletes worked there. Benedict Whitby had a job in the store's mail-order department. Sam was there too. Benedict knew I was looking for work, so he rang me up one day, asking if I was interested in a job in the warehouse. I'd worked at Pizza Hut and McDonald's and fancied upgrading my battered old Fiesta, so I thought, 'Why not?' The job involved collating envelopes and leaflets to send out marketing information to Sweatshop customers. It wasn't what you'd call challenging work, but the hours suited me just fine. Whenever they needed me over at the warehouse Benedict would give me a bell and leave a message. 'It's half-ten, son. Finish up your training. I've got a job for you. Get down here!'

After a while I switched from the warehouse to the shop floor. Working at the Sweatshop could be a good laugh, but that wasn't always the case. Sometimes I'd go out on the Friday night, come back in the early hours and wake up on Saturday, feeling shattered and knowing that I had to turn up for work at the Sweatshop that morning. Those days could be really long.

At lunchtime I'd go for a run with Benedict and Sam, but they ran insanely fast. Our usual route was through Richmond

Park, and we'd do a good 10 miles in our lunch hour. The run would start off at a good pace, then, all of a sudden, Benedict would start picking up the pace, going faster and faster. Being that little bit younger than them both, I struggled to keep up. The first time the three of us went out for a run together, I couldn't believe the pace Benedict was setting. That guy used to kill us in training; he was an absolute animal. After that I knew that training with Benedict wasn't going to be fun. It was going to hurt. My legs would be killing me by the end of a session, but I knew that was a good thing. The pain would make me a better runner.

In our first year at the centre, Alan organized a trip for the St Mary's athletes to a UKA training camp at Potchefstroom, which is about 75 miles from Johannesburg in South Africa. At 4430 feet above sea level, it's at the bottom end in terms of altitude-benefit for athletes, but it's a good intro-duction to training at altitude, and as it's only two hours ahead of the UK, it doesn't mess with your body clock. The facilities are top class, and in the winter months it's warm without being too hot. It was my first time training at altitude and I loved it. The camp had two all-weather racetracks, but we stuck to running on the grass because it was so good.

Everyone from my crowd at St Mary's went on that trip: Tom Bedford, James McIlroy . . . about a dozen of us in total. I was up to my usual tricks and games. On the Sunday evening we went into town to catch the first *Lord of the Rings* movie at the cinema. Potchefstroom is a nice white neighbourhood; I knew this at the time because I was aware of being the only black kid in the audience. All of a sudden, the power cut out. Everyone got out of their seats and started piling towards the exits. I saw my opportunity for a joke. I bolted up from my seat, ran down the aisle towards the front of the screen and started barking like a dog. I've no idea why I did that. It just seemed like a good idea at the time. Everyone in the audience started spinning around to see where the dog noises were coming from and spotted this black kid howling in front of the screen. I must have been quite a sight.

Throughout this time I still kept in touch with Alan Watkinson at St Mary's. We'd meet up for coffee and he'd sometimes come along to the campus to watch me train. Of course, he still followed my results really closely. I think both Alan and Conrad were pleased to take a back seat in terms of my career. They had helped me out a lot – Alan especially had been running around sorting things for me for years. He was probably looking forward to having a bit of a rest! He had seen me grow from a restless kid who couldn't speak much English into a determined young runner who was on the verge of racing at senior level. Life is like that. You get somewhere, suddenly everyone wants to congratulate you and take credit for your success. In your heart, you know the people who truly matter – the people without whom you couldn't have made it onto the podium in the first place. For that reason, whenever anyone asks me who the biggest influence in my life has been, I always tell them, 'My old teacher, Alan Watkinson.'

For a while back there, I was in danger of losing my way

at St Mary's. I didn't go completely off the rails, but I definitely let my focus slip from training. I was carefree. One night a bunch of us went out to Oceana. It was the usual suspects: myself, Tom Bedford, Big Frank, plus a few other lads. After I'd given a demonstration of my finest dance moves, we left the club and wandered around the streets of Kingston at gone two o'clock in the morning, six guys on the lookout for something crazy to do to make it a memorable night. It was winter and freezing cold, but as we strolled past the River Thames, one of the lads suddenly had an idea.

'Boys,' he shouted. 'I've got it . . . let's jump off the bridge!'

Everyone started cheering. Great idea! Two o'clock in the morning, freezing cold, jump in the river. Classic. Soon we were arguing over who was going to jump into the water first.

'If you do it, I'll do it,' one guy said.

'Only if you go first,' I replied.

'No, no!' Tom declared. 'Tell you what, boys. We're all going in at the same time!'

Suddenly, a few of the lads went quiet. Jumping into the Thames didn't seem like such a good idea any more. Soon everyone else had bottled out, leaving just Tom and me, who were still up for jumping off the bridge. We stripped fully naked. I handed my clothes to Big Frank and made my way to the middle of the bridge. It was a freezing night and the water looked properly cold, black and slimy. Tom and me both stopped at the edge. Well, this was it now. No going back.

We looked at each other as if to say, 'Are you really going to do this?'

Kingston Bridge is not some tiny crossing over a little stream. It's a long stone bridge that's roughly the same length as the 100-metre distance on the track. Fall over the edge and you're hitting the water with a bang. I looked down. It had to be a drop of 10 or 12 metres from the arches to the water. I didn't know what I was doing up there. I couldn't even swim properly. In the distance I could see Bushy Park. I remember shuffling further along the bridge, thinking it through in my head. 'Right, I'll aim for the edge of the river because that way I'll land closer to the bank, so I won't have as far to swim to the bank.'

We both took one final breath. One, two, three . . .

Then we jumped.

BOOOM!!!

I fell hard. Felt a sharp stinging pain hit me, like someone had slapped me across the chest. I'd hit the water flat. I saw black for a moment. Couldn't tell which way was up or down. The water was like ice. Then I came up for air. I looked around for Tom. He'd crashed into the water a metre or so away from me. I started flapping around, while up on the bridge Big Frank and the other lads were killing themselves with laughter, leaning over the arches and waving down at us both. At that point one of the boys pointed somewhere down the bridge and shouted, 'LOOK! POLICE! LEG IT!'

In a panic, Tom and me both swam frantically towards the edge of the river. Tom was a much better swimmer than me; I arrived at the bank after him, my arms splashing water all over the place. We climbed out, dripping wet and stark naked, and raced in the opposite direction from the police, using our hands to shield our privates. Big Frank still had our clothes. My teeth were chattering from the cold. I was dripping wet and chilled to the bone. Steering clear of the main road, we legged it as fast as we could down this dimly lit footpath. Then we found some thick bushes and decided to hide in them. We must have stayed hidden there for a good fifteen minutes before Big Frank and the rest of the boys showed up, laughing out loud. Tom turned to me and growled, 'Those bastards are winding us up!'

Big Frank chucked us our clothes. We quickly got dressed and headed back to the campus before the police showed up for real.

The next day I hopped on a flight to Boulder, Colorado, where I was due to train at a high-altitude training camp. I didn't feel too good at check-in. By the time I got off the plane, I was feeling properly ill. I was coughing loads. My body was sore all over. I had the chills. I couldn't even turn my head to the left or right because my neck muscles were badly strained. For the whole week I felt really bad and did as little running as I could get away with. I tried to hide my symptoms from the other guys at the camp, but one or two caught me having a coughing fit and asked what was wrong. I just muttered something about coming down with a cold. I left out the bit about jumping off a bridge into a freezing cold river in the middle of the night.

Throughout my time at St Mary's I stayed in touch with

Tania. We had remained close friends after leaving school, spending time around each other. That closeness between us – it was always there. Around this time I picked up an injury that prevented me from running. As part of my rehabilitation I had to do regular sessions of something called aqua-jogging. This basically involves performing a low-impact running motion in a pool. It's a good way to keep your fitness level up without putting pressure on the muscles and risking aggravating the injury. Tania offered to come along with me and do the aqua-jogging together. She'd stopped running by this time, but because we were such good friends she wanted to help me out and knew I would get bored going down to the pool by myself. As we still lived near to each other, we got into a routine of meeting up somewhere between our homes in the evening. Then we'd jump on a bus together and head down to the swimming pool, listening to Tupac tunes on my iPod, one earphone in my ear, Tania listening through the other earphone. Tupac was our favourite artist. By the time we got to the pool it was late in the evening and the place was deserted. Often we'd be the only ones there. The two of us aqua-jogging together. At the end of the session we'd hop on the bus again. Ride home. Listen to some more Tupac. Being injured is never fun, but hanging out with Tania made it manageable.

In the spring of 2003, I learnt that Hassan, my twin, was getting married. We had managed to speak on the phone a few times, although getting hold of him was fraught with difficulties. He had moved into a house with Mum and a few relatives, and he now worked as a mechanic at a local garage. I had to smile at that. I'd had my heart set on being a mechanic as a kid, whereas Hassan had never really given it a moment's thought. It's funny how things work out sometimes.

As soon as I heard the good news, I knew that I had to fly to Hargeisa, to be there with my family, to see my twin brother get married.

I was going back to Somaliland for the first time in sixteen years.

8
GOING BACK

HASSAN'S wedding was good timing as far as I was concerned. I'd been thinking for a while that I needed a break from the track. I'd made lots of friends at St Mary's, had some happy memories of my time there, but the truth of it was that during the first half of 2003 I'd lost some of my enthusiasm for running. That season I placed seventy-fourth overall in the World Championship Cross Country in Switzerland and finished second in the 5000 metres in the European Junior Championships in Bydgoszcz, Poland – the same race I'd won two years before in Grosseto, Italy. Chris Thompson won the race. My results had nothing to do with Alan Storey. For whatever reason, my heart just wasn't in it. More than anything, I needed a break.

First, though, I needed to save up for a plane ticket. Flying to Somalia wasn't cheap. The airport at Mogadishu had been closed down since the civil war began, meaning I'd have to fly to Djibouti City, then catch a chartered plane across the border to Hargeisa. I wasn't exactly rolling in cash. I had my lottery funding, which covered my basic costs, like food and kit. I also had a bit of sponsorship money, but that was about it. To earn more I pulled extra shifts at the Sweatshop, working at the weekends and fitting in extra hours whenever I could. It was tough, combining my training with all the hours at the shop. But eventually I had saved enough – about £500 – to buy a return ticket to Djibouti City. There was just enough left over to pay for my onward flight to Hargeisa, plus some wedding present money for Hassan and his bride-to-be.

My last race of the season took place on 8 August. I was competing at the Norwich Union Grand Prix at Crystal Palace in the 5000 metres; I came home in ninth place: 13:38.41. I'd already told Alan Storey that I'd be going home for Hassan's wedding. He was cool about it, and anyway, it was the end of the athletics season so I was due a break. The plan was, I'd go home for a couple of weeks, rest, see my family, and be back in time for the start of the cross country season.

The next day I flew out of Heathrow.

I flew minus my hair. Sporting plaits in Somaliland was a big no-no. The tradition for Somali men is to keep their hair cropped short and to grow a beard. With plaits and no beard, I'd stand out like a sore thumb around Hargeisa, so I decided the hair had to come off before I saw my family. Out came the clippers, off came the hair. After that, it just seemed easier to keep my head shaved rather than grow it again.

On arrival in Djibouti City, I caught a charter plane to Hargeisa Airport. When I boarded the plane I couldn't believe it. There were no seat belts and condensation was dripping from the cabin ceiling onto the passengers. After a shaky journey, we landed in Hargeisa and I got off the aircraft and looked around. All I remember is Hassan coming up to me, giving me a big hug and a kiss on my cheek and saying, 'My brother, my brother, my brother!'

Twelve years is a long time to be away from someone you love. It's hard to describe the joy of that moment. It felt like a part of me had been missing the whole time I had been growing up separately from Hassan. The way I see it is, we're not different people – we're part of the same person. At last, the void in my life was gone.

All I could think was, 'It's been so long. So many years.' And yet in all that time Hassan had never been far from my thoughts. I knew he would've been thinking about me a lot too. Seeing him again filled me with this sense that things were complete now. The fact that our mum was there too made it even more special. Now the three of us were together again I had this feeling that there was nothing else for me in life. The rest of it – athletics, races, my time at St Mary's – it had all seemed really important before. But standing there at the airport, I realized that all I'd ever truly wanted was to be with my family. Now they were here, I didn't want or need anything else.

I was truly happy.

So happy, in fact, that I ended up spending two months there.

There was so much to catch up on. Hassan explained that everyone in the family had been following my athletics career. You'd be surprised what people have out there. Most homes have got some kind of satellite dish that can pick up thousands of channels. People in Hargeisa probably have more TV channels to choose from than anyone in Britain! If they couldn't follow me on TV, they'd tune in to the BBC World Service for Somalia and wait for the news broadcast. People did whatever they could to keep track of my results. I was touched. That meant a lot to me, the fact that people in Somalia were taking pride in my achievements. Hassan, in particular, has followed my career very closely. To this day, he can list my time and position in just about every race I've competed in since my junior days.

Being able to be around Hassan again was such a wonderful feeling. In a way, it was like I'd never left. We instantly clicked. That was the strength of the bond between us. We hadn't seen each other for more than ten years, and then to be able to meet up and resume our friendship like we'd never been apart – it was amazing. We even got back into the habit of wearing each other's clothes. We still had the same build, and almost everything Hassan owned fitted me nicely.

Some things had changed, though. The city was mostly peaceful, but the long-running civil war meant that inflation had gone through the roof. I remember changing a small amount of US dollars and getting back this massive wedge of Somaliland shillings. It was like lugging around a brick. I saw people carrying shopping bags of money when they went out to the markets.

Hassan had changed in some ways. He now had scars across his body from an accident he'd been involved in not long after I left Djibouti to live in England. One sweltering hot day Hassan and a friend had stumbled upon this strange object lying at the side of the road. They didn't approach it because it looked like a bomb, but Hassan being Hassan, he decided to find out whether it *was* a bomb by hurling rocks at it from the other side of the road. His first couple of attempts landed wide and short. The third rock hit the target. The bomb exploded and a huge boom echoed around the street. Hassan, just a few metres away, was blasted with hot bits of shrapnel, smoke and dust.

He spent the next fortnight in hospital recovering from his injuries. The doctors decided against removing the shrapnel – it was too risky – so Hassan still has bits of metal embedded in his body to this day. Every time he goes through an airport metal detector he sets the machine off big time. I listened to this story and was like, 'No way!' Even I never did anything as nuts as that.

Other things were different too. Like the fact that Hassan now chewed *qaat*, a plant that's supposed to give you a bit of a buzz. All grown-up Somalis chew this stuff. It's like a mark of becoming an adult. You find *qaat* in a lot of countries in East Africa and in most Arab countries too. Some people see it as a drug, although for Somalis and Muslims generally, it's a social thing, like drinking coffee or having a beer in a pub in England. I couldn't help noticing that Hassan was chewing on this big ball of *qaat*. I asked him what it tasted like and he immediately offered me a bundle to chew for myself. I sort of hesitated.

'Try it, *walaalaha*,' Hassan said. 'Everyone is doing it now.'

'I don't know,' I said. 'I don't think it's all that good for you.'

'How do you know until you've tried it?'

I shrugged. Okay, I thought, why not? I wanted to see what all the fuss was about. I took a small bundle of leaves from Hassan and chewed on them for a bit. I didn't notice any difference at first. Then I put my head down to sleep – and I couldn't. My eyes were popped wide open. *Qaat* has this weird effect on your brain. You feel relaxed and happy for no real reason. Your mind starts to wander. You stare at the ceiling all night, thinking about random stuff. It makes you want to do things. You start getting ideas. I remember lying in bed, looking up at the ceiling and thinking to myself, 'Yeah, I'm gonna build this and do that . . .'

The following day I woke up with this fog behind my eyes. I hadn't slept a wink. I rubbed my eyes, climbed out of bed and headed into the kitchen. My mum was there, making pancakes for breakfast. I yawned. Mum took one look at me, pulled a face and said, 'What's wrong with your eyes? They're all big and bloodshot.'

'Nothing,' I said weakly. 'Nothing at all, Mum. I'm fine.'

Hassan and his bride, Hoda, tied the knot at a colourful ceremony held in a rented hall in the city. It was a beautiful day. Hoda – her name means 'lucky' in Somali – also happened to be a twin, although Hassan told me this wasn't a coincidence. He'd always wanted to father twins when he got married, and believed he'd stand a better chance of doing so if he married one. They now have six kids – five girls and a boy – but no twins. Hassan insisted on all of the girls having names beginning with 'H' – just like their mum and dad. Typical crazy Hassan.

Two days after the wedding ceremony, Hassan and Hoda invited all their friends on a bus tour, a chance to travel through rural Somaliland, sharing memories and taking pictures of the happy couple. The bus would stop every so often, and we'd all get off, take out our cameras and have a bite to eat. The journey took us all the way from the city to the mountain peaks, thousands of metres above sea level. The scenery was amazing. I'd never seen Somaliland from high up. We had a great laugh. Hassan and Hoda looked truly in love. I was so happy for him – for them both. Despite all that had happened, he was building a life for himself in Hargeisa, and I was doing the same in Britain. As night folded in we rode the bus back to Hargeisa: Hassan, Hoda, me, all their friends.

It was the second wedding I'd been to in the space of a few months. Alan Watkinson also got married that same year. He'd invited me and my cousin Mahad up for the wedding. In the space of a few months two of the people closest to me had gotten married. It was a great feeling. As a gift, I presented Alan with a poster, a huge blown-up photograph of me winning my first English Schools Cross Country aged thirteen. In the photo I'm wearing a club vest over a baggy jumper, and gloves to warm my fingers against the cold. The expression on my face is a mix of pain and grit and determination. At the bottom of the photograph I wrote a message for Alan: 'What you have done for me will never be forgotten.'

Athletics took a back seat while I was in Somaliland. It just felt so good to be back with my family. Two weeks went by in the blink of an eye, so when the day came for me to return to the UK, I suddenly decided that I wasn't going to leave. Not for a while longer. I'd been away from Hassan and my mum so long, all I wanted to do was stay in Hargeisa. I made no effort to contact Alan Storey and tell him about my change of heart. Couldn't have told him, even if I wanted to. My mobile didn't function in Hargeisa because I was using a pay-as-you-go SIM that only worked in the UK. I never checked my email. I pushed all thoughts about athletics and St Mary's and running to the back of my head and just enjoyed being around my family.

I did go out for a run once. I remember it being a blazing hot day. The temperature was in the high thirties, but it was still quite early and I thought, 'I should probably go for a run before I get too out of shape.' I got dressed, put on my running shoes and bolted out of the front door. Almost as soon as I started running through the streets, a bunch of kids started chasing after me. They were laughing and shouting, 'Hey, hey! Crazy man! You crazy, man!' As I said earlier, people don't run in Somaliland. I was the only guy going out for a run, so I stopped and went back home. After that, I didn't bother running again while I was there.

The good feeling lasted for two months. That was the happiest I'd been in a long while. If someone had offered me a job right there and then, I would've been seriously tempted to take it. The way I saw it, I had my family, I was happy and I didn't need anything else. I didn't want for anything in life. But deep down I knew I couldn't stay in Hargeisa. It was a dream, that was all. My life in Britain was pulling me back. I had my scholarship at St Mary's. I was starting out in athletics. I owed it to myself to see how far I could go as an athlete. I wanted to make my country, and my family, proud. As much as I dreamt about staying on in Hargeisa for good, Britain was my home now. I had to go back. In October I said goodbye to Hassan and my mum and everyone else.

When I returned home and explained to Alan Storey why I'd been away for so long, he was fine about it. He knew that I hadn't seen my brother in many years; knew what it meant for me to go back to Somaliland. There was no anger from Alan, no lectures about going AWOL. 'Did you at least stick to your training programme?' he asked.

'Yeah, yeah,' I lied, not wanting to disappoint him. 'I went running every day.'

By this point it had been a full eight weeks since I'd done any training. But it was the off-season, there were no big races coming up for a while and I figured a few hard sessions in training and I'd soon be in good form for the upcoming cross country season. That plan went out of the window in my very first training session. I went for a run and imme-diately felt this intense pain flare up in my right knee. It seems obvious that the pain was related to the fact that I hadn't been training. But no way could I admit to Alan that I hadn't done a run for the best part of two months. At first I tried running through the pain. Sometimes you get these aches and strains that go away once you get into your stride. But this pain was different. It persisted, flaring up every time I went for a run. I'd feel okay to begin with, and then four or five minutes into the session my knee would explode in agony. The pain wouldn't go away, no matter how hard I tried to run through it. And I have a high pain threshold; I can run through most things, but this pain was on another level. I didn't know what to do. I knew I couldn't tell Alan about not training in Somalia because I felt like I had let him down. On Neil Black's advice I stopped training and went for some scans to get to the root of the problem. Nothing showed up.

The medical experts tried everything. Neil was as stumped as the rest of us. My knee was explored repeatedly, but no matter what tests they ran, the answers that came back were the same: the knee was fine. There was nothing wrong with it. To this day, no one can be sure what caused that sudden knee pain. We could never get to the root of it. I tried to go out for a run again. The knee flared. I gritted my teeth through the pain. The knee screamed. I ran some more. It went on like this for a while. Agonizing runs, physio, more tests, no answer. And then, just like that, the pain stopped. I breathed a huge sigh of relief. Now I could go back to running.

But the knee wasn't the only thing interfering with my running. Mentally, I was distracted. For months after I'd returned to St Mary's, my mind kept drifting back to Hargeisa and the beautiful days I'd spent with Hassan and my mum. I'm sure Alan could see that I was a little distant, that my mind was elsewhere. People couldn't get through to me. Flying back to Somaliland had been a life-changing experience for me. Now I was back in the UK, I didn't have the same hunger for athletics. All I could think about was my family. I still put in the effort training and competing in races. But, if I'm honest, I was on autopilot for almost a year after my trip. I was going through the motions. The knee injury affected my training, I missed a large part of the winter cross country season, and maybe my motivation suffered as a result.

In mid-April 2004 I flew out to the UKA camp in Potchefstroom for some warm-weather training. Among the other athletes there were Sam Haughian, Anthony Whiteman and Neil Speaight. Anthony had competed at the Olympic Games in Atlanta and Sydney; Neil was a talented middle-distance runner who competed for Belgrave Harriers, the best athletics club in the Premiership. Sam was getting ready to compete for Great Britain in the 5000 metres at the Athens Olympics. He'd missed much of the previous track season because of injury, but big things were expected of him going into the Games. The year before he got injured, Sam had the best season of his career. He came second in the 5000 metres at the Spar European Cup in Florence, and finished fifth in the Commonwealth Games in Manchester, beating Craig Mottram, the Australian, when he clocked the 5000 with a time of 13:19.45. Sam was that good.

Potchefstroom didn't hold a lot of happy memories for Sam. The training camp is based in the grounds of North-West University. You have the camp on one side and the university buildings on the other, with Thabo Mbeki Way slicing down the middle. The first time Sam attended the camp a big bunch of us went out in the afternoon for a run on the grass around the campus, a good 10 kilometres. At a certain point, the group decided to head back, but Sam kept on running even though the light was fading. He was going at a good speed when suddenly he saw this pole, one end of a chain-link fence that had been partially taken down, just in front of him. Sam jumped over the pole to avoid crashing into it, but he jumped too late and the sharp tip of the pole gashed the inside of his thigh. He fell to the ground, blood pouring from the wound. Luckily, some exchange students happened to be camping nearby. They heard Sam's cries for help and managed to get him to hospital. The surgeon who operated on him said afterwards that if the gash had been a centimetre longer either way, he wouldn't have been able to save him. Sam came *that* close to dying.

During my stay in April, I could see that something wasn't quite right about Sam. I didn't know what was bothering him, but he wasn't his usual bubbly self. He seemed a little quiet, a bit down, like he had something on his mind. On the Friday evening, Sam and his physiotherapist, Rebecca Wills, drove down to Johannesburg while the rest of us stayed in Potchefstroom. I went to bed, wondering what had been on Sam's mind and looking forward to going for a run with him the next day.

Late that night we learned that Sam had been involved in a car accident. He was being treated at a hospital in Johannesburg. They said his condition was critical. They didn't know if he was going to make it. Rebecca had also been injured and was being treated for her injuries at the same unit. Crazy as it might sound, it didn't occur to me that Sam's life might be in danger. I remember thinking, 'Has he broken his leg? Is he going to have to miss the Olympics? Sam will be so disappointed. He's trained so hard to get to Athens.' Then we got the dreaded news that none of us wanted to hear.

Sam had died of his injuries. The news came as a complete shock. I felt cold and stunned, like someone had punched me in the guts. Sam was dead. I simply couldn't believe it. None of us could. It was like something out of a nightmare. Sam was the brightest runner among us, and suddenly he wasn't there any more.

Sam had grown up not far from me in Feltham. I'd met his mum a few times. I felt terrible for his parents. I realized they must be going through hell back in the UK. I wished I could do something to help, but in that situation you feel utterly helpless.

When the police asked for someone based at the training camp to go down to Johannesburg and identify the body, Anthony Whiteman, Neil Speaight and I volunteered. It seemed the right thing to do – the very least we could do. Early in the morning, the three of us drove to the city and made our way to the hospital. It was the longest journey of my life.

When I saw Sam lying there in the hospital, the first thing that went through my head was that I wanted to wake him up. I kept waiting for him to open his eyes and say something. But he didn't. His eyes stayed clamped shut. So many things were going through my head. I wanted to know more about what had happened. Where, when, how, why? It didn't seem possible. One minute we had been joking and laughing, talking about the future. Then all of a sudden, Sam was gone.

He was just twenty-four years old.

Anthony, Neil and me drove back to Potchefstroom in silence. The camp was eerie. Everyone was devastated by the news. None of us wanted to stay for a moment longer. We wanted to go home.

For the longest time I didn't want to talk about what had happened. I didn't say anything to anyone. Not to Alan or my friends or my family. But not talking about it didn't help. The only way you can deal with stuff like that is by talking. Gradually, I started to talk about it with people close to me, to try to come to terms with it. I didn't want to admit it at first, but Sam's death affected me deeply.

The hardest thing of all was accepting that life goes on. I found that really hard to take. I'd always imagined that when people died, life was never the same any more. But it doesn't work that way. The rest of the world goes on without you. It doesn't matter who you are or where you come from. For a time, everything felt different, but then slowly things started returning to normal. That was actually the scariest part for me. I'd see Sam's younger brother Tim around the club and instantly I'd be transported back to that night in Potchefstroom.

In the end, I realized that life is precious – that you don't have any control over certain things, and all you can do in this life is to try to be kind and decent to those around you.

To be a good person, to do the best you can. Sam was a brilliant young athlete. More than that, he was one of the nicest guys in athletics. That's the memory I have of Sam. I've tried my best to follow his example.

I still kept in touch with Tania. Our lives were pulling us in different directions, but we were still close and we still found time to chat on the phone – these long conversations talking about nothing really, like you do at that age. A year or two into my time at St Mary's I dropped hints to Tania, about the way I felt about her. I remember us talking on the phone one evening as I was getting ready to fly out to yet another training camp. I said something about wanting to pack Tania in my suitcase and take her everywhere I went. Anyway, it didn't happen. I didn't feel any resentment over it. I was just happy to be friends. I still dropped in on Tania, popping round to her house and chatting with Bob and Nadia. Tania had a boyfriend at the time, but regardless of that fact, I always had what I like to call the sweet spot for her. And Tania knew how I felt, even if I hesitated to express it. One evening in early 2005 I went over to her place for a chat. We did our usual thing. Sitting around, listening to some tunes. I didn't know it at the time, but Tania was pregnant. The fact that she didn't tell me was nothing to do with shame or anything like that. Tania simply didn't want to hurt my feelings. She didn't feel the same way about me as I did about her, and she knew that if I learned she was having a baby with someone else I'd be disappointed – because that would mean things might never happen between us. Actually, I didn't find out that Tania was pregnant until she gave birth to Rhianna that summer. None of this altered my feelings towards Tania. We kept in touch after Rhianna had been born, although shortly after that we might only speak once in a blue moon. Partly that was the stress of motherhood for Tania. Partly it was down to my training commitments and travelling. For a couple of years, things simply got in the way.

For a while after Sam died, training felt weird. I needed something to focus on, something to take my mind off Potchefstroom. The next big meet on the horizon was the 2005 European Under-23 Championships, which were taking place in Erfurt, Germany, in July. I felt good about my prospects going into the Under-23s. My times had been good in training, I'd put my knee problems behind me and I'd improved my 5000 metres personal best to 13:30.53. Earlier that year I finished sixth in the European Indoor Championships in Madrid in a personal best 7:54.08. At the Under-23 championships two years earlier in Poland, Chris Thompson had beaten me into second place. This time I was determined to win.

Erfurt was a wake-up call. I was way off the pace, finishing 4 seconds behind the winner, Anatoliy Rybakov of Russia, in 14:10.96. It didn't feel like it at the time, but losing in Erfurt was the best thing that could have happened to me. The disappointment of that defeat stung me to the core and helped to focus my mind. I flew home from Germany, thinking that something had to change.

My results in 2005 were a real mixed bag. I was trying

to make the step up from the juniors to the senior ranks and was quickly finding out that there was a big difference between the two. My first race for Great Britain had been at the World Cross Country Championships in St Etienne-St Galmier, France. I finished in thirty-seventh place in a field dominated by Kenyans, Eritreans and Ethiopians. There was also a bunch of Kenyan athletes who'd switched to Qatari nationality, which made the field even stronger.

Personally, I'm against fast-tracking the naturalization of athletes. I don't blame the runners – these guys have families to feed, and athletics careers are notoriously fragile and short-lived. It's hard for some of them to make the Kenyan team, simply because there are so many good runners in Kenya. If they go to Qatar, they can make enough money to look after their family, have a good life, and compete in the Olympics and the World Championships. But I believe the countries themselves shouldn't be allowed to naturalize athletes so easily. If you want to run for Qatar or Bahrain, you should be expected to live in that country for a number of years before becoming eligible. At the moment you have guys who are running for Kenya one minute and appearing at the Worlds for Qatar the next. That isn't right.

It would be a lie to say that East Africans weren't totally dominating the field. I saw it in competitions, and I saw it in training too. Every Sunday a few of the lads and me would do a hill session in Richmond Park. We'd meet up at Ham Common and do sessions up and down the incline just inside Ham Gate. The sun would be out, people would be jogging or walking their dogs, and the swans would be floating on the lake. Then the Kenyans would rush past us, this blur of colour tearing up the incline at a ridiculously fast pace. I'd glance at Scott Overall or Abdi Ali. We were all thinking exactly the same thing: 'Man, these guys are *gooooood*.'

The problem I faced was the same one that had affected any aspiring British or European distance runner over the past several years. From early on in my athletics career there was this general belief that the Kenyans were so far ahead of the rest of the competition that they couldn't be beaten. None of my coaches ever told me this. It's just something you absorb from a young age. The mentality at the time sort of said, 'The Kenyans are too good and you'll never beat them. The best you can do is finish fourth and just enjoy yourself.' It's the equivalent of a football team entering the World Cup and on the eve of their first game the coach telling the players: 'We'll never beat Brazil, so let's just beat the teams below us and hope for the best.' Then they meet Brazil in the quarter-final and they lose – because they expect to lose.

I started thinking to myself, 'How do I beat these guys?'

At the same time, I was ready to move out of St Mary's campus. I'd given up my studies at the college in Richmond and enrolled on a sports massage therapy course at the university. I figured that it was at least related to my career. Once I finished that course, I was ready for a change of scenery. Some of the lads had moved on. Lee had gone home to Burnley. I was sad to see him go. At the time I didn't think he was leaving for good. I thought, 'Yeah, he'll come back.' He never did, which was a shame. Lee had the talent to be a major force in cross country running, but a career in athletics isn't for everyone. You have to make a lot of sacrifices. The training is hard, painful and often boring. You miss your friends. You miss your family. At the lower end of the scale, the money isn't great. You can get injured, and even if you're supremely talented and hard-working, it doesn't always pan out. Malcolm Hassan had gone to do a sports scholarship at Utah Valley University in the US. For whatever reason, it didn't quite happen for him out there. James McIlroy fared better. He clocked 1:44.65 in the 800 metres in Rieti, Italy, after leaving St Mary's, finished fourth in the European Championships and competed for Britain in the Olympic Games, World Championships and three Commonwealth Games.

With guys like Lee and James leaving, a new intake of athletes arrived to take their places at the centre. Suddenly, I was one of the older guys. The new kids were doing the things that I'd already done when I first started at St Mary's: going on nights out to Kingston, staying up all night, going to fancy-dress parties. I felt I'd done all that stuff already, and the thought of doing it all over again didn't really appeal to me. Most of all, I was beginning to understand that I needed to calm down if I was serious about competing at the highest level. With that in mind, I took the decision to leave the campus and live somewhere else. I felt that a change of environment would be good for me. The only problem I had now was: where am I going to live?

I mentioned to my agent Ricky that I was looking for

somewhere to live. 'Well, Mo,' he said after he'd given it some thought. 'Why don't you try living with the Kenyans?'

I should explain. PACE represented numerous Kenyan athletes. Whenever they were competing in Europe, they would stay two to six weeks at a time in a house on a leafy road in Teddington. The idea of living there had never occurred to me before, but the more I started to think about it, the more it made sense. I had always been curious about what the Kenyans were doing differently that made them so much faster in competition.

'There's a room free at the house,' Ricky explained. 'The rent is cheap. It'll be a great chance for you to see how the Kenyans live and train. It might open up your eyes a little, Mo.'

The truth of it is, I wasn't fulfilling my potential on the track. And it wasn't down to my coaching or my race tactics. It was down to me not training to the same high standards as the Kenyans. Staying there was a chance for me to live like them, to do the same things. I didn't need any more convincing.

I said, 'When can I move in?'

It would turn out to be a life-changing decision.

9
EAT, SLEEP, TRAIN, REST

Fʀᴏᴍ the outside, the house where the Kenyans stay isn't much to look at. It's set on a leafy, tree-lined street in Teddington and looks like every other house in the road. Inside, though, it was a different story: it was home to some of the most talented Kenyan athletes in the world, and they had very clear ideas about how to eat, sleep, train and rest. From late 2005 for the best part of eighteen months, I lived and trained at the Kenyan house. It's a special place for me because it's where the Kenyans showed me how to live like a professional athlete. How to dedicate myself fully to athletics.

The list of people who stayed at the house throughout the year reads like a who's-who of Kenyan distance runners: Olympic Champions Noah Ngeny, William Tanui, Joseph Keter; World Champions and World record holders like Moses Kiptanui, Daniel Komen, Benjamin Limo, John Kibowen, Saif Saaeed Shaheen, Jackline Maranga, Sally Barsosio and Sammy Kipketer; Commonwealth Champions like Laban Rotich. The list goes on and on. In my first year I would see Colin Jackson, Kelly Holmes and Paula Radcliffe popping in to get treatment from the physio, Gerard Hartmann, who worked from the house during the summer. Living among these guys was an eye-opening experience, and it took some getting used to.

The first evening after I moved in, I remember getting ready to head out to the cinema with some mates. I went downstairs to see if any of the Kenyans wanted to come along. To my surprise, they were getting ready to go to bed. I looked at my watch. It was half past eight. I was like, 'No way can they be calling it a night already! It's still very early.' I left, met up with my friends. Came home about midnight. The lights were out. Everyone was asleep.

I was woken up at 6 a.m. by the sound of church music. Now, I'm not a morning guy at the best of times. Rolling out of bed at 9.30 or 10.00 a.m. – that was more my thing. Imagine my surprise when I cracked open my eyes, saw that it was still dark outside and the house was filled with the sound of a choir singing hymns to a blaring organ accompaniment. It was like waking up on the set of *Songs of Praise*.

The Kenyans went out for their first run early. They'd be up, dressed and out the front door no later than 7 a.m. They believed it was best to get the first run out of the way nice and early, when your head is clear and your body is nicely rested. Their main route was through Bushy Park. I remember shaking my groggy head clear and staggering out of bed to join them on a run. The Kenyans trained hard. And I mean really *hard*. Those first sessions, I bust a gut trying to keep up with them. By the end of the session I was knackered. After the run they spent forty-five minutes doing stretches, taking a few strides to warm down. I'd never warmed down for that amount of time. After our first training session, we went back home and the guys would rustle up some food. The Kenyans didn't go in for Tesco Value lasagnes or McDonald's burgers. They cooked simple, home-grown foods in these massive pots, typical Kenyan staples like *ugali*, a maize flour mix rolled into a doughy lump and cooked in a pot, served up with a stew or sauce to dip it in. This was new to me; I'd never tried it before. Kenyan runners swear by *ugali*: it's loaded with the carbohydrates that distance runners need.

After food, they'd sleep. In the afternoon, they trained again. In the evenings they ate, rested and went to bed early. They did this every day. It was a question of doing whatever the body needed in order to properly rest and recover from training. Late nights were harmful because they didn't give the body enough time to recover between one session and the next. It was an almost monk-like existence.

For entertainment, the Kenyans used to play chess. There was no proper chessboard, so they made one from a piece of cardboard and used bottle caps for the pieces. I'd never played chess before moving in with them. John Kibowen taught me how to play. He beat me every time. In the evenings they used to watch running videos. That's all they ever did. No TV shows, no comedy, no movies. Just videos of old Olympic races, the Golden League (nowadays called the Diamond League). At first I couldn't understand it. All I wanted to do after a hard day's training was go out to town or play some Pro Evo. Something – anything – to take my mind off running. But as I watched the Kenyans gathering around the TV to watch old races, it hit me just how little I knew about running compared to these guys. They took their athletics seriously. Running was their life. Their dedication was 100 per cent. It was eat, sleep, train, rest. Day in, day out.

My attitude didn't change instantly. The way these guys trained exploded a few myths that I'd grown up with. But it didn't take long for the penny to drop. I remember going out for a run one morning with John Kibowen, Benjamin Limo and Sammy Kipketer. (I should explain: none of the other athletes was based at the house all year round. Once the season in Europe was over and they had no more races to compete in, the guys would return to Kenya, so there was a high turnaround in the house. Kibowen and Kipketer might base themselves at the house for five or six weeks. When they were done racing, they'd fly back to the training camp run in Kaptagat, in the Kenyan Rift Valley, and their rooms in the house would be taken by, say, Boniface Songok and Micah Kogo – a younger runner who was beginning to make a name for himself on the circuit by winning several road races in Europe. A few months later, Kibowen and Kipketer would return to the house from Kaptagat, and so on.)

After training and a lengthy warm-down the four of us returned home. I was thinking, 'Yeah, I'll go out tonight.' I was getting ready to go when Kibowen slapped on a video of an old Golden League meeting. I can recall sitting on the living room sofa, itching to go out and have some fun with the boys. Suddenly I asked myself, 'For real, what am I doing here?' Here I am sharing a house with the guys I'm supposed to be competing against in track races and cross country championships. But while they're watching races, learning about different race tactics and events, I'm getting ready for a night out in Kingston. What was I thinking? How could I ever hope to beat the Kenyans in a race, if I wasn't taking my career as seriously as they did? 'If I want to beat these guys,' I told myself, 'then I've got to do exactly what they're doing.'

It was like a switch had been turned on inside my head. Like that, I knew what I had to do to win. I would have to work even harder than before. No more late-night trips to the cinema or dancing at Oceana. No more jumping off bridges. I couldn't be doing with any of that. Not unless I was happy finishing fifth or sixth for the rest of my career. And no way would I ever be happy with that.

It wouldn't be easy. I knew that much. If it was easy, so the argument goes, then everyone would be a distance runner. But now I was willing to go that extra distance. I didn't just want to be the number one British runner. I wanted to be the best distance runner in the world.

From that day on my attitude changed completely. I went to bed early. I trained hard. I ate more healthily. I took naps in the afternoon after running through Bushy Park. I got in plenty of rest. I drank water, which I never used to do: I used to drink tea. I would have six or seven cups a day, taken with three or four lumps of sugar. Water didn't taste good to me. I was like, 'Who drinks this stuff? Tea is way better.' On race days at the club, Conrad used to tell me to make sure I drank lots of water before the race. If the conditions were hot, I might have a few sips. That was my limit. I might have been dehydrated during the odd race, but I was so used to not drinking water that I never really noticed it.

The late nights I'd enjoyed at St Mary's were a thing of the past. I even changed my mobile phone number so that people couldn't get hold of me and tempt me into going out. It was a bold decision, but the way I saw it, I didn't have any choice. I had to make the running work. What else was I going to do? I had no back-up plan, no qualifications for anything else. It was running or nothing.

Around this time I had also switched athletics clubs, moving from Windsor Slough Eton & Hounslow, who were in Division One, to the Premiership club Newham & Essex Beagles. I'd had great fun at Windsor and made some really good friends at the club, but I felt there simply wasn't enough of a challenge in Division One for me to keep improving as an athlete. In contrast, there were some really tough competitors in the Premiership. The strongest club in the country was Belgrave Harriers, based in Wimbledon and with eleven Premiership titles to their name. Their alumni included the likes of Philips Idowu, the triple jumper from Hackney who competed in the Olympic Games in Beijing and the World Championships, winning gold in Berlin in 2009 to add to the gold he won in the Commonwealth Games in Melbourne in 2006. As well as Belgrave there were clubs like Birchfield Harriers and Shaftesbury Barnet. For me, competing for Newham & Essex was a step up in competition. The field was full of top-class athletes who'd represented Great Britain at various levels. The club members included the likes of Christine Ohuruogu, the 400 metres specialist who later won gold in the event in Beijing as well as gold in two World Championships, Osaka in 2007 and Moscow in 2013. The change of club scene was exactly what I needed.

In training I started keeping up with the Kenyans, matching them. It got me thinking, 'If I can match these guys in training, then why can't I do it in competition?' It wasn't long before I had a chance to find out. The following March, 2006, I was selected to run for Great Britain in the Commonwealth Games in Melbourne, Australia. This was my first major outdoor senior track event representing my country. I couldn't wait to get out there and race.

There's a question mark over every athlete making the step up to the senior level. People are watching you and thinking, 'This guy might have posted some good results in the juniors, but can he do the same in the seniors?' Until you do it, the doubts don't go away. I was conscious of the same question mark hanging over me when I flew out to Melbourne two months ahead of the games in order to acclimatize. I would be staying at a house owned by Nic Bideau, Sonia O'Sullivan's partner. Nic was also an athletics coach – he used to manage Cathy Freeman, and at the time I travelled to Melbourne he was looking after Craig Mottram.

Craig was a big deal at the time, one of the stars of the 5000 metres. He'd already competed in the 2000 Olympics, running in front of a home crowd in Sydney at the age of just twenty. A few months before I flew out to Australia I'd watched Craig win bronze in the 5000 metres at the World Championships in Helsinki. Watching that race, I was like, 'Woah!' For a white guy to finish in the medal places ahead of the likes of John Kibowen and Eliud Kipchoge, another great Kenyan runner, was an incredible feat. White guys simply weren't supposed to beat the Africans on the track. The Kenyans called him 'Big Mzungo' – Big White Man. In a way, Craig's achievement in Helsinki eclipsed that of my Kenyan training partner Benjamin Limo in winning the gold. It made a lot of other athletes – me included – sit up and take notice. Here was someone special.

I already knew Craig a little before the training camp in Melbourne. During the summer, for European meetings, he would base himself in Teddington, same as the Kenyans. I'd often see him at Kingsmeadow running track in Kingston. Alan Storey would take me over there on Tuesday afternoons for a session, and Craig would be there too, training under Nic. Because of the connection between Alan, Sonia and Nic, I'd sometimes join in with Craig. Not often, just once or twice. I was curious. Here was a guy who'd put himself on the distance-running map. He'd done good things at 5000 metres and I wanted to know what his training was like, what he did differently from me. I've always thought, no matter how good you are as an athlete, you can always learn something new, always get better. It's part of my job. I'm always interested in what other athletes are up to – what they're doing in training and why. These guys are my competition, after all. It's my responsibility to know what each and every one of them is capable of. Craig was one of the guys I looked up to. I was a bit in awe of him at first. Seeing him win bronze in Helsinki taught me that the Kenyans were beatable. That if Craig could do it, then I could too.

I flew out to the training camp in mid-January 2006. The games were taking place from 15 to 26 March. The idea was I'd spend two months in Melbourne acclimatizing, training alongside Craig and another Australian distance runner, Collis Birmingham. The three of us would train together at the high-altitude camp at Falls Creek, about four hours' drive from Melbourne. It seemed like the perfect preparation.

When it came to training with Craig, I felt he was using me to help him without him wanting to help me improve as an athlete. Normally when a group of athletes do a track session they will share the pacemaking duties, rotating who runs at the front, where it takes more effort to run at a particular speed. During one rep, an athlete will go in front and lead the group through laps of, say, 62 seconds. For the next rep that runner will go to the back of the pack, and another guy will lead the group at the required speed. You see it a lot in cycling where the front guy does all the work and the others sit in his slipstream.

But judging your pace is something you only get better at over time. Your body instinctively knows what pace it's going at. You can feel it. It's sort of like driving a car. The first time you're behind the wheel of your new motor, you've got to constantly check the speedometer to see what speed you're doing. After a few drives you start getting used to the feel of the car. All of a sudden you don't have to look at the speedometer any more. You just instinctively *know* that you're doing 50mph. I'm much better at it now – pacing, that is – but back in 2006 I was useless. Couldn't tell how fast or slow I was going. I'd start off really fast and would have no idea how long it was taking me to clock a lap.

As the young buck in training, I was supposed to share the pacing duties with Craig but as he was so much faster at the time I was afraid to take the lead – and when I did my pacing was all over the place. I would help out for the first few reps but I struggled to run consistent splits. If we were supposed to go 62 seconds in one rep I'd go 60, and the next I would be at 64. By the end of the session, it was easier for me to just follow Craig. I didn't know what I was supposed to be doing. The longer this went on, the angrier Craig was getting.

'Slow down!' he called out. 'Faster! No, no! Slower!'

In a way, I could sympathize with Craig. When I was at the front, the pace was up and down, all over the place. When I followed him it was much easier, but then he was having to do all the work. At the time my main focus was to keep up with him and not get dropped. No doubt Craig was wondering what I was doing, keeping up with him at the end of a session but not helping with the pace. Simply put, I wasn't helping him out. All I was doing was making him more and more annoyed. Towards the end of the session Craig exploded.

'Why don't you lead?' he shouted. 'If you can keep up with me, why don't you lead instead of sitting on my tail!'

I didn't understand what I'd done wrong. I just looked

at Craig and shrugged. 'What's his problem?' I thought to myself. Looking back on it, I realize he was understandably pissed off with me for not doing my job properly. That was a lesson well learnt.

Waiting to make my first appearance in the 2006 Commonwealth Games was a nerve-racking experience. I remember being in the call room in the bowels of Melbourne Cricket Ground, waiting for my turn to enter the stadium. I was competing in the same event as Craig: the 5000 metres. I could hear the noise of the crowd, people roaring and cheering. Some of the other athletes looked white with fear. That was the most nervous and tense I've ever felt before a race. I'd never competed in front of anything like that crowd before. This was a huge step up for me, a huge test of my abilities. I didn't want to let my country down.

As I walked out onto the track with the other runners, I was confronted by this wall of noise. I'd never experienced anything like it. Camera flashes going off everywhere. A hundred thousand people screaming their support for Craig Mottram, the local hero. He was undoubtedly the star attraction of the games. They had come to see him mixing it up with the East Africans. I don't remember much about the actual race, except that I finished in a disappointing ninth place. 13:40.53. Craig came second, behind another Kenyan athlete, Augustine Choge, with World Champion Benjamin Limo third and Joseph Ebuya fourth.

I knew I could've done better than ninth. I let myself down. I trained too much, too hard during my time at the camp in Falls Creek. I was doing everything the same as

Craig. The runs, the gym work, the recovery sessions. In the end, I put in a lot more work at the camp than I should have done. There was no need for me to follow Craig's routine, to match him in training. He was older than me. He had been a professional athlete for longer. I should have reined myself in. Instead I went into the Commonwealth Games feeling tired, and I paid the price.

I was determined to make up for my poor showing in the summer. In my heart I knew I could do a lot better than 13:40. I'd shown that much in training. At the KBC Nacht of Athletics in Belgium in 2006 I had the chance to prove it.

There are two major athletics meetings held in Belgium. One is the Diamond League meet in Brussels. The other is held in Heusden in July. I was competing in the 5000 metres. Micah Kogo was there. So too was James Murigi and Gamal Belal Salem, a naturalized Qatari born in Kenya. All three were athletes I'd trained with in Teddington. Also on the start line was an experienced indoor runner, Mark Bett, and Ali Abdalla of Eritrea. Micah Kogo won the race. I came home in sixth place. But that didn't matter. I'd clocked a time of 13:09.40. Prior to that race my best time at 5000 metres was 13:30.53 in Solihull at the British Milers' Club event the previous summer. For me, that was a massive leap in performance. Not only had I significantly improved my time, it was also fast enough to make me the second-fastest British runner after Dave Moorcroft. It was the big break-through I was looking for. I had made a statement. I was starting to get respect on the circuit. And at the European

Championships in Gothenburg the following month, I had the chance to do even better.

Gothenburg was my first major track appearance since Melbourne. I was determined to make up for my poor showing. More than that, I wanted to go for the win. I felt I had a good chance of success at the Europeans. I would be better prepared this time. And there would be no East African runners to compete against. I viewed Gothenburg as a big opportunity to win a medal and earn some serious respect on the senior circuit.

In the 5000 metres heats I finished third behind Eduard Bordukov of Russia and Khalid Zoubaa of France. Three days later, I woke up to compete in the final. It was raining that afternoon. I felt a little nervous before the race. Ahead of the final, Paula Radcliffe gave me some important last-minute advice.

'Go out there and be brave,' she told me. 'Just believe in yourself.'

I remembered those words as I stepped out into Ullevi stadium. People in the crowd were waving the Union Jack. The field was strong. Spain had a tradition of producing good distance runners, as did France. The European field was generally considered very strong heading into the championships.

The main threat, I knew, would come from Jesús España. He had good speed and was the man to beat. The way people think of me now, as the distance runner with good speed in the sprint finish? That's what people thought of España back in 2006. I had a strategy all planned out for beating him. My aim was to take the sting out of him by constantly pushing the pace, winding it up, making him run harder. By the time the last lap came around, España wouldn't have the mileage left in him to sprint ahead of me. I didn't worry about anything else. I just had to focus on my game plan.

The race began. At the start the pace was quite slow. That suited me just fine. I slowly wound it up. With about a mile to go, I surged to the front of the pack, winding up and winding up. Going faster and faster. The race was going to plan. The pace was picking up. Then the bell rang. One lap to go – everybody kicked on. Thirteen guys gritting their teeth in pain, giving it everything. I was still leading the way as I steered into the back straight. Then I saw someone coming up on my shoulder. I recognized him as the Turkish runner Halil Akkas. I couldn't afford to let him pass, so I dug in and sprinted away from him, running as fast as I could. I was flying now. With just 150 metres to go, this race was mine to lose. As I came into the home straight, I thought that I'd done enough to fend off my rivals.

Then I saw this blur of red surge past me. Number 245 pinned to the back of his jersey.

España.

Somehow he managed to open up this tiny gap ahead of me. We're talking inches. I dug in hard. I was going flat out, straining every sinew to catch my rival. With the finish line in sight, I managed to close the gap between us. The inches disappeared. We were neck and neck as we raced towards the line. Then España did something incredible. He found the strength to kick on and nudged a fraction ahead of me as we reached the line. He'd clocked in at 13:44.70. I finished on 13:44.79. One hundredth of a second between us. España had edged the gold. I was gutted.

At the end of the race he put his arm around me. 'Don't feel so bad,' he said. I could barely hear his voice above the din of the crowd. 'Okay, you lost today. But your time will come.'

I tried to smile back at him. I did a lap of honour to thank the crowd for their support, but I didn't really feel like doing it. I was hurting inside. The fans were great: they had travelled a long way and the least they deserved was a show of my appreciation. They were cheering me and clapping and shouting, 'Well done, Mo!' as I went round. I waved back, trying to look pleased. Maybe I should have been happy with that silver, but deep down I was bitterly disappointed. I couldn't stop thinking about how close I'd come to winning that gold. If I'd been well beaten on the day, I might have been able to deal with it. But with 200 metres to go, I'd believed the gold medal was in the bag.

Tactically, España had run a good race, making sure he had enough speed left in the tank to kick on with a couple of hundred metres to go. I hadn't done well enough at the kick. After Gothenburg, I decided that I needed to work on my speed. Up to that point in my career, I didn't believe in my speed at the sprint finish. I knew I was fast, but I would never plan a race around bursting ahead once I'd heard the bell. Instead, I'd wind it up gradually with two or three laps to go, slowly increasing my speed so that, as the finish line drew near, I'd be pulling clear of the group. Clearly, if I wanted to get better, I needed to get faster.

Once I got over the disappointment of losing out to España on the home straight and processed my defeat, I realized that there was a silver lining to my performance. It was the first sign to me that I'd made the right choice by moving in with the Kenyans. I'd made a lot of sacrifices: going out with my friends, staying out late, pursuing other interests off the track. But I finally felt as if all my hard work was beginning to pay off. That feeling of standing on the podium with a medal round your neck – it was totally worth it. It was worth everything. I wanted more of the same.

On the back of finishing second at the Europeans I secured a good contract with adidas. When I heard how much adidas were going to pay me, I had to sit down and catch my breath. It wasn't millions, but it was way more than I'd earned in athletics up to that point. From now on I wouldn't have to pull shifts at the Sweatshop. I traded up my old Fiesta to a red Peugeot 206. Now I was really going places.

With the track season over, I went away to South Africa for a month in a training camp in Durban. I came back home in time for the start of the cross country season. It was late November 2006 and I felt in great shape heading into the next race, a 9 kilometre course in Dunkirk, France. I won the race, beating Micah Kogo. That result caused a huge stir. At the time, Micah was the number one in the world at 10,000 metres. Beating him was a big deal for me personally, and it put me in good form going into the final major event of the year: the European Cross Country Championships in San Giorgio, Italy.

I wasn't the hot favourite at San Giorgio. That honour went to the Ukrainian, Sergiy Lebid, who had dominated European cross country for years. He'd won the title five times in a row, from 2001 to 2005, and everyone fancied him to walk away with it a sixth time. I told myself, 'I need to beat Lebid if I'm going to stand any chance of winning this thing.' I'm sure he was looking at my result in Dunkirk and thinking, 'I've got to watch out for this kid.' That definitely gave me a little bit of an edge going into the race. You want your opponents to be worried about what you can do. It gives you a psychological boost.

San Giorgio is a great cross country course. It's not too hilly – just a few man-made hills around the track – and it's mostly flat, which suits my running style. It was cold that day, the kind of cold that eats into your bones. No snow, just mud. Lots and lots of mud. Beforehand Alan Storey told me, 'Wait as late as possible before making your move, Mo.'

I started working my way through the pack and building up my speed. With two laps of the course to go, I swept ahead of the lead group. Soon I'd created a big gap between myself and the second-placed runner. I'd gone a bit earlier than Alan would have liked, but I felt comfortable with it. I was having to work really hard, digging deep. A quick glance over my shoulder going into the last lap, and I couldn't see Lebid anywhere. The Ukrainian favourite was way back in the chasing pack. I knew then that I'd won for sure. I was unstoppable.

I won the 9.95 kilometre race with a time of 27:56, a good 10 seconds ahead of Portugal's Fernando Silva. Juan Carlos de la Ossa of Spain was third. Lebid finished way down the list in eleventh. I hadn't just beaten Lebid; I'd crushed him. It was the first time he'd missed out on the European title since 2000.

This huge feeling of relief washed over me when I won. Living with the Kenyans – training as they did – it had worked. I'd made a real breakthrough at San Giorgio. Winning that first major title on the world stage is something every athlete dreams of. I'd always known that I had it in me to win races at the senior level, but as long as that first title evades you, these little doubts linger at the back of your mind. The ones reminding you about all those other outstanding junior athletes who never quite stepped up. You'd overhear people saying, 'Oh, yeah, I remember so-and-so. He was good as a junior. He went to the world juniors but he never broke through as a senior. Whatever happened to him?' That wasn't going to be me. Now I had the title to prove it.

It was the perfect end to a good year.

10
THE CAMP

'FARAH!' the Kenyan athletes would say whenever the time came for one of them to return home. 'You simply must come to Kenya, Farah.' For some reason, the Kenyans always insisted on calling everyone by their surname. 'It'll be fun. You can see my house. I will introduce you to my family. You can see where I grew up.'

It goes without saying that Kenyans are some of the most hospitable, welcoming people you'll ever meet. They pride themselves on having good manners and always being polite and softly spoken. Almost as soon as I'd moved into the house, John Kibowen, Benjamin Limo and the rest were on my case to visit them. I liked the idea of heading out to Kenya and seeing how they trained at altitude. I knew that PACE ran a camp in Kaptagat for the Kenyan athletes it represented, but it was unheard of for Brits to train there. The main problem was finding a slot in my schedule to get out there for a month or six weeks because 2006 was a busy year for me. In terms of my training, I knew I'd made the right call in living with the Kenyans. To improve further, I had to keep doing even more of the same things. More sessions. More attention to my diet. More recovery.

Then, in 2007, I made another huge stride in my career. At the World Cross Country Championship in Mombasa,

Kenya, I finished eleventh – an unbelievable result and the best of my career to date, especially considering the unbearably hot weather, with athletes dropping like flies throughout the race, and the fact that I'd suffered food poisoning in the Durban camp before the race. Eleventh place made me the highest-placed European in the race.

Even better was to follow. In August I travelled to Osaka in Japan for the World Championships. Competing in the 5000 metres, I finished sixth behind Bernard Lagat, Eliud Kipchoge, Moses Kipsiro, Matt Tegenkamp of the USA and Tariku Bekele, Kenenisa's younger brother. This was another big step forward to add to my very positive performance in Mombasa. The only disappointment was that I was still falling short of winning or even getting a medal. A pattern was starting to emerge. I was finishing ahead of the Europeans, but behind the leading pack of Kenyans, Ethiopians and Eritreans. Coming so soon after beating Micah Kogo in Dunkirk and winning the European Cross Country Championship in San Giorgio, I knew I had the talent. I had no doubt I was on the right track with my training, but I had to take it to the next level. I knew then what I had to do.

I had to go to Kenya.

I ran four more races after Osaka, a 3000 metres race in Zurich in early September, the 3000 and 5000 in the World Athletics Finals in Stuttgart, and a 3 kilometre road race in Newcastle. At the end of the month a deal was arranged with UK Athletics that enabled me to travel and train in Kenya. UKA generously agreed to pay for my flight, and I'd stay in Benjamin Limo's house in Kaptagat.

I couldn't wait to get out there. My belief has always been: if you want to be the best, you've got to learn from the best. The Kenyans and Ethiopians were dominating the distance events. I'd learnt so much just from living with each of them for a few weeks in Teddington; I'd learn a whole lot more by living with these guys in their own back yard.

From the moment I arrived at Kaptagat, Benjamin Limo and the other guys made me feel at home. They didn't have to do that. These were world-class distance runners who'd beaten me time and again on the track. They didn't have to give me the time of day. Some of them I didn't even know that well. And yet they welcomed me with open arms. That's very typical of the Kenyans; they have a humble, gracious mentality.

Kaptagat is a tiny village set high up in the mountains, at almost 2500 metres. It's also near the equator, so it's dry and sunny all year round. Many of the great Kenyan athletes lived and trained in Kaptagat: Vivian Cheruiyot, Daniel Komen, Sally Barsosio, Elijah Lagat, Moses Tanui, Brimin Kipruto. The village is totally isolated. The roads are dusty, red dirt trails criss-crossing the rocky hills. The people live in shacks. Kids run around barefoot. Up there in the mountains is as basic as you can get. You're on the edge of the Rift Valley, surrounded by this vast wilderness of acacia trees and tall elephant grass. If you want to go to the shops, their nearest town is Eldoret, a good 25-minute drive away.

There's no hot water in Kaptagat. If you want to wash,

you have to boil water in a big pot. There's no such thing as an oven, either. Cooking is done over an open fire, and we'd collect firewood for this purpose at the end of training each day. The food was usually chicken – preferably a live one that the Kenyan runners would catch. I remember sitting down to my first meal at the camp, my belly growling with hunger.

'Hey, Farah!' one of the guys called out. 'You must eat lunch with us.'

'Yeah, yeah, cool,' I replied quickly. 'What's for lunch?' Thinking they were going to rustle up a tasty stew, or maybe a serving of *ugali*.

'Chicken!' the guy replied. I frowned. I didn't see any chicken meat anywhere. Then he pointed to a chicken pecking at the soil by his feet and grinned. 'I think this one will do nicely!'

When there weren't any chickens to hand, the guys would cook big pots of *ugali*. I shared a room with three other athletes training in the village, following their routine. I ate when they ate, I slept when they slept, and I trained when they trained.

At first, adjusting to life at the camp was a bit of a culture shock. I had to make do without the luxuries we all take for granted in the West. They had satellite TV with a lot of sports channels but there was nothing else, no Internet, no shops, restaurants or cinema. I had to drink bottled water because my stomach couldn't tolerate the tap water the Kenyan guys were drinking. Kids ran alongside me, keeping up the pace and shouting, 'How are you?' Others shouted,

'Mzungo! Mzungo!', which means 'white man' in Swahili but they also use it for anyone who is a foreigner.

I soon started to realize that being so isolated was one of the most important things about Kaptagat. Running is deeply embedded in the culture of the place. Everyone who lives there knows about running. You're high up in the mountains to train and do nothing else. You're not there to pick up your post, pay bills, run errands or meet up with mates. It's athletics 24/7. Over 100 miles of hard running, week in, week out. And once I understood that, I began to reap the benefits.

As a distance runner, you learn that it's important to rest more and do less. That might sound counterproductive, but it's all about quality over quantity. The philosophy of the training camp is that the more basic the facilities, the better. There were often fifty or more guys out training at any one time. Many had luxurious family homes in town but preferred to live in a basic camp to maintain their focus and discipline. They worked hard with no distractions. As soon as my time at the camp was up, I knew I wanted to go back there in the future.

The next year, 2008, a very decent hotel cropped up in the neighbouring town of Iten, so I decided to base myself there. You can't miss Iten. There's a colourful sign hanging over the road leading into the town that reads, 'WELCOME TO ITEN: HOME OF CHAMPIONS'. There are more comforts in Iten compared to Kaptagat. I stayed at the Kerio View hotel, which had a good restaurant, Internet and satellite TV where I could watch Arsenal games. It was just like a European hotel. Another athlete, Lorna Kiplagat, also had a training centre there, with a gym, a sauna and a dormitory block. American high school kids would stay there and train on the cinder tracks. Monday to Friday I'd make the trek to Kaptagat or the track in Eldoret. At the weekends, I'd head back to Iten. It was a good routine.

After that first trip to Kaptagat, I made going to the camp a regular part of my schedule. Once I'd been three or four times, people back home started to realize that other UK athletes could benefit from training at the camp. Before long, more and more British athletes began training at altitude in Kenya, and now UKA has an annual camp for 30–40 athletes in Iten, but I was the first to get out there.

I missed the cross country season in 2007 after suffering a stress fracture in my hip, which meant I wouldn't be able to defend the title I'd won in San Giorgio the previous winter. While recuperating, I decided to leave the Kenyan house. After eighteen months living there, it was time for me to move on. I relocated to a room in a property London Marathon rented, also in Teddington, a three-storey red-brick house that accommodates six young athletes at a time. The location was perfect – it was literally across the street from St Mary's. Although I would no longer be living with the Kenyans, there was never any real danger of me slipping back into my old habits. I stuck to the same routine as I'd done at the Kenyan house. Going to bed early. Getting plenty of rest. Eating healthily. Training hard. Now I'd seen what I could achieve by dedicating myself purely to running, I was determined not to let my performances slip. There'd be no more dramatic breakthroughs like the one at Heusden, I knew. From now on it was going to be hard, incremental improvements of 1 or 2 per cent here and there.

For a couple of years after Tania had given birth to Rhianna, we had almost lost touch. Things picked up again in early 2008, by which time Rhianna was two. One day I stumbled upon Tania's profile on Facebook – she had recently joined the site and was friends with one of my friends, which is why her profile popped up. Eager to hear from her, I sent Tania a friend request along with a message asking her to get in touch. She quickly responded and popped round to the London Marathon-rented house to see me. At first, things felt a little strange. We hadn't seen each other for a long time. Tania was a mother now, living in rented accommodation with Rhianna and holding down a steady job. She had split up from Rhianna's biological father. The relationship between them had completely broken down by this point; he wasn't on the scene with regards to Rhianna. As a result, Tania was having to raise Rhianna on her own, paying phenomenal childcare fees and juggling the demands of a full-time job as well. And I was striving to make my name in athletics. So much had changed. But soon we were chatting away and joking around like before. Some things hadn't changed – such as the way I felt about Tania.

Despite being a young mother (Tania was nineteen when she gave birth to Rhianna) and the difficulties of raising a child on her own, she was doing really well for herself.

She had a great job, was earning good money and drove a nice car. When I first saw how well Tania was doing, I couldn't believe she was able to achieve all that whilst juggling the pressures of being a single mother. I started to look at her in a completely different light. Here she was paying her way, doing everything for herself, not looking for any help. She didn't mope around feeling sorry for herself. She just rolled up her sleeves and got on with it. It was clear to me that we shared that same sort of mentality – the willingness to graft, to raise and look after yourself and earn your keep in this world. We were cut from the same cloth.

We were soon spending a lot of time together. Every week Tania would come over to my house after I'd finished training. The two of us would crash on the sofa and watch *Prison Break* together. We absolutely loved that programme. We'd watch five or six episodes back-to-back. It became our weekly ritual. We were sitting on the sofa one evening, watching an episode of *Prison Break*, when I casually put my arm around Tania. She didn't brush it off. That was the moment I thought to myself, 'I'm in there!'

Even before we were officially a couple I was keen on meeting Rhianna. I kept on at Tania all the time. Telling her, 'I really want to meet your daughter.' We arranged to meet up at Bushy Park, where I often trained. Rhianna was two at the time. We met at the kids' playground and the two of us hit it off immediately. Kids tend to warm to me anyway, because I have that childish side to my character. And Rhianna's very easy to get on with. From that moment on we had this immense bond – a bond that has never been broken. The rest is history.

People say that nothing compares to the Olympics. They say it so many times that it's become the ultimate cliché. The thing is, it's true. Nothing compares because the Olympics is the biggest show on Earth. For me, making the Great Britain team was a massive deal. The Olympics is the world stage. Billions of people are watching you. You win a local athletics meet . . . great, well done. Five seconds later the race is forgotten about and you're thinking ahead to the next event. The Olympics is different. Kids don't dream about winning the Worlds. They dream about winning gold in the Olympics. I was the same.

One of my most vivid memories is watching the men's 10,000 metres in Sydney. I was studying at Isleworth at the time, and for practically the whole week I'd been watching the swimming and the gymnastics, counting down the days until the athletics began. I remember being hooked to the TV when the race started. Watching legends like Haile Gebrselassie and Paul Tergat tearing around the track, matching each other step for step. Tergat kicking on in the final 200 metres and looking like he was going to win, then Gebrselassie doing this amazing sprint finish and nudging ahead of Tergat to take the gold by 0.09 seconds. After watching that race, I told myself, 'I'm going to do as well as I can in running and I want to become Olympic champion.'

I was going to train as hard as I could for Beijing. Running on such a big stage meant so much to me. I was determined to do my country proud. To prepare for the 5000 metres, me, Micah Kogo and 12:55 5000 metres runner Boniface Songok went to train at altitude at a camp in Flagstaff, Arizona. All three of us were preparing for the Olympics and as Ricky Simms (who coached Micah, Boniface and all the Kenyans) and Alan Storey worked closely together we agreed that we would all do the same programme.

I already knew both Micah and Boniface from the house in Teddington and training in Kenya and had become good friends with them. Both had lived there for a while at the same time as me. Most Kenyan athletes come from rural areas, small towns and villages, but Boniface didn't act like that. He was into cars and technology. He spoke good English, he had interests outside running, perhaps more so than some of the other guys. As a result, I found it easier to socialize with him. I got on really well with Micah too. He liked to tell me how, when he was a kid, he had to run because it was the only way he could get to school.

Flagstaff is a small city along Route 66. It has everything a runner needs for a training base: all-weather tracks, sunshine, fitness centres and breathtaking scenery. The city is surrounded by huge mountains and forests, and you can go running on dirt trails or along rolling mountain roads. It's perfect. The three of us – me, Micah and Boniface – stayed in this massive rented house in the city and concentrated on the programmes we'd been given by Alan Storey. Some of the sessions he'd set were really hard and long. In addition to my track work I was going to the gym and lifting weights. Micah and Boniface had wondered about this. Going to the gym was not something the Kenyans did too much of. They do exercises or circuits but don't spend a lot of time in the gym. Not their thing. But Micah and Boniface wanted to know more. So we struck a deal: I'd take them to the gym in Flagstaff and teach them about weights and strength training, and in return, they'd teach me about running. As I've said before, you never stop learning. There's always something new to pick up from an athlete. Boniface and Micah were brilliant runners and it'd be stupid of me not to try and learn as much as I could from them.

They agreed on the spot.

Each day, the Kenyans taught me about pacing, doing the reps, working your way through a group, pushing towards the end of a race. We went on runs together where they'd start off slowly and then quickly pick up the pace rather than slowly winding it up. Those runs were hard work. After we'd finished our sessions on the track, we'd head to the gym, do some weights. Pushing each other to the limits. I didn't realize it at the time, but in my quest to be in top condition for Beijing, I was making the classic mistake of overtraining.

We didn't just feel tired: we looked it. Boniface and Micah had that look about them the whole time – slumped, as if they'd just woken up. I imagine I looked basically the same. It's true that it's the coach's job to monitor the condition of his or her athletes ahead of competition and map out the sessions accordingly. But Alan was back in the UK. He had no idea how hard we were pushing. It wasn't his fault. We were sending back amazing training times but he couldn't see how tired all three of us were. An athlete is the worst judge of whether or not they're tired, so we were totally blind to the fact that we'd badly overcooked it. The bottom line is, if you're doing lots of fast sessions, like me, Micah and Boniface were in Flagstaff, then you need to get lots of rest to compensate for the strain you're putting your body through. But instead of resting properly, we'd hit the gym and lift weights. If we'd had any idea of the damage we were doing, we'd have told Alan and he would probably have set us a less physically demanding programme. But our heads were in the sand, so we stuck to Alan's gruelling sessions.

Honestly, I didn't realize how bad things were until I took part in the Payton Jordan Cardinal Invitational in Stanford, California, on 4 May. Stanford was a warm-up towards the end of our time at the camp. If you're generous, you'd describe my performance in the 10,000 metres as 'okay'. I led the race for a while but ended up well down the field in fifth. Craig Mottram won, kicking on ahead of me with 800 to go to finish with a time of 27:34.48. It wasn't the worst result in the world, but to lose the race in the final kilometre like that was disappointing. I knew I was capable of a better run. Disturbingly, I'd felt tired coming into the last 800 – more tired than was normal. I was starting to feel the effects of overcooking it in Flagstaff.

It wasn't just me: Boniface Songok also had a pretty poor race, placing fourth in the 5000 metres, behind Bernard Lagat, when he'd been expected to finish in the top two. It was painfully obvious that we'd been pushing each other way too hard at the camp in Arizona. Now we needed to rest. Instead, we were having to compete. And as a result, our performances were suffering.

I spent six weeks at Flagstaff, then I bid goodbye to Boniface and Micah and returned to the UK. Back in Teddington, I did a few sessions. Nothing too intense. Now I was back at sea level rather than altitude, I started to feel like I was getting some of my strength back. At this moment I was on what I call 'the edge': about to hit peak form. But the edge is a dangerous place to be. Too many hard training sessions, and I'd tip over the edge and into a bad place. My body kept telling me that I needed a few days to rest, to take it easy and recover from Flagstaff. But instead I continued to train hard.

Back in Kenya, Boniface Songok and Micah Kogo were preparing to compete in the Olympic Trials in Nairobi. (You might be wondering why the Kenyans needed to qualify for the Olympics through trials while I didn't. There are two standards, 'A' and 'B', based on certain times. For the 5000 metres the 'A' might be 13:15 and the 'B' might be 13:20. Each country can send three athletes for an event, two at the 'A' standard and one at the 'B' standard. In a country like Kenya, where you've got dozens of guys who meet the 'A' standard, they host trials to determine who's going on the plane and who stays behind. In Britain the situation is different. I was the only British athlete to set an 'A' standard time in the previous twelve months, so I was allowed to run the 1500 metres in the Trial. My place in the 5000 metres was already assured.) In his trial, Boniface finished outside the qualifying positions, coming fourth. His Olympic dream was over. That was a big shock. Micah just about scraped his place on the team, finishing third behind Moses Masai and Martin Mathathi to qualify for the 10,000 metres.

Despite the warning signs, I kept up my intense pre-Beijing training programme. I was doing block sessions, big reps of 1000 or 1200 metres, amounting to a total of 12–15 kilometres. That's a lot of work, but at the time I thought it was the right approach. I wanted to be as strong as possible going into the Olympics. Athletics is a fragile sport. You train hard for four years, waiting for your chance to compete on the biggest stage of all, and then your dream can be wrecked in the time it takes to click your fingers. Maybe you get tripped up on the third lap. Maybe you didn't put in enough hours on the track. Maybe you haven't researched your opponents properly. This was my first Olympics. For all I knew, it might be the only one I ever got to compete in. A lot can change in four years. I was determined not to let this moment pass me by.

Three weeks before the Games began, I put in an unbelievable session alongside some of the other guys preparing for the 5000 metres. I kept pace with Moses Kipsiro, the Ugandan who'd won bronze in Osaka the previous year. On the last lap I actually surprised myself by running faster than him. Matching a world-class runner like Kipsiro, I told myself, meant that I was doing something right. I came off the track filled with a sense of excitement. Thinking to myself, 'That's probably the best session I've ever done.' I was pumped and ready to go.

The truth was, I'd peaked too soon.

Training is like running up a hill that has a sheer drop on the other side. You have a good session, you get further up the hill. Then you have more good sessions. Suddenly you're close to the peak. But if you push it too hard for too long, you go over the top and fall off the edge. You crash. That's what happened to me in the build-up to Beijing. I was only aware of this in hindsight. At the time, I didn't think anything was wrong. I flew out to the training camp in Macau to link up with the rest of the Great Britain team, full of confidence about my chances in the 5000 metres. Alan travelled with me this time, as he was part of the official UKA delegation. It was good to have my coach there. The mood in the camp was vibrant, friendly, relaxed. I caught up with people I hadn't seen for a while on the circuit and tried to ignore the tiredness that was working its way deep into my muscles. 'I just need some more rest, that's all,' I tried to convince myself. While I was in Macau I did just a few light sessions. I didn't want to push it. But then, after one supposedly easy session, I came away thinking, 'That was a lot harder than it ought to have been.'

I rested up some more.

I delayed my departure to the Olympic village in Beijing to the day before my heats. As an athlete, the last thing you want to be doing is hanging around, counting down the days to your race. Staying in the village is a weird experience. You're in this bubble, cut off from the outside world.

You're barely aware of being in a foreign country. If you asked me, 'What's Beijing like?' I couldn't tell you because the simple truth is, I don't know. I spent my entire stay in Beijing cooped up in the village, sharing a room with the marathon runner Dan Robinson. When I wasn't sleeping, I hung out in the entertainment centre, playing the arcades or having a go on the air hockey table to take my mind off the upcoming race.

Still, I was incredibly excited. The Olympics! The pinnacle of my career so far. I loved everything about it. So many athletes from all over the world – every country imaginable. I remember getting my Great Britain kit. You're given loads of kit, including a Great Britain suit and everything. There's this sense of occasion. You're part of something special. I really got into that. I kept my kit as a souvenir – I've still got it at home somewhere.

The morning of the heats I woke up feeling pretty good. I still wasn't 100 per cent, but at least I seemed to have shaken off the tiredness that had troubled me in Macau. I was racing in the second heat, alongside Edwin Soi of Kenya, Moses Kipsiro and my old rival from the European Championships, Jesús España. A good field, but I still favoured my chances of reaching the final. Before my race I'd been in the call room at the stadium, watching the first heat on the live TV feed. Matt Tegenkamp, the American, had qualified in first place, with Eliud Kipchoge and Tariku Bekele second and third. Those guys were guaranteed a place in the final three days later. Now it was my turn. All I had to do was finish in the top four places in the race to be sure of my place. Even if I finished fifth or sixth, the three fastest losers advanced to the final too.

I lined up at the start of the race. I was nervous, but I was also feeling confident.

The race starts. The crowd cheers. I get off to a good start. With five laps to go, I take the lead. My legs are aching. Muscles pumping. I'm gritting my teeth through the pain. I'm pushing, running hard. The effort I'm having to put in is ridiculous. I'm running 64- or 65-second laps, and it feels more like I'm running 60-second laps. That's how much effort I'm putting in. Two laps to go. Just two laps, then I'm in the final.

And that's when everything starts to go wrong.

One guy shoots past me first. It's Edwin Soi. Then Kipsiro cruises clear of me. Kipsiro, who I'd matched stride for stride on the track only a few weeks earlier. I can't believe what is happening. My place in the final is slipping away before my very eyes. Then Cherkos races ahead of me. Then España. As I come into the last lap it hits me: *I'm down in fifth. In the heats.* This is bad. Really bad. I know in my head that I need to wind it up now if I'm going to claw my way back into the qualifying positions. But I can't do it. There's nothing left to wind up. I'm kicking hard, giving it everything I've got, but it feels like I'm wading through treacle. Every muscle is heavy. Physically, I'm spent. I've done such a high volume in training that on the day of the race my tank is empty. I'm like a car running on fumes.

I have nothing left to give.

I'm still kicking as an Eritrean passes me and I cross the

line in sixth place. For a moment I'm stunned. I can't believe it. My time is 13:50.95. It's not even good enough for me to sneak into the final as one of the fastest losers. My Olympic dream is over.

My mind is racing. I look across at España. He's finished fourth – *fourth!* – qualifying him for the final. I always try to show the greatest respect for my competitors, all athletes do, but the same thought keeps churning over in my mind as I watch España celebrate. 'Even this guy has made it! I should've beaten him easily.' There are no 'should haves' or 'might have beens' in athletics. There's only what happened. And what happened is, I'd blown my chance of a medal in the Olympic Games.

Every defeat hurts. But some defeats hurt more than others. If some raw nineteen-year-old who's never been on your radar kicks on and sprints past you like it's nothing, then you accept it. It's hard to swallow, but you can process it. The same if someone accidentally trips you up. Things happen in a race. There's a difference between what is in your control and what's outside it. When you lose a race because of something outside your control, okay, that's one thing. But when you lose a race because of something you did have control over – like how hard you trained – that's harder to process. That defeat in Beijing hurt me more than any other.

I had let myself down. I had let my country down. Wearing that Great Britain jersey meant so much to me, and I'd arrived in Beijing full of hopes of winning a medal for my country. Now I'd failed even to make the final of my event.

All those months of training – all that effort – it had all been for nothing.

I didn't want to stick around Beijing for a moment longer than I needed to. I just wanted to be alone. Later on I found out that Boniface Songok had done exactly the same thing as me. He'd returned to Kenya ahead of the Olympic trials and kept up the intensity in training, not allowing his body to recover. When it came to running in the trials, his body was shot. That's why he'd failed to make the team. Likewise, Micah had been wiped after Flagstaff. But unlike Boniface and me, he'd listened to his body and dialled down on the training in Kenya, doing only light sessions and making sure he got plenty of rest. Micah went on to win the bronze medal in the 10,000 metres in Beijing. Moses Kipsiro placed fourth in the 5000 metres. For me, there was only one reason Boniface didn't qualify at the trials and Micah got an Olympic medal. It was the same reason I'd under-performed in the heats. We had over-trained.

I remember sitting on the flight back home, staring out of the window, feeling utterly deflated. I was more down than I'd ever been before in my life. To lose a race by running badly or getting your tactics wrong, or not putting in the effort, that's one thing. I could deal with that. But to have given everything for a whole year and get nothing in return, that's really hard to take. It would be some time before I managed to put Beijing behind me.

Looking out of that window, I told myself: 'I'm never going to feel like that, ever again.'

11
GOING IT ALONE

MENTALLY it was hard for me to focus after Beijing. I just wanted the season to be over. I was tired. My body needed to rest. Back in Teddington, Ricky explained to me that a rest would simply have to wait.

'Your contract with adidas is up for renewal,' he said. 'And we have a problem. You haven't run sub-13:15 all year.'

'So?'

'If you don't run sub-13:15 at 5000 metres by the end of the season, the retainer on your new contract automatically goes down. You'll be taking quite a hit.'

I should explain. A runner's main income is through a shoe contract: that's how you put food on the table and pay the bills. The way the contract works is that you get a retainer, a basic salary to retain your loyalty, but there are several bonuses built into it based on whether you win medals or perform well or race certain times. If, for example, you win bronze in a World Championship 5000 metres, that bonus kicks in for your next contract. Suddenly, you're making more money. But if you fail to maintain those standards the following season, you don't qualify for the bonuses and your next contract goes back down to the original retainer. In 2006 I'd run that 13:09 race at Heusden in the

Netherlands, so the following year my contract went up. But in 2008 the fastest time I'd clocked at 5000 metres was 13:25.01 at the Golden Spike meeting in Ostrava in the Czech Republic. Nowhere near good enough, so we were talking about a big drop in income. Athletics isn't Premier League football. Most athletes most of the time are on a pretty modest income. Coming so soon after Beijing, I wasn't sure I had it in me to run a sub-13:15 race. Physically, I was wiped. Mentally, I needed a break. I was in nothing like the condition I wanted to be in. In Beijing I'd clocked 13:50.95 in the heats. Now I was being asked to shave more than 35 seconds off that time. I told Ricky that I didn't know what to do.

'Look, Mo,' he said. 'You may as well run one more race at 5000 metres. The Diamond League meet in Brussels is coming up. For the next two weeks just jog slowly, do some strides and get plenty of rest. Why don't you go to Brussels, give it your best shot and see what happens? You've nothing to lose.'

If I raced and failed to make the time, then it didn't make a difference to the contract situation. I'd still be dropping down to my original retainer. If I did clock a time under 13:15, then I'd keep the increased retainer for the following twelve months. Also, having to race so soon after Beijing meant that I didn't have time to dwell on that defeat. Now I had to focus my mind on the event in Brussels. Two weeks after the Olympic Games, I took to the track again.

My last chance to run sub-13:15 in 2008.

The Diamond League meeting in Brussels is also known as the Memorial Van Damme and it takes place at the King Baudouin Stadium. This was a good arena for me: the previous year I'd run my personal best of 13:07.00 at the same meeting. Now, more than ever, I needed to run a similar time. It wasn't just about the money, although I was concerned about what would happen if my retainer went down. For me, this was a chance to begin the long process of putting my Beijing nightmare behind me. I'd be foolish to suggest that doing well in Brussels would make up for failing to make it through the heats at the Olympics. It wouldn't. But at least it'd be a start.

I wasn't sure I had it in me to run sub-13:15 so soon after Beijing. I wasn't in a good place. But then a funny thing happened. On the day of the meeting in Brussels, I did better than I'd expected. Way better. I went out there, ran the race and finished fourth. My time?

13:08.11.

Clocking that time was a bittersweet moment for me. My immediate feeling was one of relief. I'd saved my adidas retainer. I'd given it my best shot and it had worked. But at the same time I was like, 'You must be kidding . . . *13:08*!' That time would have easily qualified me for the 5000 metres final in Beijing. I was only two seconds behind Eliud Kipchoge, who won the silver in Beijing, and I beat Moses Kipsiro, who finished fourth in the Olympics. If only I'd run that time two weeks earlier. If only I'd properly rested in the run-up to the Olympics instead of over-training and working myself into the ground. If only . . .

If anything good came out of my performance in Beijing, it was that I learnt to listen much more carefully to the needs of my body. It's very easy to over- or under-train. Getting it spot on going into a major competition is one of the most difficult tasks for an athlete. You don't want to go in underprepared. But if you overcook it, you'll perform just as badly. There's a fine line. The more you race, the more you begin to understand your body and how it responds to different approaches to training. What works for someone else doesn't necessarily work for you.

In November I had the chance to go on a trip to a training camp in Ethiopia. Kaptagat (and Iten) had been so good for me that I was keen to check out more camps. It wasn't just the Kenyans who were doing great things in distance running. The Ethiopians were right up there too. Kenenisa Bekele had won Olympic gold in the 5000 metres and 10,000 metres in Beijing. His younger brother, Tariku, was also making a name for himself. I was keen to see what they might be doing differently.

You have to make a lot of sacrifices in athletics. I was lucky that in Tania I had someone who was understanding about the commitments I had to make to become a better runner. Shortly before I travelled to Ethiopia Tania won a prize for being one of the top ten salespeople in her company. The prize was a trip for two to New York. Tania really wanted to go – we had only recently got together and New York would've been a nice way to celebrate. But I had to make this trip to Ethiopia to train. Tania was a bit gutted. We missed out on a really lovely trip, but she understood what I needed to do. There were some things that we wouldn't be able to do as a couple, things that would have to take a back seat, because everything had to fit around my training.

I flew out to Addis Ababa with a few other Europeans, including the French steeplechaser Bouabdellah Tahri, Lidia Chojecka from Poland and Scott Overall, my old friend from Windsor Slough Eton & Hounslow. Also there was Mustafa Mohamed, another distance runner from a Somali background. I'd raced against Mustafa several times on the circuit, including the European Cross Country Championships in San Giorgio, when he finished third. He was already racing for Sweden by that point, having moved there from Mogadishu in his early teens. In 2007, the year following San Giorgio, when I'd been unable to defend my title because of injury, Mustafa took silver behind Sergiy Lebid. As well as being a good cross country runner, Mustafa specialized in the 3000 metres steeplechase. He's a softly spoken, quiet guy, unassuming, but warm and friendly. We had that shared experience of leaving Somalia at an early age. There's quite a few Somali-born athletes who had to move for one reason or another. Mukhtar Mohammed, for example, also runs for Great Britain and gave up a promising career as a footballer with Sheffield Wednesday to pursue his career on the track. There are Somali-born guys representing Holland, Belgium, Canada, the USA – all over.

The camp in Ethiopia was nothing like the one in Kenya. Instead of basing ourselves in a remote village, our camp was located in the north of Addis. We were basically running around the outskirts of the city, passing run-down shacks and piles of rubble. People would stand at the sides of the roads watching us train. The trails were narrow, steep and winding, and were also pot-holed and scattered with rocks, so I had to watch my step. The narrowness meant that the Ethiopians went out in tiny groups of one or two, unlike in Kenya, where sixty or more runners might go out together.

Maybe because of this, I got the impression that the Ethiopians were less welcoming than the Kenyans. Somehow they came across as more private. It's not that they were cold towards us or anything like that. They just very much kept themselves to themselves. They didn't like outsiders training with them. I found this strange. In Kaptagat I'd jump in on a training session and the Kenyans were more than happy for me to join them. Afterwards we'd share a meal, talk for a bit. There was none of this in Addis. I ended up training alone. As I picked my way up a steep, rocky incline, I might pass an Ethiopian runner, perhaps a pair, but I was never invited to join in their session. Not all the athletes were stand-offish, though. Meseret Defar, the 5000 metres runner, invited some of us to her house for dinner. The gold medal she'd won in Athens took pride of place on the wall. Meseret cooked us a traditional meal of *injera* flatbreads with a chicken stew and some vegetables. That was lovely of her, but I couldn't help wondering why she was the only one who made us feel truly welcome at the camp. Looking back, I think it's because we were male athletes. We weren't competition for her, whereas the men probably perceived us a threat – European runners who'd come to their backyard to learn their training secrets.

After the European Cross Country in Brussels in mid-December I went back to Kaptagat/Iten for my winter training. I needed to get Beijing out of my head. Going into the 2009 season, I was desperate to get a win under my belt. I knew that the better I ran, the more my mind would begin to clear, the more I could put the Olympics behind me. I got off to a great start, winning the Aviva International Match 3000 metres in Glasgow on my seasonal debut in late January and setting a new British record time of 7:40.99, just beating John Mayock's record by a tenth of a second. The next month I ran even faster in Birmingham, shaving more than 6 seconds off my time in Glasgow with 7:34.47 and moving me up to second on the all-time European list. The only British athlete ever to run faster than me outdoors at that distance was Dave Moorcroft. Winter training had gone well, and I felt in great shape going into the European Indoor Championships in Turin.

Big pressure came with the Europeans, though. On the back of my good performances in Glasgow and then Birmingham, people were hanging the gold medal around my neck before I even got to Turin. As for me, Beijing was lingering at the back of my mind, and I was conscious that Turin was the first major competition since then and I simply had to win. I had to work hard in that final. I led from the gun, but Bouabdellah Tahri was right on my heels throughout the race. I could hear him. We'd trained a lot together, knew each other's weaknesses. Tahri had finished fifth in the 3000 metres steeplechase in Beijing, so he was no mug. But with five laps left I finally broke him and kicked on to win in a time of 7:40.17, a new championship record. Jesús España, who'd beaten me in 2006, was third. Crossing the line, I had this overwhelming sense of relief. Winning a big title from gun to tape isn't easy. You can't afford to let your concentration slip. I told the press that after the year I'd had, I was simply pleased to have won a big title. I wanted to try and build up some momentum over the next few months. The World Championships were coming up in August and I was desperate to do well against the Kenyans and Ethiopians.

In the back of my mind, though, doubts were beginning to form about my training programme. Something had to change – I knew that much.

Alan Storey was more than simply my coach. He was someone I respected and listened to. I still believed in Alan, still thought he was the right person to take me forward. But I was starting to think more independently about my training needs. Asking myself, 'Is this right for me?' I'd always placed complete faith in Alan, followed his programmes to the letter, done whatever he'd asked of me. Now I started to question things. Nothing major – just small things here and there.

There's no denying that I'd made really big strides under Alan. I'd stepped up to the senior ranks, got silver in the Europeans, won the cross country title in Italy and become one of the best distance runners on the European stage. But something wasn't right. On the biggest stages – Osaka,

Beijing – I was falling short. Despite pushing hard in training and making big sacrifices, living and training with the Kenyans, I was still finishing behind them in the major competitions. I believed I was capable of beating them. I looked at guys like Micah Kogo and told myself, 'Here's someone I'm regularly matching in training, yet he's won Olympic bronze, broken the world record for 10k on the road and is the number one 10,000 metres runner in the world. I've beaten him in Dunkirk, so why aren't I doing it in big events?' What was most frustrating for me was that, in some ways, I trained harder than these guys. Not only was I busting a gut on the track, but I was putting in sessions at the gym, making more changes to my diet, paying attention to nutrition, going to high-altitude camps. In simple terms, I was putting in more effort than the Africans but getting less out. Something had to change.

I reached a personal low point at the 2009 World Championships in Berlin. I went into that competition thinking that I had a realistic shot of a medal in the 5000 metres. At first glance, the field was strong: Kenenisa Bekele was there, and Bernard Lagat. So too were Moses Kipsiro and Jesús España. That's not how I saw it. 'Kipsiro, I've beaten him in training,' I thought. 'España, I've beaten him in competition.' Lagat and Bekele were top class, but looking across the line, there was no one else I wasn't capable of beating on my day.

I finished seventh. I actually pulled away at the beginning of the final lap but fell away coming into the last bend. Bekele, Lagat, Kipsiro . . . they all placed ahead of me. I couldn't help thinking back to the last World Championships in Osaka. Back then I'd finished sixth. Two years on, I was placing seventh. In my opinion, I'd actually gone backwards. That was hard to stomach. Throughout this period, I never lost faith in my ability. I never doubted myself, not for one minute. But I knew something needed to change. At least Rhianna and Tania were there to help take my mind off things. It was the first time they had travelled abroad to watch me run and it was a big deal for me, to have them both cheering me on, me wanting to make them proud. I was conscious of that while I was competing. It made me feel good, knowing that I had family up there in the stands.

I returned to Teddington, spent a week by myself, thinking things over. By the end of that week I'd reached a decision: I didn't want to be coached by Alan Storey any more.

This wasn't a decision I reached easily. On the one hand, I knew I needed a change. On the other, this was Alan Storey. He wasn't just my coach. He was my friend – someone I felt close to. We'd been through a lot together, and when someone has done a lot for you, leaving them can be really hard. Normally when my mind is made up to do something, I just do it, easy. But when it came to Alan, I spent a long time weighing it up. I thought about what had worked in training for me, what hadn't worked. I looked back over my performances under Alan and asked myself what I could have done better, or differently. Leaving Alan, I knew, would change everything for me. But in my heart I also knew that it was the right thing to do if I was serious about beating the Africans.

Different athletes respond differently to the same training programme. What works for one athlete doesn't necessarily work for the next guy. As an athlete, it's up to you to be honest about the areas you need to improve on. It's like this: Alan Storey got me 98 per cent of the way towards becoming a World and Olympic champion. But I felt I needed someone else to come in and give me that 2 or 3 per cent to get me over the line.

I sort of drifted away from Alan for a while after Berlin. We talked less and less. I went off to Kenya as usual. Instead of following Alan's programme, I decided to try coaching myself. Going it alone. Sometimes I would train with athletes in Iten, guys like Moses Masai, who got a bronze in Berlin. Then other times I'd jump in workouts with some of the other groups training on the track in Iten. At this stage I was mainly building up my mileage. I knew what I had to do. It wasn't rocket science. Some of the runners training at Iten then were actually Kenyans who'd been naturalized as Qataris. They were being trained by Renato Canova, an Italian coach employed by the Qatari Athletics Federation. They were staying in the same hotel as me and sometimes I would join in with their workout rather than driving to Eldoret or Kaptagat to train.

Renato was a former schoolteacher, and he'd been coaching professionally since 1969. He had a good reputation on the circuit for his work with the Kenyans. He'd coached some of the most famous distance runners of the past few years: Saif Shaheen, Moses Mosop, Wilson Kiprop and Christopher Kosgei. The sheer intensity of his sessions took me by surprise. I had thought that the sessions under Alan were tough, but they were nothing compared to what Renato's group were doing. He insisted on doing a high number of reps, running circuits of flats coupled with uphill sprints to build up my strength. Everything was done at a faster speed than I'd been used to. We'd have a few hours' rest at midday. Then, in the afternoon, we'd head back to the track and do some more running work.

Renato liked to talk a lot. In that respect, he was your typical flamboyant Italian. Very expressive, very passionate. When it came to debating what was best for me in training, Renato could be quite forceful. I'd disagree with him on something he'd said, or question something, and he'd be like, 'No, no, no, Mo! You mustn't do it like that. Do it this way instead!'

Renato Canova wasn't the only one dispensing advice to me in Iten. At the same time I would join in on the odd session with guys coached by Jama Aden. Jama was also working for the Qatari federation. (As the Qatari runners were mostly naturalized Kenyans, it was easier for the athletes to stay on and train in Kaptagat/Iten, where conditions were ideal for training, rather than relocate to the desert.) Like me, Jama was born in Somalia and we had known each other for years. He ran for his country before becoming a world-renowned coach. He had family in Sheffield. Jama had mentored one of my personal heroes, the great Abdi Bile, another Somali athlete, winner of the 1500 metres in the 1987 World Championships in Rome and the 1989 World Cup in Barcelona, when he beat Seb

Coe. To get advice from the man who'd coached Abdi Bile was a privilege. We had the same arrangement as with Renato – very informal, just jumping into workouts with their groups or giving bits of advice here and there over cups of tea in the Kerio View. I was very grateful for the help. There was nothing in it for Renato and Jama, really. But they loved the sport and loved helping an athlete reach his potential.

Now I was getting the experience of training with different groups, I realized that what the Kenyans or the guys under Jama and Renato were doing was different from my training programme under Alan Storey. On the back of that, I knew that my instincts were right, that things simply hadn't been working for me 100 per cent back home. But there was a downside to going it alone. I'd think too much. When someone else is mapping out your programme, you follow it and that's it. Maybe you suggest one or two changes here and there. But basically, what your coach says goes. Now, at the end of a good session, instead of focusing on my rest and recovery, I'd already be thinking ahead to the next session. I was doing a lot of what I had done previously with Alan, but with the freedom to add in elements that I thought were missing. I was having to filter all the advice being given to me, trying to figure out what worked for me and what didn't. Instead of concentrating on my rest, I was questioning myself: Was that run too hard? Did I go too slow? How did I look on the workout today? What should I do tomorrow? I needed someone I really trusted to be there and tell me these things.

It would have been ideal to have Alan there with me. But

the truth is Alan couldn't travel with me wherever I went. He had numerous commitments in his role as Head of Endurance for UK Athletics, which meant he had to base himself in the UK for much of the year. Although he gave me as much time as possible, he simply wasn't able to completely oversee me in training. What I really needed was someone who could be there with me all the time. And I didn't have that.

Prior to going to Kenya I had mentioned to Dave Bedford that I was moving away from Alan. I'd gotten to know Dave pretty well down the years through his son, Tom, and the fact that London Marathon sponsored the endurance programme at St Mary's. He could see that I was not satisfied with the way things were going in my career, finishing seventh at the World Championships. During one conversation, the talk turned to my plans for the next year. I told Dave I wasn't sure what to do.

'Well, Mo,' said Dave. 'We both know that you're capable of a lot more than you've done in the past year. Maybe it's time for a change? Forget track. Why don't you try running the marathon instead?'

I remember hearing this and thinking, 'If I switch to road races, that means turning my back on the track.' Was I prepared to do this? It would be a huge decision. I spoke to Ricky and we talked it through. There were reasons to make the switch, and reasons *not* to make the switch. The last twelve months had been pretty rough. Beijing, then Berlin. I wasn't closing the gap on the Kenyans and Ethiopians, despite my best efforts. Guys like Bekele were still way ahead of me. I wondered: Could I never get any better than fifth or sixth on the global stage? But at the same time I honestly felt that I hadn't achieved everything I was capable of on the track. If I turned my back on the track now, would I regret it, knowing that I could have done more, that I could have done better? Running in the London Marathon appealed to me, but it was something I imagined doing later in my career. This moment might have come too soon.

In the end, I decided that if I was going to make the switch, I'd only do it if I could be trained by the best guy in the business: Alberto Salazar. If Alberto said no, I wouldn't make the switch.

'I'll speak to Alberto,' said Dave. 'Look into setting up a meeting. But listen – if Alberto agrees to be your coach, will you make the switch?'

'Yes,' I said.

Although I had never met him, I knew about Alberto. He's one of the most famous distance runners in the USA, but he's less well known in Britain. Alberto was born in Cuba, but moved to Weyland, Massachusetts, at a young age and began competing in high school track-and-field events. He wanted to emulate the achievements of the legendary US runner Steve 'Pre' Prefontaine, who had died tragically young in a car accident. Alberto had an older brother, a college runner who competed in some of the same National Collegiate Athletic Association (NCAA) races as Pre. As a result, Alberto would hear about what Pre and the Oregon runners were doing, having a pre-race meal of peaches on toast, going for 3-mile runs to warm up on the day of their races, and he'd do the same things. Alberto then went on to become one of the greatest marathon runners in the world. He ran his first-ever marathon at New York in 1980 in a time of 2:09.41 and ended up winning the race. He won two more New York Marathons, in 1981 and 1982, added the Boston Marathon title in 1982 and twice broke the American 10 kilometre road record. Alberto also had this reputation as a true fighter. He trained hard – harder than anyone in the business – and he wasn't afraid to put his body through hell. In 2007 he suffered a heart attack on a practice field at the Nike campus. His heart stopped beating for 14 minutes. Miraculously, Alberto survived. He returned to coach the US Olympic team in Beijing.

Many in athletics considered Alberto to be something of a genius. I knew that if I had him as my coach, I stood the best possible chance of winning at the 26.2 mile race – the marathon. For me, there was no point switching from track to road if my results were going to be the same. Track, road – in the end, whatever surface I was running on, I just wanted to win. I was conscious of the fact that there would be tough competition in the marathon. I knew about guys like Martin Lel, who won the London Marathon three times and New York twice; Sammy Wanjiru, the Olympic Champion and a London and Chicago winner; Haile Gebrselassie, who held the world record and was still going strong; and newcomers like Tsegay Kebede. Alberto had achieved amazing results with the likes of Kara Goucher (bronze in the 10,000 metres at the Worlds in Osaka) and

Dathan Ritzenhein (a three-time USA Cross Country winner). For me, hanging up my spikes only made sense if I had Alberto coaching me at the marathon. It was that or nothing.

In mid-October the World Half-Marathon Championships were taking place that weekend in Birmingham. Alberto was in town to watch Dathan Ritzenhein compete, and Dave asked if I would like to travel up to meet him? Alberto, not Dathan. I said yes.

We met in a hotel in Birmingham city centre. The IAAF (International Association of Athletics Federations) had taken over the hotel for the weekend and everywhere you looked there were athletes and coaches and agents. Dave introduced me to Alberto. Of course, I'd seen him around on the circuit, but this was the first time we had properly met. We talked for a bit, but it soon became clear that Alberto wouldn't be able to coach me.

'It's not possible,' he said. 'Not at this moment in time, anyway.'

'Why not?' I asked Alberto.

'Three reasons.' Alberto counted them off on his hand. 'You're sponsored by adidas. I work with Nike. It's none of my business who you're sponsored by, but I can't coach an athlete who's under contract with a rival sponsor. And somehow I doubt adidas would be very happy with that arrangement either.'

I nodded. Fair enough. 'What's the second reason?'

'You're British. Strictly speaking, the Nike Oregon Project is about promoting American distance running.'

The Nike Oregon Project, with Alberto directing it, had

been specifically created by Nike to improve the prospects of US distance runners. American distance running, as in Britain, had been in a bad state for a long time. Alberto had previously brought over a couple of Kenyans to help train the American athletes, but that hadn't worked out. Since then, the project had focused purely on US runners.

'That's two reasons,' Alberto went on. 'Third, I personally don't think you should be running the marathon yet.' He turned to Dave Bedford. 'I've seen Mo a couple of times. The kid has got great potential on the track if he works on one or two things. For me, he gives up the track now, it's too early.'

I left the hotel thinking, 'Alberto doesn't want to coach me, so what am I going to do now?' I had a big decision to make on my future. Dave Bedford was still pushing for me to switch to the road. I was about to go to Kenya to start my winter's training. I weighed everything up and felt I had unfinished business on the track. My mind was made up. I wasn't going to run the marathon. Not yet, anyway. If I had given up track then, I would have felt like I had failed. There would be plenty of time for the marathon in the future. I wanted to give the track one more shot.

And this time I wanted to break the British 5000 metres record.

12
UNFINISHED BUSINESS

I MOVED in with Tania after returning from Kenya in late 2009. The lease on the place she was renting had come up for renewal and I thought, 'Why don't we just move in together rather than living in separate homes?' Things had been going really well between us and I was ready to take our relationship to the next level and share a home together. I was spending a lot of time at Tania's anyway, so we were practically living together by that point. Maybe if that lease hadn't come up for renewal, the idea of living together wouldn't have occurred to me. But now that the opportunity had presented itself, we decided to take it.

Not long after moving in together, we attended the wedding of one of my close friends, Mustafa Mohamed. He married his Swedish wife in Gothenburg; it was the first time Tania and I had attended a big function together as a couple and being there, seeing how happy Mustafa and his wife looked, brought up the subject of marriage in my mind for the first time. I was in love with Tania, things just felt right between us and I thought to myself, 'I want this. I want to get married.' Within two weeks of returning home, I decided to pop the question. We were watching TV one night, talking about this, that or the other, when I just casually dropped it into the conversation.

'Do you want to get married?'

Tania looked at me for what felt like the longest moment. She probably wondered if I was joking. To be fair, it wasn't exactly the conventional down-on-one-knee proposal.

'Are you asking me to marry you?' she asked at last.

I nodded. 'For real.'

I was serious. It clicked. Tania smiled.

'Let's do it!' she said.

We set our wedding date for the following April. Everyone was thrilled for us. Tania's parents, Bob and Nadia, were over the moon. In the meantime, I knuckled down to the business of smashing records.

13:00.41. Dave Moorcroft's 5000 metres British record had stood since 1982. I hadn't even been born then. For me, breaking the record was the biggest thing. Ever since I'd edged closer to 13:00 in Heusden, I'd been obsessed with it. I believed – I *knew* – that I could break it. And twenty-seven years is a long time. But this was about more than simply beating Dave's record: running a sub-13:00 was something I'd never done before, and it would put me in the mix with the world's leading distance runners. Kenenisa Bekele had clocked 12:37:35 in the Netherlands in 2004 to set a new world record. Championship races are tactical and the pace is usually slower. But running under 13 minutes would give me a psychological boost going into the big competitions.

People have this idea that athletes set their aims for things that are a long way away: the Olympics, the Worlds. That isn't how it works. For sure, a young runner might dream of running in the Games, but there are loads of steps to take before getting to that level. So you don't look too far ahead. You focus on something closer. Making this time or winning this race meeting. Inch by inch, you edge towards your big goal. At this point, I wasn't thinking about the next World Championships or Olympics. The only thing I could think about was getting back out there on the track and beating that record.

My year didn't get off to the greatest start. On Christmas Day 2009, I went to Richmond Park to do a hill session on my own. It was a freezing cold morning. I was running up and down repeatedly on this one hill when I noticed a couple with a baby in a pushchair walking up the same hill. They were taking up nearly the entire path, and as I was having to run around them, I couldn't train properly. After three or four attempts to run around the couple I got a bit fed up and approached the man.

'Sorry, mate,' I said. 'Would you mind moving just a little bit to the side of the path so I can run past? I'm training.'

The man refused. I'm not sure why, but he appeared to have got the idea into his head that he had right of way on the path. I wanted to get my sprint sessions done so I asked the man politely again if he would consider moving. He still refused. Things quickly escalated into a heated argument – from both sides. Neither of us would budge. We both believed we were in the right. All of a sudden the man stepped towards me, as if he wanted to fight. He was much taller and bigger than me but I did not want to back down so I took a step towards the man. We were in each other's faces. Then it all kicked off. Before I knew it, we were having a full-blown fight, rolling around on the ground, trading blows. Onlookers had to pull us apart before things got really bad. Meanwhile, Tania was at home preparing for our first Christmas Day under the same roof when I called her.

'Come down to the park,' I mumbled incoherently. 'Come down, quick as you can.'

Tania couldn't understand me so I passed the phone to an onlooker.

'I think you'd better come down,' the man said to Tania. 'There's been a fight. He's okay, but you'd best get down here.'

Several minutes later the police showed up. A few minutes later Tania arrived. She'd rushed down to the park from our flat. I was caked in mud from where I'd been rolling around on the grass. There were nicks and cuts all over my face and I sported a massive bruise on my head. I wasn't badly hurt or anything but you could tell that I'd been in a scuff. Nothing came of it; there were no arrests made or anything like that. The other guy looked the worse for wear too and although I told the police that he had attacked me first they were reluctant to press charges, because the guy looked as if he had come off worse in the scrap, despite being much bigger than me. Thankfully things calmed down after that and I came home, cleaned up and changed and forgot about it. We all had Christmas dinner, but it's fair to say my day got off to a bad start.

Earlier in December I had run the European Cross Country Championship in Dublin and finished second on the 9.97

kilometre course. In early January 2010 I ran the 4 kilometre Great Edinburgh International Cross Country and placed third. On both occasions I collapsed at the finish line. At the time there was a lot of speculation that I'd suffered some kind of dietary problem, with reports claiming that I had lower than normal levels of iron and magnesium. In Ireland I'd been locked in a duel with Alemayehu Bezabeh, an Ethiopian athlete who now represented Spain. Bezabeh was running fast in Dublin – and I mean *fast*. I ran as hard as I could, trying to beat him. Ricky likes to say I have the heart of a lion, and I was pushing harder and harder, right to the very limits, practically killing myself to finish ahead of this guy. I started feeling dizzy. But no matter how hard I ran, I couldn't catch Bezabeh. I don't even remember crossing the line.

Three weeks later in Edinburgh the same thing had happened. I got off to a blistering start. At one stage I'd put almost 100 metres between myself and the second-placed runner. Towards the end of the course I had the same dizzy spell. Something wasn't right. I faded badly and was close to collapse at the finish line. Paramedics rushed over to me immediately.

It wasn't the first time I'd felt dizzy in a race. In my junior years I had tried sticking faithfully to Ramadan during the athletics season. I remember running in the European Cross Country Championships Juniors race one year when I suddenly felt faint and started experiencing these dizzy spells as I went round the course. Somehow I made it to the finish line before collapsing through sheer exhaustion. It wasn't hard to figure out what had gone wrong: the race was in the middle of Ramadan and I'd fasted in the days leading up to it. Chris Thompson had been competing at the same championships. He came over and checked up on me. When I explained what had happened, he was stunned that I'd been able to run in the first place. For me, I was never going to say, 'I can't do Ramadan, I'm an athlete.' But obviously collapsing in races was no good either. I had to find a balance, so I began fasting in the lead-up to Ramadan, breaking the fast during race meets and then catching up with the fasting days I had missed out at the end of the season.

After the race in Edinburgh a bunch of tests were run, but the results were inconclusive. There were a lot of factors to consider: at both races the weather had been freezing cold; I hadn't been eating properly and I was still feeling the effects of having run too hard in Dublin. I'd had a couple of off-days. That was it. Despite this, I felt in good shape. On New Year's Eve, between these two events, I'd run a great race at the BoClassic International in Bolzano, Italy, finishing just 4 seconds behind Edwin Soi and Imane Merga. After Edinburgh I flew out to Kaptagat/Iten for high-altitude training. In March 2010 I won the British World Cross Country Trial and went on to place twentieth at the World Cross Country Championships in Poland.

In April I got married.

On the big day Tania was a lot more nervous than she thought she was going to be. We both were. As Muslims we were married in the traditional way, in a private ceremony at a nearby mosque. A week later we had the official celebration. Everyone we knew was there. All our friends and Tania's family. Steve Cram was there with his partner, the former athlete and BBC commentator Allison Curbishley. Paula Radcliffe and her husband Gary Lough were there too, along with Hayley Yelling, Jo Pavey, Mustafa Mohamed and his wife. Ricky, Marion, Grainne and Mike Skinner, one of my former training partners who also worked at PACE, were all there. Steve Vernon, Scott Overall, Alan Storey and some of the old St Mary's and Loughborough crews attended the wedding, along with Darren Chin. My groomsmen were Tania's brother Colin, Scott Overall, Kevin Quinn – another running mate – and Ricky. Alan Watkinson was my best man. It was a beautiful day apart from one small hiccup – we forgot to arrange for someone to capture the wedding on video. Happily, Darren came to the rescue and whipped out his mobile phone. He's living the dream in Jamaica these days, so the only footage that exists of my wedding day is somewhere in his pocket.

Tania's grandmother was there too. 'I knew it!' she said at the wedding, reminding us of the time I popped round the house as a kid with a gift for Tania and she had been there. 'I knew all along that he had a thing for my grand-daughter!' Apparently the signs were always there. When Alan Watkinson gave his best man speech, he recalled a time when he gave me and Tania a lift to a training session at the athletics club. According to Alan, the two of us were arguing in the back like husband and wife. It was clear from the start that there was a strong chemistry between us.

The following morning we left for our honeymoon in

Zanzibar, off the coast of Tanzania. Tania had the wedding blues and was pretty depressed on the flight out. Zanzibar was entirely my choice for the honeymoon. Mustafa Mohamed had gone there for his honeymoon six months earlier with his wife, staying in a top hotel overlooking the beach. He came back raving about the place, telling me how amazing it was, this quiet, secluded spot, far away from anything touristy. It sounded great.

When we first arrived in Zanzibar, it looked a little less great. On the drive from the airport we had to pass through several dodgy areas, and at one point Tania turned to me and said something like, 'What are we doing here?' Things got better when we arrived at the first hotel. (We stayed in three different hotels on the trip.) It was just like Mustafa had sold it to me. Right on the beach. Pristine white sand. Blue skies. Deep blue water. Palm trees. Not a soul in sight.

During the days we'd go for walks along the beach. We did a few water sports too, including a deep-sea diving trip. A group of about six of us strapped on oxygen tanks as the diving instructor explained that there was enough oxygen in each tank to last forty-five minutes. We went down quite deep under the surface and started exploring the reef. About twenty minutes in, I suddenly couldn't breathe. Alarm bells went off in my head. I didn't know what was going on; I was terrified. I bulleted to the surface and ripped off my breathing mask. The diving instructor inspected my tank to see what had gone wrong. To his amazement, my tank had run out of oxygen. Because I have much bigger lungs than the average person, an oxygen supply that was supposed to last forty-five minutes lasted less than half that for me. The instructor couldn't believe it at first. He told us it was unheard of for anyone to use up their oxygen supply so quickly.

It was a great holiday. A beautiful honeymoon. We did a lot of chilling out and relaxing, staying up all night and enjoying the feeling of being newlyweds. We even got up to the odd bit of mischief. At one of the hotels we became good friends with the night-time supervisor, a lovely guy called Robert. One night we were up into the early hours and both craved some food. No one was about, so Robert let us sneak into the hotel kitchen at three o'clock in the morning and told us we could cook up whatever we wanted. Brilliant. What with all my travelling and training in camps, being able to spend some quality time with Tania meant a lot to me. Although one of Tania's pranks backfired a bit. We were lazing around the pool one day when Tania asked me, 'Is your watch waterproof?'

I nodded. 'Yeah, it is,' I replied, frowning. 'Why?'

Without a moment's hesitation Tania pushed me into the pool. It was for a joke and I would have been laughing along with her – had it not been for the fact that I was fully clothed at the time and my iPhone was in my shorts pocket. Tania had no idea. But stored on my phone were all of our text messages from when we had first gotten together and started dating. I scrambled out of the pool and frantically dug my iPhone out of my pocket. It was dripping wet. A total write-off. At first Tania couldn't see why I was so upset. Then I explained about the texts. It wasn't Tania's fault. She wasn't to know I had my iPhone on me. And we soon forgot about it and went back to enjoying ourselves.

By the time it came for us to fly home, I was itching to get back to training. I'd hardly done any running in Zanzibar, and as a result I'd put on a bit of weight. To look at my frame you wouldn't believe it, but I do put on weight really easily. Tania noticed it straight away on our honeymoon. We were both eating the same portions, but I was the one putting on the pounds. As a junior runner, I'd been able to scoff McDonald's burgers all day long, but these days I can't get away with it. Now I have to watch my diet very carefully: after the London Olympics I did a lot of media work and didn't train properly for a while, and in the space of a few weeks I ballooned from 52kg, the leanest I'd ever been, to more than 60kg. It was ridiculous. Leaving Zanzibar, I wasn't in race shape.

The original plan was for Tania and me to fly back to London together, and then I'd head on to Stanford, California, in time to compete in the Payton Jordan Cardinal 10,000 metres. On arriving at Nairobi airport, the first leg of our journey home, we discovered that half of Europe was covered by a volcanic ash cloud and all flights had been cancelled. We wouldn't be going anywhere; we were stranded in Nairobi. There was nothing to do except book a room in a nearby hotel and sit it out. Luckily, Tania's dad, Bob, worked in the travel business and had the inside scoop on when the flights were going to start again. For a few days we were on edge, wanting to know what was happening, when we could leave. Neither of us was enjoying our enforced stay. Tania wanted to get back as Rhianna was due to start school in a couple of weeks. I wanted to get across to California and race – and I would have gone had it not been for Tania. She felt that, considering the shape I was in, racing in Stanford wouldn't be a good move for me. I'd not trained properly and if I went over to Stanford and lost badly, that would dent my confidence going into the European Championships. Since we were already in Kenya, Tania thought it made more sense for me to go up to Iten and train there instead. She made a compelling argument. After all, I already had a load of clothes left at the camp from my previous training block there. All I had to do was get a short forty-five-minute flight to Eldoret and catch a taxi to the camp.

In the end I changed my plans and decided to head up to the Rift Valley, while Tania would return home to England at the first opportunity. At last the cloud cleared and Bob managed to get Tania on a flight bound for London. We said our goodbyes at the airport. That was really, really hard for us both. We had only been married for a few short weeks. All we wanted to do was spend more time with each other. Now we were going to be separated for the next six weeks. It hurts, but these are the sorts of sacrifices you have to be prepared to make in order to achieve everything you're capable of. We've both made countless sacrifices for the sake of my career. And believe me, it's painful to stand there in the departures lounge at Nairobi airport and watch your wife fly home alone from her honeymoon.

At this point I was being coached by Alan Storey again. After my problems in Dublin and Edinburgh I reached out to Alan to ask his opinion. We started talking more often again and as I was getting into my track season preparations, I felt that I needed Alan's help once more. I needed more structure, some kind of framework to allow me to concentrate more on running than over-thinking my programme. I explained that I wanted the freedom to source advice from others, including Ian Stewart, who had taken over from Alan as Head of Endurance at UKA. I didn't want to be tied completely to his methods because while some of them worked well for me, others were less successful. Alan was okay with that. Both of us wanted the same thing – for me to win races – and sometimes when a coach can see that things aren't going well, they'll take a step back and let the athlete explore different things. I wanted a structure, but I also wanted the flexibility to try different things, to add more quality to the track workouts and reduce the volume. The two of us came to an arrangement whereby Alan was my main coach. He'd write a training programme for me. I'd go away and think about it. Then I'd use that programme as a framework, adjusting it depending where I was or who I had to train with.

That volcanic ash cloud turned out to be a blessing in disguise. Rather than flying to Stanford only to get beaten, I spent six weeks working hard in Kenya to reach peak fitness.

When I came back, I was ready for the 2010 European Championships.

My form was excellent going into Barcelona. After returning to Teddington, I based myself at a training camp in Font-Romeu, a small town high in the French Pyrenees, close to the Spanish border. Paula Radcliffe had been using Font-Romeu as her base for several years. You can instantly see why: the village is nearly 2000 metres above sea level, there are loads of flat trails ideal for endurance training, and plenty of steep inclines to do hill sessions. Font-Romeu is a typical Alpine village: lots of ski chalets, lots of restaurants. I kept up my training regime, doing hill sprints up the steep mountain climbs and going for grinding runs on the trails.

Physically, I felt strong. I took part in a couple of warm-up meetings. I won the 10,000 metres European Cup in Marseille on 5 June. Two weeks later I won the 5000 metres at the European Team Championships in Norway. I was well up for it.

Then – out of nowhere – my Achilles started hurting.

I remember going out for a run and feeling this sharp pain shoot up and down the back of my ankle. I was diagnosed with Achilles tendonitis. This is common among athletes. Most distance runners suffer an irritation of the Achilles at some point in their career. It's caused by the constant impact of sprinting movement, which in turn overworks the tendon. There are only two things you can do: manage the pain, or go under the knife. I'd trained hard for the European Championships. Surgery wasn't an option, but the injury was constricting my running gait. Every time I stepped onto the track, I got this sudden pain and tightness in my Achilles. I wasn't running as freely.

I gritted my teeth and trained through the injury as best I could. It's a weird one, the Achilles. The pain isn't severe enough to stop you from training, but it inhibits you just enough to play on your mind. You're aware of it with every stride. I did everything I could to minimize the pain. Wearing spikes aggravated the tendon, so at the beginning of each training session I'd have to wear racing flats until it was well warmed up and only put on spikes for the last few reps. It wasn't ideal. Achilles tendonitis is not something that just goes away, and it's hard to perform to your best when you're worrying about an injury. I decided to try and get through the championships, then begin proper treatment of the injury.

On the Tuesday I raced in the 10,000 metres. It was a hot night inside the Olympic Stadium. I'd done my homework on the competition and knew that Ayad Lamdassem, a Moroccan now running for Spain, was my biggest threat. My friend Chris Thompson was also on the starting line. Back in 2003 Chris had beaten me to win the 5000 at the European Under-23s in Bydgoszcz. Now, seven years later, we were lining up together as seniors. Athletics is funny like that. You can be best friends with someone off the track, but once that gun goes, it's every runner for himself.

The gun cracked. The shot echoed. The race started. Lamdassem and me soon pulled away from the chasing pack. After that, it was a straight tussle between the two of us. I was pushing hard but, unlike at Beijing, I had some gas left in the tank this time round. I had trained better, smarter. As long as I stuck close to Lamdassem, I knew I had the pace to beat him on the sprint finish. He knew it too. With 500 metres to go, I saw him glance up at the screen. He saw me hovering on his shoulder, pushing hard, waiting for the loud clang of the bell to sound the final lap.

At 400 metres to the line, I kicked on. Fifty metres further on, 350 to go, I stormed past Lamdassem. I knew he couldn't catch me. Not now. I was stretching. Increasing the gap between us. I was in control of the race. With 200 metres to go, Lamdassem faded. I charged towards the finish line, arms outstretched. Lamdassem crossed the line in fourth. Chris thundered ahead of him on the home straight to claim second, shading silver ahead of the Italian Daniele Meucci on the line. A one-two for Great Britain.

This feeling of pure joy washed over me, like nothing else I've ever felt. The clock told me that I'd run the race in 28:24.99. The time was irrelevant. All that mattered was the medal. My first major title. Right then, it hit me: 'I'm the first Briton to land 10,000 metres gold at the Europeans.' I had gone where no British runner had gone before. When I'd run in the Europeans in Gothenburg in 2006, no British runner had even competed in the 10,000. I was delighted for Chris too. He had been through more than his fair share of injuries. In the 5000 metres in Gothenburg, the same race where I lost to Jesús España on the home straight, Chris had staggered home in last place. To come back from that was an incredible achievement. After the race Chris grabbed me and planted a kiss on my head. He told someone he was going to celebrate with a beer. No one deserved it more than him.

Winning that race went some way towards easing the pain of Beijing. After the race I was inundated with text messages. One of them was from Arsène Wenger, the Arsenal manager, congratulating me on my win. Coming from Wenger, that meant a lot. But there was no time for me to celebrate. I had two days to rest and recover before the 5000 metres heats took place.

I still had unfinished business with España.

I breezed home first in the second qualifying heat, finishing ahead of España and another Spanish runner, Sergio Sánchez. Earlier Chris Thompson had also made the cut for the final, coming fourth in the first heat behind Alemayehu Bezabeh and Hayle Ibrahimov of Azerbaijan. I went back to the hotel, rested up some more, and returned to the Olympic Stadium for the 5000 metres on Saturday 31 July. This was the one I wanted the most. Four years had passed since I lost to España in Gothenburg. Four years I had to wait for this opportunity. Revenge was on.

I had everything riding on this race. España was the favourite because he was racing on home turf and had the backing of 50,000 Spanish fans crammed inside the stadium. I was determined to avenge my defeat in Gothenburg. I told myself, 'You've got nothing to fear.' In 2009 I'd beaten España in the 3000 metres at the European Indoors in Turin, and finished ahead of him in the 5000 metres at the World

Championships in Berlin. But this was the first time we had been direct rivals in a big race since that day in Sweden.

Bezabeh, one of three Spanish runners competing in the race and the Ethiopian-born athlete who had run insanely fast at the cross country race in Dublin the previous winter, when I'd collapsed at the finish line, took an early lead. Soon España was nudging out in front and Bezabeh slotted in behind him. At that point I was back in fourth. España was going at a decent pace – not too quick. He wanted a fast race, thinking that I was still recovering from running the 10,000 metres. But I didn't feel tired. I wound it up. Then I wound it up some more. Slowly, I started to rein in España. With four laps to go, Bezabeh still led and I was in second place, with Ibrahimov in third and España down in fourth. Three laps to go, I glanced up at the screen, saw España trailing behind. His head was rocking from side to side with the strain as he dug deep and pushed really hard. Now I kicked on. I'd gone a little earlier than I intended, but suddenly I was striding ahead of Bezabeh, stretching the field. Bezabeh faded. I had to keep digging, keep the pressure on. Now Ibrahimov was breathing down my neck, with España just behind him. I was hurting a lot but I was riding the pain, telling myself over and over, 'No way. You can't let him sprint past you. Not this time.' I dug very deep and put in a 59-second lap as I came to the bell. Suddenly, I was stretching down the back straight, giving it everything, constantly checking to see how big the gap was between España and me. Ibrahimov pulled closer. España was gone. He was spent. I kicked again from the front.

I started pulling away from Ibrahimov and the small gap between us quickly opened into a big one. As I came sprinting around the home straight, I was far clear of the other runners. Ten metres of beautiful blue track between España and me. I swept across the finish line and for a moment I couldn't believe I had won. The first thought that flashed through my mind was, 'It was worth it, then.' Those six weeks I had spent away from Tania and Rhianna after Zanzibar, when I had to watch my wife go home by herself, the sacrifices I had made – it hadn't been for nothing, in the end. It was totally worth it. I later found out that my last mile was sub-four minutes.

Losing a race in athletics is not like losing a football or tennis match. There's no second chance, no opportunity to make amends the following week. You have no choice but to wait, and then wait some more. Me, I'd been waiting four years to make up for Gothenburg. As soon as I won, a feeling of absolute joy washed over me. I sank to my knees, kissed the track, and whispered a prayer. I always drop to my knees and say a prayer after a race. I can't remember what I said that day, I was so pumped up.

Gothenburg was history. Jesús España came over to me as I finished praying. Ever the gentleman, he was the first runner to congratulate me. He gave me a hand and helped me to my feet.

'Well done,' he said. 'You deserve it.'

'Thanks,' I said back.

In Gothenburg the better man had won. This time, I deserved it. I'd trained hard and worked at my preparation and won the race. España raised my right arm in victory to the crowd. Everyone cheered. I was just ecstatic to have won the race. It was an incredible moment in my life, the pinnacle of everything I'd been striving to achieve up to that point. Only four other guys had done the European distance double, and they were all legends in their own right: Emil Zátopek, Zdzislaw Krzyszkowiak, Juha Vaatainen and Salvatore Antibo. I was the first to achieve the feat since 1990.

Winning the double in Barcelona thrust me into the limelight for the first time. The races had been shown live back home in the UK and my achievements had made the headlines of the national newspapers. None of this was apparent to me at first. Me, Tania and Rhianna celebrated together as a family after the championships, enjoying a bit of down time together in the city. It was only when we flew back to London that it dawned on us, just how big a deal I now was. Loads of news crews and journalists and photographers were waiting for us at the airport. That was quite a shock. We hadn't expected to get mobbed as soon as we stepped off the plane. Athletics is not the Premier League. We don't have the round-the-clock coverage other sports enjoy. And for me, the attention on us was something I'd never experienced before in my career. I did the rounds on breakfast TV, as well as the national media circuit. The sudden attention on me took some getting used to. One evening me, Tania and Rhianna headed over to Nadia and Bob's to eat pizza and watch some TV and generally relax. Imagine our surprise when we turned up to find a news van parked outside their house! No one knew we were going there. But the media didn't know where I lived and had stationed a van there on the off-chance that I'd pop over to see the in-laws. This was my first real taste of national recognition. From spending years under the radar, I had the media all over me.

In the midst of all this coverage, the secretary to Ivan Gazidis, the chief executive of Arsenal, contacted me with an invitation to attend the first home game of the season against Blackpool as an honorary guest. For a die-hard Arsenal fan, this was the greatest news ever. I brought Tania and Rhianna along to the match with me. We got to sit in the director's box, which is invite-only. Everything was specially laid out for us and everyone at the club, from top to bottom, was as nice as you could imagine. Before the game Ivan presented me with an Arsenal shirt with 'Farah' on the back. Wenger also came up to the director's box before the match and said hello to me and my family. Wenger being one of my heroes, meeting him blew my mind. He's an extraordinarily humble and decent man. At half-time I was invited to walk out onto the pitch and display my two European gold medals to all the fans. Arsenal won 6-0. Walcott scored twice. Great result, and a great day all round – one of the best days of my life, and one I'll never forget. I mean – how many Arsenal fans get to actually meet Wenger?

With this new recognition came heightened expectations. In the wake of Barcelona people started to view me as a realistic medal prospect for the London 2012 Olympic

Games. The press now asked me questions such as, 'How do you feel about your chances in 2012?' Stuff like that. Up to that point in my career, I hadn't been viewed as someone who was remotely a threat for the Olympic Games. The European Championships changed all that. I got a taste of winning – a taste of success and what it brings. I wanted more.

I had one target left to achieve before the season was over: the British record.

Throughout the Europeans I'd been feeling my Achilles. The tendon was still inflamed, it wasn't getting any better and the advice from Neil Black was that I shouldn't push it and run in Zurich. Neil feared that if I attempted another race, I might do lasting damage to the tendon. Ricky shared his concerns. They were in agreement: running in Zurich was a bad idea. I listened to them, nodded, but I was adamant that I wanted to go there and compete. I understood that they had my best interests at heart. I'd won the European double, why not end the season on a high note rather than risk further injury? But I was determined to run. I thought, 'I'm in good running shape. Only the Achilles is holding me back. One more race, then I'll get the injury sorted.' I still had my eye on Dave Moorcroft's British record. That had been my goal at the start of the year. I didn't want the season to end without having achieved it.

My last race of the 2010 season took place on 19 August at the Diamond League meeting in Zurich, the penultimate meet in the calendar. It's usually hard for an athlete to produce their best form coming off the back of a major championship. Big races do take it out of you. You spend months in training with the aim of peaking at the big competition, and to carry that through to the next event and the one after that is difficult, mentally and physically. But I sort of knew that if I carried myself well leading into Zurich, I had a good chance of going close to the British record. I had no idea how far under 13 minutes I could go if I actually did it. But my first target was to run under that time. I arrived at the league meeting feeling strong, lean, fast and ready to give it my best shot.

Achilles aside, I was in the shape of my life. Barcelona proved that. This was a big moment for me. A huge test. My last chance to run sub-13:00 before the curtain came down on my season. It had been a good year. The best so far. Getting married, winning at the Europeans. I wanted to smash that record and end the season on a high note.

As soon as I began warming up for the race in the call room, my Achilles flared up. Neil had warned me about the dangers of running in Zurich. I hadn't listened to him. Now this. Here I was, about to take my place on the start line of the 5000 metres race, and I was practically hobbling on one leg. I couldn't pull out of the race. Not now. I did what I could to manage the discomfort, not wearing my spikes until the very last minute.

The 5000 that day was a good field. It had all the big names. Tariku Bekele had a season's best of 12:53. Fellow Ethiopian 12:53 runner Imane Merga was there, and Olympic medallists Eliud Kipchoge and Edwin Soi, plus two other good Kenyans – Vincent Chepkok and Moses Masai.

Chepkok had run 12:51.45 in Doha in May. Masai, he'd won bronze in the 10,000 at the 2009 Worlds in Berlin. These guys were world-class runners. Chris Solinsky, the muscular American who was the first non-African to run sub-27:00 at the 10,000, was there, along with Galen Rupp, an up-and-coming American runner. My mate Chris Thompson was there too. It was a major race. A lot of unbelievable talent on that start line. All the Diamond League meets that year had been fast. Sixteen guys had run sub-13:00.

The early pace was blistering. For the first few laps I lurked at the back of a huge pack as the pacemakers led the way. Early on in the race, I knew that my pace was good, and as I started working my way through the field, I was almost 3 seconds ahead of the time Dave Moorcroft had run in Oslo. The guys at the front began winding the pace up. I kept digging. After 4000 metres I'd moved 4 seconds clear of the British record. All I had to do now was keep going. Keep pushing. But the next 600 metres was brutal. The pace was unbelievable. I was struggling with my Achilles. I dug deep and pushed through. By the time the bell rang, I knew I was only a few strides up on the record and I'd have to push really, really hard on the last lap. I fought through the pain. That last 200 metres was agonizing. I pushed harder than I'd ever done before.

I finished fifth.

My time? 12:57.94.

I'd shaved almost 3 seconds off the record.

Breaking that record was a big, big deal for me. When Dave Moorcroft had run 13:00, twenty-seven years earlier, it had been a new world record. He was well clear of the pack and effectively ran a solo race. I came fifth behind Tariku Bekele, and my time was the 177th fastest ever, which shows just how much distance running had moved forward in the intervening years. I'd always had that inner belief in my ability to run sub-13:00, but results-wise I'd not always performed. Admittedly, Beijing and the months after it had been tough. Breaking the British record was, for me, part of the recovery process – of proving to myself that I had what it took to compete with the very best. And to do it late on in the season and coming off the back of Barcelona, which had been a physically and emotionally draining experience, was something special.

It's weird, but once I broke the record, running under 13:00 felt like nothing to me any more. It changed my feeling about who I am. It gave me the confidence to mix it in with the likes of the Bekele brothers and the Kenyans. It hadn't happened overnight – there had been plenty of ups and downs and bumps to get to this point – but shattering a long-standing British record showed me that if I got the training right and applied myself properly, I could run with the best. Most importantly, I believed in myself.

Now, I thought, anything is possible.

Immediately after the race, I went to another meeting with Alberto Salazar. Ricky had arranged for the three of us to have dinner at a hotel in Zurich. A year had passed since I'd sat down and talked with Alberto in Birmingham. In that time, I'd tasted success. I had the utmost respect for Alan, but it was hard for him to coach me properly when he was in London and I was halfway around the world. I was doing some sessions with groups in Kenya, some sessions with groups in the UK, some sessions on my own in Font-Romeu. I needed one coach and one training group that would be with me 24/7, 365 days a year. I was having to process all this information, figure out what worked for me and what didn't, at the same time as trying to concentrate on running well in each training session and getting a proper rest afterwards. I'd been carrying on like this the whole year and I was getting frustrated with not having my own coach at the track all year round. By the end of the season I'd had enough. I couldn't face another year acting as my own coach, playing roulette with my career. I didn't want to live in Kenya all year and there were no strong groups in the UK. I needed a single person to oversee my training. Someone who could set me sessions, watch my sessions, tell me when I needed to push harder or slow down, without me having to scratch my head and ask myself, 'Is this right or wrong?' Alan was doing his best, but things had changed between us and we both knew that I needed to move on.

I had the beating of the European field. Breaking the British record convinced me that I was on the edge. I was *this* close to fulfilling my potential. Now I needed someone who had the expertise and ability to squeeze that 1 or 2 per cent more out of my running. For me, there was only one person for the job: Alberto Salazar.

I was keenly aware that Alberto had already turned me down once. Some of the stumbling blocks he'd mentioned in Birmingham still existed – the sponsorship issue, and the fact that his Oregon Project was purely focused on American distance runners. But at the same time, we were coming at this from a different angle now. I wanted Alberto to coach me on the track, not train me to run the marathon. Alberto had said that I had potential on the track; now I was starting to realize it, and I wanted Alberto to be the guy who got me over the line.

That meeting in Zurich went really well. Alberto liked the idea of working with me. We had a long chat. He explained a few things to me about the Nike Oregon Project and the group he worked with, what would be expected of me if I joined the group. I had to fit in with what he was trying to achieve in Portland. That was key. And I had to be prepared to work incredibly hard. I was ready for that. I'd heard about the Oregon Project; I knew training under Alberto would be more gruelling than anything I'd ever done before. Of course I'd heard the stories about his scientific approach, using underwater treadmills and cryo-saunas, for example, but the fact remains that Alberto possesses an incredible work ethic – a disciplined and relentless desire to improve. If he thinks there's an aspect of your running that needs to be corrected, he'll leave no stone unturned in his search to find a solution.

'And, of course,' Alberto added, 'you will need to move to Portland.'

I nodded. I'd understood from the get-go that if I wanted to be coached by Alberto, I'd have to relocate to the USA with my family. London was our home, and Rhianna had just started school, but being coached by Alberto would give me the best possible chance of beating the Ethiopians and Kenyans in major competitions. When news of my move to Portland went public, there were a fair few comments in the media, asking why I was changing coach with less than two years to go until the Olympics. Others questioned the wisdom of leaving Alan Storey permanently when 2010 had been such a successful year. That's not how I saw it. Sure, changing coaches is always a risk. But there's a big difference between winning the Europeans and winning the Worlds or the Olympics. At the European Championships, I wasn't competing against a huge pack of East African runners. If anything, the fact that I finished fifth in Zurich behind Tariku Bekele, Merga and Chepkok emphasized how much further I had to go in order to win on the world stage. The easier thing would have been to stay in England and keep the same set-up. But doing the easy thing isn't what wins you medals. I knew that moving would be difficult, both for me and for my family. But it's like I said. You have to make sacrifices in order to be successful. If I had to move away from my home to get better, then that's what I would do.

We reached an agreement that Alberto would become my new coach, subject to resolving the sponsorship issue. My contract with adidas still had a few months to run, which meant I had to stay put for a while before I could link up with Alberto in Portland. Adidas had matching rights on my next contract. We were very open and honest with them about the situation. There was no pressure from Alberto or Nike to make the switch to Portland. It was entirely our decision. In fact, by agreeing to join Alberto's group at the Oregon Project, I was putting myself in a weak negotiating position, since Nike knew I had to sign up to them before I could work with Alberto. I had no choice but to accept whatever offer they put on the table.

But the sacrifice was worth it. From now on, Alberto was the guy in charge. I wouldn't have to be both an athlete and a coach any more. I could focus solely on running. Alberto would be the one calling the shots.

2010 had been a good year. The next year was going to be even better.

13
THE PROJECT

From my house in Teddington to Bushy Park is a distance of approximately 700 metres. Whenever I'm going for a run in the park, I'll begin my warm-up by jogging at a light pace from my front door to the park gates. Two days after returning home from Zurich, I laced up my trainers and headed out the front door, intending to put in a good session at the park. I was on a big high after Zurich. I had the British record under my belt and a new coach to work with in the not-too-distant future, provided my sponsorship issue was resolved. When you're in good form like that, you don't want your season to end. But as I set off down the street, I could immediately feel that something was wrong.

My Achilles.

The tendon had been sore and stiff throughout the summer. Now it was so bad I couldn't jog on it. At first I tried running through the pain. I just about made it to the park gate. There I stopped and thought, 'This is too much.' I couldn't run any further. I turned around and limped back home. 'That's it for a few days,' I thought. A couple of days' rest, that's what I needed. I put my feet up for two days and rested the tendon. The pain faded. Then I went out for another run.

Soon as I started running, the stiffness came back.

'This isn't happening,' I thought. The 2010 Great North Run up in Newcastle was in early September, less than two weeks away, and I was desperate to compete.

At the end of the athletics season, when all the big track competitions are over, there are several major one-off races held around the world. As a distance runner, your aim is to finish the athletics season, then compete in a few big road races. One of the big public races is the Great North Run, held on a Sunday in September. On the Saturday there's the Great North CityGames, staged in Gateshead, on a purpose-built track near the city centre. It's free to watch and they host a number of events including the long jump, pole vault and mile race. I was scheduled to run the mile. On the back of my wins in Barcelona, I was now ranked the number one distance runner in Europe, and one of the best in the world. That made me a big draw for the road races. Suddenly Ricky's phone didn't stop ringing as organizers queued up to add me to their events. For me it was a chance to compete in one of the biggest road races in Europe. Now my Achilles was threatening to disrupt all that.

I went to see Neil. He had a look at my Achilles.

'Do you think it'll be all right to do a run in, say, two weeks, a week and a half?' I asked casually. I'd run with the injury in Barcelona and in Zurich. One more race would be okay, surely?

Blackie laughed. 'No chance, Mo! You need to give it some serious rest.'

I had no choice but to withdraw from the CityGames. Then I rested up, under strict instructions from Blackie not to do any running work for two whole weeks. Meanwhile, Blackie did his best to treat the injury, giving me deep-friction massages, which involved applying a degree of pressure to the sorest part of the tendon with the pads of his fingers and squeezing hard to help speed up the natural repair of the tendon. I have a high pain threshold, but those massages were something else. Hands down, it was the worst pain I'd ever experienced. It felt like someone twisting a knife inside my Achilles.

This was a deeply frustrating time for me. I was in brilliant shape coming out of the track season, and I was looking forward to carrying my good form into the road races. To make matters worse, I was restless from not being able to run, constantly fidgeting and making a nuisance of myself around the house. I was like a kid during the school holidays, full of energy but with no way of burning it off. After two weeks of rest and treatment, Blackie gave me the green light to start running again. The next morning I got up, itching to get down to Bushy Park and run. As soon as I stepped outside, I felt the soreness in my Achilles again.

This was getting serious now. The injury wasn't responding to rest. Neil took me to see an Achilles specialist who'd flown in from Sweden. He was a leading expert in his field – what this guy didn't know about Achilles injuries wasn't worth knowing. He carried out a thorough investigation of my foot, and afterwards he and Blackie decided that the best course of action was to give the tendon a further two weeks' rest. If the soreness hadn't eased up by then, the specialist recommended surgery. This was bad news. Going under the knife would mean missing several months of training, at the very least. And there are no guarantees with Achilles operations. Some athletes have the operation and never fully recover. It's a big risk. Blackie and I were in agreement that surgery was a worst-case scenario. But we both knew that if the injury didn't show signs of improvement, there was no other option.

For two weeks I did everything I possibly could to help the tendon heal. I gritted my teeth through several agonizing deep-friction massages. I did sessions on an exercise bike. I hopped on one leg in the physio room. I performed calf raises to strengthen the muscles. I even cut the heels off my trainers in order to reduce the pressure on my tendons. Nothing seemed to work. The tendon was still sore. On the Friday we went back to see the specialist for another consultation. It wasn't looking good. 'Two days,' the specialist said. 'If the tendon shows no sign of improvement over the weekend, then we'll arrange for you to fly to Stockholm on Monday. You can have the operation there.'

On the Saturday, the tendon started to feel a little less painful. On the Sunday, I went out for a light jog. This time, the soreness wasn't quite as bad. There was a little bit of feeling there and it still hurt, but it wasn't as bad as it had been after Zurich. On the Monday, the specialist took another look at my Achilles. 'The tendon has improved,' he said. 'You won't need the operation.' I breathed a massive sigh of relief. I'd been less than twenty-four hours away from having to go under the knife. The tendon never quite recovered – Achilles tendons rarely do – but it was good enough to run on again. To this day, it still feels quite sore.

I spent Christmas and the New Year at the camp in Iten, and kicked off the 2011 season in style with victory in the Great Edinburgh Cross Country – the same event where, twelve months earlier, I'd nearly collapsed close to the finish line. With the Achilles injury pretty much behind me, I pulled clear of the lead group with two laps to go to finish 30 metres ahead of Galen Rupp, who was a member of Alberto's Oregon Project. Ayad Lamdassem, who I'd beaten in the 10,000 metres in Barcelona, trailed in third. At the end of the month, I flew out to Portland, Oregon, on a recce mission to meet the other guys Alberto worked with and to find out more about the project.

At this point, very few people knew that I was going to be working with Alberto. Outside my immediate family, Ricky and Neil were the only two people aware of my trip to the US. Going out there, I wanted to keep things under wraps because I wasn't sure what would happen. We'd had that meeting in Zurich with Alberto, but I wasn't signed up yet and, as far as I was concerned, I had to see the set-up with my own eyes before committing. If I liked the feel of things out there, I'd rubber-stamp everything with Alberto and bring the family over. At least, that's what I had in mind. In fact, the opposite was true. Like a footballer trying out with a new club, *I* was the one on trial, *not* the Oregon guys. The group coached by Alberto is very tight-knit, and bringing in an outsider is a big deal. At the end of my trip, if the guys on the team gave me the thumbs-up,

Alberto would take me on. If not, I'd be out – simple as that.

Alberto put me up for a few days in the spare bedroom of his house. He's an interesting guy, Alberto. Like me, he holds his faith close to his heart. Alberto is a devout Roman Catholic, a two-beers-an-evening kind of guy who wears a tracksuit and a baseball cap. He also happens to possess the wickedest sense of humour on the circuit. Some coaches like to imagine they're funny, but Alberto is the real deal. He knows how to make people laugh. While I was staying at the house, he introduced me to his wife, Molly. They both went out of their way to make me feel at home, and I quickly warmed to Alberto. As a coach, he takes an interest in you above and beyond mere athletics. He cares about you on the human level. You have this feeling that you can talk to him about pretty much anything that's on your mind, and he'll give you a sympathetic hearing. My first night in the Salazar household, we talked about all kinds of stuff.

On top of everything else, Alberto also happens to be a forward-thinking coach when it comes to distance running. Naturally, I was full of questions about the Oregon Project when I first arrived. 'What kind of sessions do these guys do?' 'How many reps do they do?' 'What about preventing injury?' The next morning Alberto invited me down for a tour of the project headquarters to find out more.

The idea for the Oregon Project was born in 2001, during a conversation in a deli between Alberto and Tom Clarke, the President of Business Development at Nike. They were both disgusted at the state of American distance running.

The Boston Marathon had just taken place and the highest-placed US runner was sixth, and certain commentators were celebrating that like it was some kind of achievement. In response, Tom and Alberto came up with the idea of creating a special camp for training American distance runners with the potential to win Olympic gold and the big marathon races. Nike would provide the funds, and Alberto would oversee the project and provide his coaching expertise. They were going to put distance running back on the map, and Alberto was the guy who would make it happen.

The Nike campus, where the Oregon Project is based, is located in Beaverton, about 6 miles west of downtown Portland. A woodchip trail encircles it, and there's an all-weather track surrounded by dense trees with mountain peaks visible in the distance. This is where I'd be putting in hard work, training with the other guys in the group. Once Alberto had finished giving me the grand tour of the facilities, he introduced me to the rest of the team.

My main training partner would be Galen Rupp, who I already knew from competing against him in cross country and track events. Galen was three years younger than me, and the star of the Oregon Project – the guy they called the 'project's project'. He'd been training with Alberto since the age of fourteen and became a project member straight out of Central Catholic High School in Portland. Like me, Galen had preferred playing football as a kid. Like me, he was also very fast: in his high school freshman year he was running 200 metres in under 30 seconds. And also like me, Galen had almost no interest in running before his coaches persuaded him to start running on the track. We had a lot of things in common off the track as well. We both enjoyed playing FIFA; we both loved pancakes; we had the same taste in music, even down to the fact that we both had the same track playing for the first dance at our weddings ('Differences' by Ginuwine). We looked at each other and were both like, 'What are the chances of that?!?'

Alberto also introduced me to the rest of the project members: Alan Webb, a middle-distance runner who'd been an American high-school prodigy; Kara Goucher and her husband Adam; and Dathan Ritzenhein, who took bronze at the Birmingham half-marathon in 2009 when I had first met Alberto, although he wasn't in Portland at the time. It was a small, tight group. I went out for runs with Galen to get a feel for the intensity of training I'd be doing. In the evenings the entire group went out for a meal downtown. Being around Alberto, Galen and the other guys, everything just seemed to click. It felt right. I could see that Alberto was creating something special here. I thought, 'This is the place to be.'

On the third day Alberto told me that he'd be flying down to Albuquerque in New Mexico to see how things were going with Dathan. I'd join him later, but for the next few days I would stay on in Portland and get to know the other project members a little better. Alan Webb had a spare room, so I crashed there. I spent some more time hanging out with Galen. On the fourth day I caught a flight to New Mexico and met Dathan, and was there for a day or two. The more time I spent around Alberto and his group, the more I wanted to be a part of things.

I flew back to London, pumped with excitement. Talking to the guys in the group, seeing the facilities, spending time with Alberto, everything had confirmed to me what I'd already known: moving to Portland was the right thing to do. When I got back home, I sat Tania down and told her all about the trip. She could see that I wanted to make the move. Even though it meant moving away from our friends and her family, Tania was happy for me; she was willing to do whatever I felt was right for my running career. The move was more difficult for Rhianna. She'd just started school and was beginning to make friends. Uprooting her and changing her life was the biggest obstacle we had to overcome. But while I was in Portland, I'd done my research about where we'd live, the schools in the area that might be suitable for Rhianna. I had it all planned out. We also had to consider the fact that even though we'd be moving to the US as a family, there'd inevitably be long stretches of time when Tania and Rhianna would be pretty much on their own while I was off at training camp.

Ultimately, both Tania and I felt the move was the right one for me. It really wasn't that hard a decision to reach. Sure, we'd have some adjustments to make to live in another country. But Tania had seen me finish sixth or seventh in the field behind the Kenyans so many times, she knew as well as I did that something had to change. She had just one question.

'Do you genuinely believe this guy will help your career?'
I nodded. 'A hundred per cent.'
'Then, okay.'

That sealed it, really. We took Rhianna out of school and in February 2011 moved into a rented three-bedroom apartment in Portland. I say 'apartment' but it was more like a decent-sized house. The Londoner in me was stunned by how big people's homes were in the US. Portland was pleasingly chilled, a very relaxed city. Everyone was so nice to us when we moved in. People had time for us. It's the opposite of somewhere like New York, where everyone is busy all of the time. It turned out to be a good age for Rhianna to move too. When you're five years old, you can adapt easily and you don't really think too much about things. She treated the move like one big holiday. And Rhianna was already well travelled by that age; flying on a plane for her is like jumping on a bus.

Having said that, relocating was a stressful period for me and my family. When we headed out to the US, I was under the impression that our visas would be issued shortly after we settled in. In reality, merely beginning the process of obtaining a US residential visa takes a while. We had a top, top lawyer appointed by Nike and working on our behalf to handle the visa process during our initial months in the US. We kept waiting to hear. We kept hearing nothing. While we waited for our visas to be issued, we were stuck in a sort of limbo. I couldn't officially become a member of the Oregon Project because I wasn't with Nike and I wasn't a US citizen. Alberto appreciated the unique situation, so I was still allowed to train at the Nike campus – but because I wasn't formally a Nike athlete, I would turn up for training twice a day dressed head to toe in adidas kit. (My contract with adidas had expired but my new one with Nike hadn't started yet.) This was the Nike world headquarters, a massive campus with thousands of employees, and under normal circumstances, it's forbidden to walk around with so much as another sponsor's logo on your socks, let alone with a logo splashed all over your hat, your top, your leggings and trainers. I stood out like a sore thumb and if it had been anyone else, I would have been ejected. Thankfully Alberto put in a word with the top guys at Nike, including Phil Knight himself, the CEO and founder of the company. He told them that I was with Alberto, that I would eventually be signed up to Nike once my visa situation had been sorted out. Although that didn't stop people coming up to me during my first weeks on the campus and saying, 'What are you wearing?'

The wait for our visas dragged on. Rhianna couldn't enrol at school. I was getting frustrated with the delay. Weeks turned into months. Tania started to worry about how much school Rhianna was missing. In early May the lawyer advised us that in order to get our US visas we would need to leave the country and present ourselves at the US Consulate General Office in Toronto, where we had an appointment (the closest US embassy to Portland was actually in Vancouver, but they had no appointments for the next two months, which is why we made the longer trip to Toronto). All we had to do was turn up at the consulate, hand over our passports and have an interview. Then they'd stamp our passports and we'd be allowed to return to the US. The lawyer informed us that the process should take no longer than four days. That was the timescale we were given. We packed our suitcases with enough clothes for four or five days, booked a room at a nearby hotel – and off we went.

We arrived at the Consulate General on University Avenue for our scheduled appointment with all our paperwork in order and one of the best lawyers in the US handling our case. But instead of being invited in for an interview, the staff immediately handed our passports back to us, along with a piece of paper which more or less said that the consulate could not process our visa application because we were being investigated by the FBI. This was a shock. We hadn't been expecting this. Tania scanned this piece of paper and sent it across to the lawyer. He was stunned. It turned out that the reason why we were under investigation was because my passport stated that I was born in Mogadishu, which was a hotspot for terrorism at the time. The authorities had taken one look at my passport, noted my place of birth and decided that I needed to be investigated, ignoring the fact that I had been vouched for by Nike and had competed in the Olympic Games. We were then told that our applications couldn't be processed until the FBI had done a full background check on me. They would also need to investigate Tania and Rhianna because they were also on my application. The lawyer said the process could take up to ninety days. In the meantime we wouldn't be allowed back in the US.

By this point we were panicking hard. It wasn't as if we could simply go back to London. Our home was Portland now. All our clothes and possessions were there. And this was a World Championship year. I had some big meets coming up and I needed to train. I was losing fitness fast, so Alberto put me in touch with a local athletics coach. I rented a car and drove out to meet him. He showed me around the city parks, pointing out the good running routes. I did a few training runs here and there, but it wasn't the same. I needed to train at high altitude. Eventually we decided, as a family, that there was no point sitting it out in Toronto for ninety days. It was in my best interests to jump on a plane and head to Font-Romeu so I could train at the high-altitude camp. That was literally the only option we had: train there, wait out the ninety days until the FBI investigation was complete. Then fly back.

We were within hours of booking that flight and finalizing our plans to leave Canada, when out of the blue I got a call from Alberto. As luck would have it, Alberto knew a guy in the FBI. This guy happened to be a huge running fan and he'd heard of me. Alberto had said to the guy, 'Look, I understand what you're doing and why you have to do it, but this guy is different. He's an exceptional case. He's my athlete. He's come here to train with me, and he's going to be one of the best runners in the world. Please take that into consideration.' Fortunately for us, Alberto's contact in the FBI was sympathetic to our case. As a running fan he recognized that I wasn't just some random Somali guy looking to set up shop in the US. Alberto personally vouching for me did the trick. We got a call from him to say that everything had been sorted. Shortly after that the Consulate General rang us up and said, 'Come down to our offices and bring your passports with you.' Within five days, we had our passports stamped. We all breathed a huge sigh of relief. As a family we'd gone through every emotion in the world during those two weeks, holed up in a hotel room in Toronto, not knowing where I could train or when Rhianna could start school. At last, we were ready to go back to the US and begin our lives there for real.

By the time we returned to Portland, Rhianna had missed about four months of school. That's a significant amount of time for a child of her age. This was frustrating for me and Tania as parents: Rhianna wasn't getting any education and she was missing out on making friends and socializing with other kids the same age. So when her first day at school finally arrived, it was a big, big event in the Farah household. It felt like all three of us were going to school that day. As soon as we woke up that morning I started taking loads and loads of pictures: Rhianna having breakfast, Rhianna packing her bag. The school was right around the corner from our house and we filmed her every step of the way, walking from our front door to the school entrance. It was a special day for us. We were all on cloud nine. For me and Tania, it was one big celebration – our daughter having her first day at school and making new friends. As parents we were so happy for her.

To begin with, training under Alberto was tough. He had me doing fast and short reps on the track instead of the longer, slower reps that I'd been used to in the UK. I'd never done anything that short and fast before. For the first couple of weeks I'd drive home feeling utterly knackered – so tired, in fact, I could muster just about enough energy to drag myself out of the car, stagger up the drive and put the key in the front door. As soon as the door cracked open I'd literally collapse on the ground and crawl through the front door on my hands and knees. Alberto was pushing me to breaking point, to the extent that my body simply couldn't handle it – in a good way, of course.

Besides the track and the sessions on the underwater treadmill (a regular treadmill submerged in a big hot tub, which we used for the second run of the day to take the pressure off our legs) and the use of anti-gravity treadmills (where the treadmill is sealed inside a chamber to allow you to do overspeed training, running faster and with less resistance), Alberto's attention to detail is painstaking. He's obsessed with making sure that every little thing is just so.

I'll give you one example. In 2010 I was a good runner – good enough to win the Europeans – but my core wasn't stable enough. If you look at my races from that year, I'm rocking and rolling slightly. Alberto's thinking is that running side-to-side is a waste of energy and loses you valuable seconds over the course of a 5000 or 10,000 metre race, so he spent a lot of time teaching me to run fully straight rather than leaning to one side. He taught me how to improve my running stride. Before Alberto, my arms used to come up too high, which made me less aerodynamic. He showed me how to run more efficiently by having my arms only come up to the point where my fingertips were level with my chin before I'd bring them back down. He worked more on my lean at the end of a race. Little things like this, when you add them all up, make a big difference to your time.

A lot of my training was done alongside Galen. He showed me the ropes in those early days at the campus and we soon struck up a good friendship – and a healthy rivalry. Galen always used to beat me in training. In fact, he still does. There's no conflict between friendship and rivalry as far as I'm concerned. You can be good friends with someone off the track, but as soon as that gun goes, it's every man for himself. When the race starts, I'm not taking any prisoners. Galen is the same. We might be competing in the same event, but if he was having a hard day I'd help him out and vice versa. When we weren't training, we'd play FIFA or chat about music and stuff.

For three months I worked hard in training. In fact, I did some of the best work I'd ever done, and started seeing the results almost immediately. In March, I'd already shown a glimpse of what was possible by winning the New York half-marathon. It was the first half-marathon I'd ever competed in and it's fair to say that nobody expected great things from me going into that race. I was quietly confident about my chances of winning, but I was only the third favourite for the race. Everyone expected Gebre Gebremariam to win. Gebremariam was a World Cross Country champion, having won the title in Jordan two years earlier. In 2010 he'd won the New York Marathon in a time of 2:08.14. He was in great shape at the time of the half-marathon and my chances of beating him were generally considered to be slim.

For the first few miles I ran a conservative race. I didn't

want to go full-on in my first half-marathon. Then Galen went down like a ton of bricks right in front of me, almost taking me out with him. I narrowly avoided a collision by hurdling over Galen at the last moment. For a split second I thought I was out of the race. But I recovered my stride and carried on running, managing to keep pace with the lead pack without ever pushing on. Some of the other runners were pushing the pace hard and had I been a less experienced runner I might have been tempted to go with them. But I called on my experience and resisted the temptation to push with them. 13.1 miles is a long way and you don't want to go too hard, too early. As the race progressed, several other runners dropped off, leaving a pack of five of us racing towards the end. With 400 metres to go, it was a straight duel between me and Gebremariam. Then Gebremariam made his move. For a moment he eased forward and I thought he was about to pull clear of me. I didn't panic. I stayed level on his shoulder until the last 200 metres. Then I put my foot down. In the process Gebremariam tried to block me off, moving to the left to stop me going in front of him. I had to take a big detour in order to get round the guy – while sprinting at full speed. Over the last 100 metres I opened up a 2-metre gap on Gebremariam. I held him off and crossed the line in first place.

The New York half-marathon was a big win for me. My performance made all the big marathon race organizers sit up and take notice. They started to think, 'This guy could be a serious threat at the full marathon distance.' I also clocked the fastest time ever for a British man at the distance.

It would have been a new British record – by about thirty seconds – but because a section of the course was ever-so-slightly downhill, they were unable to ratify the result. Still, a win on my first-ever half-marathon was a great result. And Galen managed to salvage his race after falling over to finish third, making it a great day for both of us, and Alberto, as head of the Oregon Project, who could celebrate having two guys on the podium.

In June I travelled down to Eugene, a city about 100 miles due south of Portland, to compete in the Prefontaine Classic Diamond League meeting, held at Hayward Field on the University of Oregon campus, the same track where 'Pre' had broken the American 5000 metres record. The 'Pre Classic' is considered one of, if not the biggest track meet of the year, anywhere in the world. It's specifically a Nike meet, and all the top athletes in the world are involved, in every discipline: the sprinters, the long jumpers, the discus throwers and the distance runners. Basically, the cream of the crop is there. And that goes for the 10,000 metres too. Anyone who was anyone was in that race: Imane Merga, Moses Masai, Zersenay Tadese and Mark Kiptoo. There was absolutely nobody absent from the line-up. In athletics we call it 'fully loaded': it's the term we use for a race with the strongest possible field with nobody missing. Going into the 10,000 metres, on paper I was probably halfway down the list in terms of where people expected me to finish – Tania included. A lot of people had said to me before the race, 'You'd do well to come about fifth. If you're in the top five, that's a great result for you, mate.' I guess that was a fairly realistic prediction. Compared to the other guys in the race I hadn't come close to them; I'd never beaten any of them before. I hadn't even clocked any quick times that were seriously threatening them.

If you listen to the commentary for the race, my name isn't even mentioned until twenty-two minutes in. The commentator also happened to be the head of marketing for athletics worldwide at Nike. He knew everything there was to know about athletics, and had a pretty good idea about who stood a chance of winning the race and who didn't. Sure, I'd won the European titles, but on the world stage nobody is that fussed about the European Championships. It's all about how you perform at the Worlds and the Olympics. That's where it's at. And no one in their right mind expected me to finish top five at the Pre Classic. It was only after I started to creep up on the leading pack and I came into the camera shot that the commentator and everyone else in the stadium started to take notice of me. At that point I was neck-and-neck with Merga. He'd been the hot favourite for the race. Beforehand everyone had predicted that Merga would win. With 200 metres to go, I suddenly found this kick. It came from nowhere. I shot away from Merga, kicked on and won the race.

For me to win that 10,000 metres race was absolutely phenomenal. Nobody had seen it coming. All around Hayward Field, jaws hit the floor. The crowd went absolutely nuts. It was a local crowd and they were excited to see a British guy beating the Africans at their own game. In addition, the fans knew I was training and based in Oregon, working with Alberto, and they viewed me as one of their own. In the other races that evening, the crowd showed their respect, but the noise was nothing like that generated when I crossed the finish line. They went ballistic for me. That race was the turning point of my career on the world stage – the race where I went from being an outsider for the top five to becoming a world-beater. All of a sudden, I was a threat.

My victory at the Pre Classic tasted extra sweet because I had also set a new British and European record of 26:46.57 in the process. Chris Thompson, one of my main rivals as a junior, had said at the beginning of the year that he was going to go for the British 10,000 metres record. Over the course of the year, this friendly competition unfolded between me and Chris as to who could break that record first. In previous years we'd both edged closer and closer to it, shaving a second off each other's time with every race. Chris would run 27:28. I would then come back and run 27:27. Then Chris would clock 27:26. And so on. It was almost as if we were competing with each other to seize that record. It was a big target for both of us. To not only win the 10,000 metres in such a strong field, but to break the record in the process, which I'd been trying to do for two years, and to pip Chris Thompson to it as well – it was an all-round amazing feeling and fully vindicated my decision to switch coaches and work with Alberto.

In July I broke another British record competing in the 5000 metres at the Diamond League meeting in Monaco, where I ran 12:53.11 – a new personal best and almost four seconds faster than my time in Zurich. That time was good enough to elevate me to second place on the all-time European list for the event (behind only the Moroccan-born Belgian runner Mohammed Mourhit). It was also the fastest 5000 anyone had run in 2011. More importantly, I had beaten Bernard Lagat. To this day, Lagat is considered one of the all-time greats of middle-distance running. In his prime he was the best in the world, twice a gold medallist at the World Championships. Lagat was in great shape going into Monaco and for me to beat him was a massive shock and a significant boost ahead of Daegu. I had already asserted my credentials at the 10,000 metres at the Pre Classic. Now I was making my presence felt at the 5000 metres too, and against different competitors (some guys compete in the 5000 metres but not the 10,000 metres, including Lagat). Going into Monaco, you would have been laughed at if you'd put your money on me to win. With another win under my belt, my confidence skyrocketed. After the Pre Classic and Monaco, I now had the feeling that I could beat everyone. So far that year I had won every 5000 metres race I'd entered. I went into the World Championships determined to win.

Building up to the Worlds, there had been some talk in the press, a few people publicly questioning my decision to relocate to Portland. 'He's just won the European Championships,' they said. 'Why risk it all now so close to the Olympics, when everything seems to be going so well?' It was an easy argument to make, but it ignored the fact that before 2011 I'd consistently placed behind the leading distance runners in the world. I owed it to myself to ask: 'Will I get to the very top of my sport by continuing on the same path, by doing the same things?' The obvious answer was no. My results in the Eugene and Monaco meetings told me that I'd made the right choice. I was going into the World Championships at Daegu in South Korea in the form of my life.

Unlike the Worlds at Osaka and Berlin, where I simply wanted to do well, this time I *knew* I could do well. I wasn't finishing sixth or seventh any more. I was winning races. Training had been great. Now it was time to make it happen on the big stage. I was still known as a European athlete; everybody on the European circuit knew my name. But I still had it all to prove on the world stage, mixing it with the likes of the Bekele brothers. I told myself, 'There's no way I'm going home without a medal.'

This time, I simply had to win.

I went into Daegu as one of the hot favourites. With that expectation came a degree of pressure. Now people were expecting me to do well. On the evening of 28 August 2011, I entered the Daegu Stadium to take my place in the 10,000 metres final. Of my rivals for the title, Tadese and Merga were ranked in the top three in the world, but I'd already beaten them once that season at the 'Pre' Classic. Sileshi Sihine, nicknamed 'Mr Silver' because he'd taken silver twice in the 10,000 at Athens and Beijing, and three times in the World Championships, was another runner I had to watch out for. Kenenisa Bekele was there too, although he'd been struggling with injuries for some time and hadn't run a race for nearly two years. Galen was also there, our friendship on hold while we prepared to race. There were several other runners I didn't know much about: Yuki Sato of Japan, Juan Carlos Romero of Mexico, and an unknown Ethiopian runner named Ibrahim Jeilan.

As a professional athlete, it's my job to do background research on the guys I'm up against. Before a race I'll watch videos of my main rivals, figuring out whether their strength is in sprinting or endurance. I'll look for any weaknesses too – every athlete has one, even me, although I'm not about to give that away. I do enough research so that by the time I line up at the start of the race, I'll know what every single runner on that start line is capable of. And as I took my place on the line that day, I knew the main threat would come from Imane Merga, the World Cross Country holder. He'd won the 5000 metres at the Diamond League meeting in Rome earlier that season. Tadese, Sihine, Bekele – they were definitely threats. A big race like that, you can usually pick the winner from one of four or five favourites.

I lined up next to Galen on the start line and gave a quick wave to the British fans in the crowd. The race had a two-tiered start. A little bell rang to silence the crowd. I took a deep breath. BOOM!

As usual, I started at the back of the field and began working my way up to the leading pack. The first lap, the pace was in the mid-60s. Fine by me. I was happy to let it go along at this rate, knowing that I could go really hard on the last two or three laps and produce 55 or 56 seconds across the last 400 metres. Soon the lead group was reduced to Galen, me and the Africans: Tadese, Merga, Mathathi and Jeilan. At the halfway point Bekele was spent and he had to drop out. Tadese nudged out in front. The pace in the big races is often quite slow; everyone is running it tactically, and some runners are afraid of what the other guys will do. I was working hard, but the pace wasn't fast enough to split up the rest of the field. Then I started winding it up. I surged past Tegenkamp. With two laps to go, the pace picked up and runners started falling away. Now I moved up into fourth place. Still winding, still pushing. Waiting for the moment to attack. All of a sudden, Tadese slipped back. He was out of the picture.

'Now,' I thought. 'Now's the time to kick.'

With 500 metres to go, I bolted past Merga to take the lead. The clang of the bell told me we were coming into the last lap – 400 metres to go. I was having to dig really, really hard – harder than I've ever had to dig before. But it worked. I opened up this big gap between myself and the chasing pack. I must have been 10 metres in front of Merga and the rest. The finish line was in sight. At that point I thought I'd done enough to win the gold.

Out of nowhere, this guy just tore past me.

Jeilan.

In the blink of an eye, the young Ethiopian had wiped out the big gap I'd worked so hard to build and took the lead. I had to dig even deeper now. I dug hard. I worked hard. I gave it everything I could to try and catch Jeilan, sensing that gold slipping through my fingers, like sand. It was too late. I'd kicked on too soon. I was helpless as Jeilan sprinted ahead and won the race. As I made it over the line I slumped to my knees in disbelief. 'I've lost.' That thought kept repeating inside my head. 'I can't believe I've lost.' At the very moment when I felt like I had the 10,000 metres gold in the bag, Jeilan had beaten me. I had clocked a time of 27:14.07. Jeilan ran it in 27:13.81. There was less than three-tenths of a second in it. Gutting.

When I looked back at my race, I realized that I'd made a fatal mistake. Tactically, I called it wrong. In my honest opinion, I kicked too early. I should have saved my kick for 400 metres instead of going at 500. At the point when I kicked, I wasn't even thinking about Jeilan. I didn't have a clue about this guy. He hadn't competed at any of the previous races I'd been in, so I hadn't had a chance to see him and what he was capable of. I wasn't the only one who made that mistake: none of the commentators considered him a realistic shot for the title in Daegu. I hadn't done my homework on him, and I ended up paying a high price.

I had three days until the qualifying heats for the 5000 metres. Mentally I was fatigued, dejected – almost depressed. Thankfully Rhianna and Tania were in Daegu with me during the competition, and having them there helped take my mind off the result. For a couple of hours after the race I had athletes coming up to me and saying things like, 'Unlucky, mate,' or 'Maybe next time, Mo.' That's the problem with staying in the village during an Olympic Games or World Championships. You're surrounded by athletes and if you lose, you're reminded of your failure constantly. I'm sure all the people coming up to me had good intentions and were trying to cheer me up. But I didn't want to be constantly reminded of the fact that I had just lost a massive race. I needed to get out of that environment. So I decamped to the hotel where Tania and Rhianna were staying, outside the village. I just stayed in the hotel room with my wife and daughter, watching movies and trying to take my mind off the result. Psychologically that helped a lot. I wasn't allowed to dwell on losing the 10,000 metres. Rhianna and Tania took me out of that bubble. I was able to do normal things, watch TV and put my feet up, forget about everything else. Those three days were crucial for me in terms of recovering for my next race. If I hadn't had that downtime with my family, I might not have been able to overcome the mental pain of losing in the 10,000 metres.

Three days later I returned to the stadium to compete in the qualifying heats for the 5000 metres. I wanted to put things right after the 10,000. Now, more than ever, I had to win. Running a 5000 race so soon after putting in a big effort at the longer distance is hard. It normally takes my body seven to ten days to recover fully from the effects of running a 10,000 metres race. In the Olympics and World Championships, you're lucky to get half that recovery time. The only thing to do is rest as much as possible and give your body the best chance to recover.

Qualifying went well. I finished my heat comfortably second behind Merga, then I spent the next three days resting before the final. I had a lot to think about.

Analysing my race in the 10,000, it seemed to me that I'd been tactically spot on before those last two laps. I needed to relax, forget about losing to Jeilan and concentrate on running a good race in the 5000 – only this time I'd play it right going into the last 600 or 700 metres. Again, there was some strong competition on that start line. Bernard Lagat was there, along with Dejen Gebremeskel of Ethiopia and Eliud Kipchoge. Merga was there, of course, and Isiah Koech. For me, Lagat was the big threat. I'd beaten him in the 5000 in Monaco, but this time I wouldn't be underestimating anyone.

Before the race Alberto gave me a pep talk. One thing I've always done, and which I did in the 10,000 metres and didn't help me at all, was that in the closing stages of the race, the last hundred metres or so, I have this tendency to over-stride. I have a naturally long stride, and rather than run like a sprinter on the last stretch of a race, with a short and choppy stride, I'll over-stride. Watch a replay of the 10,000 metres and you'll see that Jeilan's legs are moving much faster than mine as he overtakes me heading towards the finish. Alberto noticed I had a long stride early on in our training sessions and repeatedly drummed the message into my head: 'Chop your stride, chop your stride. When you come to the last hundred, run like a sprinter. Don't run like a long-distance runner. *Sprint!*'

Alberto had one other important piece of advice for me. 'When the bell sounds on that final lap and you're going round for the last time,' he said, 'hold the inside lane. Do not let anyone take the inside lane. If someone else takes it on that last lap, the race is over. You will not come back from that. Whatever you do, hold off the other guys.'

Just like the 10,000, the 5000 metres final got off to a slow start. I tucked in amid the pack and began working my way through. Winding it up, bit by bit, inch by inch. With three laps to go, I had drawn level in the lead group alongside Merga and Abera Kuma, another Ethiopian. Those last three laps were the most important laps in my career to date. Now to finish the job.

Lagat had started out specializing in the 1500 and 3000 metres before stepping up to the 5000. That meant he was capable of some serious speed. Gebremeskel, too, had a strong sprint finish on him. Kick too early and either of those guys had the tools to punish me. With two laps left, I hit the front. I wasn't kicking on yet. Just winding it up. The bell sounded. Then I remembered the advice Alberto had given me prior to the race: *Hold the inside lane.* At the sound of the bell, I had the inside lane. I was determined to hold onto it, no matter what. Lagat desperately tried to get to inside of me. We were practically elbowing each other, fighting for that inside spot. Lagat was trying and trying. I still managed to hold him off. That's what cost Lagat the race and won it for me: holding the line. If you think about it, the inside lane is the shortest distance around the track. If you're further out, you've got to run a longer distance around each lap. On the last lap, that's going to cost you. I kept recycling the same thought over and over inside my head: *Hold him off, hold him off.* I had that phrase on repeat. With 200 metres to go, it was a sprint to the finish line. I focused on not over-striding, just as Alberto had told me. Everything came down to this moment. I was pushing and digging.

Working it. I'd come so close to gold once, I wasn't going to let it get away from me a second time. Lagat tried his best to catch me, but I had the edge on that home straight and I crossed the line in first place. I'd done it!

World Champion!

I pumped my fists in the air. All the pent-up frustrations of losing the 10,000 metres, the sacrifices I'd had to make and the hard work I'd done to get to this point – it all came out. I got down on my knees and kissed the ground in celebration. I couldn't even stand up. I just rolled onto my back. Looking up, I saw Lagat kneeling beside me. He gave me his hand and helped me to my feet.

'Enjoy it,' he said above the din of the crowd. 'This is your moment. Just enjoy it.'

If it wasn't for Alberto, I believe I would have lost the race. His instructions were the difference between me winning and losing. Without a doubt, Alberto telling me to hold that inside lane was the best bit of advice anyone had ever given me. Before moving to Alberto I'd possessed the athletic ability to win races. Now I had someone to process the tactical side of running a race. That was huge. To this day, holding that line has become one of my trademark moves.

After that race Dave Moorcroft described me as 'the greatest male distance runner Britain has ever seen'. Coming from someone who had held the British record for so long, those words meant a lot. Ivan Gazidis texted me after the race, telling me how proud everyone at Arsenal was of what I'd achieved out there in Daegu. He'd also sent me a text after the 10,000 metres, telling me not to worry, to keep my head up and that the whole club was still proud of me. He had also noticed that I'd been running in special bespoke spikes bearing the Arsenal club logo and colours. I'd personally requested the spikes from Nike and they struck a chord with Ivan, who invited me down to the club again as an honorary guest. This time, though, I was going down there as a world champion.

With my season over, I had a couple of weeks off training and I decided to take Tania and Rhianna on a trip to Somaliland to visit my mum and brother. Bob had used his travel contacts to book us on a flight to Hargeisa via Dubai. At least, that's where we thought we were headed. The computer system had told Bob that the final destination was Hargeisa. He had a confirmation slip that said 'Hargeisa' on it. Our tickets said 'Hargeisa'. We landed in Berbera, on the Somaliland coast, two and a bit hours' drive up from Hargeisa, fully expecting to catch a connecting flight to the capital – without realising that there was no landing strip in Hargeisa because the airport had been closed for reconstruction. (It still is.) Fortunately, my mum, my brother Hassan and pretty much the entire extended family and the village were already aware that we wouldn't be taking a connection to Hargeisa and had arranged for several cars to come to Berbera, pick us up and take us back to Hargeisa. We got off the plane at Berbera to be greeted by this huge convoy of cars. It seemed like the entire village had gathered at the airport. The local Somali media was out in force, along with the local mayor and the sports minister. At the front of this huge crowd of people were my mum and my brother.

It was so wonderful to see them again, and to finally introduce them to Rhianna and Tania. Rhianna especially – she'd waited a long time to meet them both, repeatedly asking me: 'Dad, when am I going to get to see your brother? Dad, where's your mum? Why can't we visit them?' It's tricky for a child to grasp that your family lives far away, that you can only visit them when you're able to take the time off from training.

What should have been a roughly two-hour drive from Berbera down to Hargeisa turned into a four-hour tour of the country. The word got out across the coast that I was coming to town. People literally lined the streets every step of the way of our journey. A lot of them wore T-shirts that had 'MO FARAH' on the front above a picture of me holding the Union Jack. That was a poignant sight. It was as if the local people were saying: 'You're one of our own,' while accepting the fact that I'm British now. They don't resent the fact that I fly the flag for another country. To them, that didn't matter. We stopped several times along the way to Hargeisa, getting out and saying hello to the fans, having my pictures taken. Tania was amazed at the reception I got. She said to me it seemed to her as if Michael Jackson was in town. It was that level of hysteria and attention.

Everywhere we went, people were inviting us into their houses for dinner. It was a humbling moment. Queues would form outside my mum's front door as people waited to greet me. And Tania and Rhianna could see the love people had for me there. Tania's suitcase had gone missing when we landed at Berbera, which meant she had nothing but the clothes on her back. In any other country that might not be a disaster, but in Somalia women are expected to dress a certain way – to cover up head to toe. And it wasn't as if she could pop down to the local shopping mall to pick up some clothes. There is nothing like that in Somaliland. Thankfully Hoda, Hassan's wife, stepped in and lent Tania her wardrobe for the week. That gesture is typical of Somali culture – people welcome you into their family as one of their own.

It was wonderful for my mum and Hassan to finally meet my wife and daughter. Even better, there was a good vibe between them. Obviously, there was the language barrier, but we all managed to have a good laugh. More often than not I would be there to translate, but on the occasions when I wasn't in the room or happened to be out, Tania and my mum and Hassan would use sign language. Tania knew a couple of Somali words, and Hassan knew a couple of English words, so between them they managed to get by. Tania couldn't help but warm to Hassan. As for my mum, she's the kind of person who, once you get to know her, really opens up. Mum couldn't speak a word of English but she still had Tania cracking up. Tania said to me, 'Your mum is a real joker. Now I know where you get it from.'

As for me and Hassan, we were soon up to our old tricks. We insisted on wearing the same clothes for the entire time we were there. I had brought two of everything with me to Hargeisa for that exact reason: one pair for me, one for Hassan. It was like reliving our childhood all over again. Hassan also shaved his head in honour of me, so we now had the same bald head. He even went as far as to grow a goatee similar to the one I had at the time. We were almost identical, aside from the fact that Hassan had a little bit more weight on him than me. If we'd shared the same physique, we would've been nearly impossible to tell apart. In fact, there was one particular evening when Tania was waiting outside the hotel. I'd popped back inside to fetch something from the room. It was quite dark outside owing to the poor lighting and Hassan happened to emerge before me. Tania spotted Hassan and started chatting away to him as if he was me. For a few moments she genuinely believed she was talking to me. She only realized it was Hassan when he started laughing. We have different laughs; it's one of the few ways you can tell us apart.

I got to meet Hassan's kids too. He had five of them (he has six now). We have that thing where his family is my family, his kids are my kids. Even after all those years apart, we still share that closeness. I've always done what I can to support Hassan and his family, and he's always there for me, for all of us. We're one big family really.

I'd brought home a video playlist to show my mum all my best runs over the last few years. The first race was from the 2010 European Championships. I'm there at the end of the 10,000 metres race, holding my head in my hands, in agony from having to dig deep. Mum abruptly looked away and started crying. At first I thought she was crying because she was so proud of what I'd done, but then she turned to me with tears in her eyes and said, 'Can you not get a normal job?'

'What?' I spluttered. '*Hooyo*! Mum, this is what I do!'

'It's too painful,' she replied. 'Watching you running around the track like that. You're going to kill yourself! When are you going to stop?' She tutted and shook her head in that way mums do. 'I mean, look at you. So skinny! You need to eat, put some fat on you. Why don't you stop running?'

We stayed in Somaliland for ten days. I felt it was especially important for Rhianna to establish a connection with my family. At the same time, I wanted my daughter to appreciate the things she had, to understand that you have to earn what you want in this life. In Somaliland she could see people doing without things that we take for granted in Britain, but they did so without complaining and feeling sorry for themselves – for them, it's just how life is. Nonetheless, Tania and Rhianna were shocked by the hardships they witnessed.

One day during my stay there Hassan took us to visit an orphanage in Hargeisa. East Africa was in the middle of what was being called 'the worst drought in sixty years' and the UN had declared a famine in Somalia. Tens of thousands of people had died of starvation resulting from the drought, and millions more were affected in Djibouti, Kenya and Ethiopia, leaving many thousands of children in the region without parents. What we saw at the orphanage was heartbreaking: twenty infants to a room, three newborns having to share a single crib. The living conditions were appalling. It was very dirty and unhygienic and the orphanage had a total of around 150 kids from newborn babies right up to the age of twelve. Seeing the conditions those children were living in inspired both Tania and me to do something about it. We couldn't just leave and not do anything. What we had seen at the orphanage stayed in both our consciences for a long time after that. To this day we still think back to the children in that orphanage. You're not human if you see that scenario, walk away and go back to your life and don't give it a moment's thought, knowing that there are kids out there, living like that.

Leaving Somaliland that year was hard. On the plane leaving for home I was close to tears, knowing that I wouldn't see my family again for a while. Tania and Rhianna could see that I was on the verge of crying and tried to cheer me up by taking the piss, saying things like, 'Look! Daddy's about to cry for the first time ever!' It's part of how we deal with things in our family. If one of us is feeling a bit down, the others will start ribbing and trying to lighten up the mood.

When we returned home we set up the Mo Farah Foundation, with the aim of providing life-saving aid and equipment to some of the 9.5 million people facing starvation and disease in East Africa. We'd pondered setting up a charity for a couple of years. Now I was in a position where I had some influence to help generate donations and support. Setting up the Foundation wasn't easy. We basically had to start from scratch. I was obviously putting a lot of my time and energy into training, so Tania stepped in and did a lot of work on the admin side, registering the Foundation as a charity and making sure all the documents and paperwork were in order. Neither of us had any experience of charities, and we were pretty much having to learn on our feet. As you might expect with handling public money, there's a lot of red tape around setting up a charity. It's heavily regulated and it takes time and resources to get established.

A short while after setting up the Foundation we heard the tragic news that Adnan, the teenage son of friends of ours, was suffering from an aggressive form of cancer and had been given just weeks to live. Adnan had previously been in remission, so it was very distressing to hear that his cancer had come back. We were in Portland at the time and Tania and I badly wanted to do something for him. We knew Adnan was a big football fan so we asked Ivan Gazidis if he could procure a couple of tickets for Adnan and his dad to go and watch a game in London. Arsenal went one better than that and gave them a whole box for the day, laying on the VIP treatment for Adnan and his dad. Thomas Vermaelen, the club captain, and Kieran Gibbs came up to say hello to him at half-time. Sadly Adnan was at death's door and in a very fragile state, but it was lovely of the club to help out in that way.

Two weeks after the cancer returned, Adnan died. At the time of his passing, he had £500 in a savings account and Adnan had told his dad that he wanted the money to go towards providing water for children in Africa. Our Foundation had zero donations, having literally only just been set up – we were still finding our feet. Adnan's dad found out about the Foundation and provided us with our very first donation – £500 donated from Adnan. It was a very moving gesture. With that money we were able to build our first project: a well that provided water to more than

500 people in a remote Somali village. The cost of the project came to a shade over £500. We named the well after Adnan.

As the end of 2011 approached, I began to prepare for the following season. I knew that if I could steer clear of injury, I was capable of reproducing the form I'd enjoyed that year and hitting the same heights. I had already gone on an unbelievable journey: from enrolling at Feltham and barely speaking a word of English, to life at St Mary's and living with the Kenyans in Teddington, learning from each of my coaches and travelling the world. I'd pushed myself to the limit in training camps from Australia to Colorado, from Kenya to Ethiopia and France. I'd made tremendous sacrifices over the years and put in a lot of hard work. In that one moment in Daegu, when I had crossed the line in first place, everything had come together and it had all paid off. At last I could say, 'I'm a world champion now.' And saying that would never get old.

The next year, my journey would take an even more amazing twist, at the 2012 Olympic Games in London.

14
THIS IS IT

ON 6 July 2005 I was behind the wheel of my car, driving up to a race scheduled to take place in Manchester that weekend, listening to the radio and chilling to some tunes. Then the news came on: 'The International Olympic Committee has announced that the 2012 Olympic Games will be held in London.' I was like, 'Amazing! We've got the Olympics!' People were celebrating wildly in Trafalgar Square. Tony Blair was calling it a great day for the whole country. But it wasn't like I was thinking, 'I'll be competing then.' As an athlete, you only look as far ahead as your next race or your next training session. Of course it was my ambition to compete for my country in the Olympics, but it's dangerous to look into the future, so I didn't really give it much thought at the time. It was seven years off – way too far ahead to even think about.

At the end of 2011 I headed out to my usual training camp in Iten. I had a different feeling as I began training there: this year, the Olympics were happening. In seven months' time I'd be competing in front of my home crowd in the biggest sporting event in the world. The reality of it began to sink in. And I had an even greater motivation to succeed when I discovered that Tania was pregnant.

I learned about the pregnancy a few days before I was

due to fly from Iten to Glasgow, towards the end of January. Owing to the eleven-hour time difference between Kenya and the US West Coast, we don't get many chances to talk while I'm in the camp. As soon as Tania wakes up in the morning she'll call me – just before I'm about to hit the sack. Then as soon as I wake up I'll call Tania, which is just before she goes to bed too. First thing in the morning, last thing at night. We were chatting away on Skype one night (my time) when Tania told me the good news. I was over the moon. Having said that, those first few months were hard for both of us. I was having to train in Kenya, Tania was suffering from morning sickness to the point where she could barely get out of bed and Rhianna was getting home from school, fixing herself some food and almost looking after herself. There was no other family in Portland to help out. I wanted to be there for Tania, but all my effort had to be poured into getting ready for the Olympics. The Games only come around every four years. This might be my last shot at Olympic gold. I had to throw everything into my training.

At first, we didn't know we were having twins. Quite early on in the pregnancy there had been some complications and Tania worried that she might be miscarrying, so she went to the doctors and had a special early scan, which showed up not one healthy embryo, but two. Tania brought a copy of the scan with her when she and Rhianna came to stay with me for a week in Albuquerque at the end of February. Learning that I was going to be a father to twins filled me with indescribable happiness. As a twin myself, being a father to twins was really special. We broke the news to Rhianna in Albuquerque as well. She was thrilled – now she'd have two little sisters to play with.

By this time Tania was ten weeks pregnant but we still hadn't told anyone else the news. Tania didn't emerge from the hotel room the whole time she was in New Mexico – her morning sickness was that severe. Everyone at the camp was growing concerned. People asked me if Tania was okay. I tried to play it down. The secret broke when Rhianna happened to be playing outside with Paula Radcliffe's daughter, Isla. Paula and her husband Gary were staying in the room next to ours at the hotel and Rhianna got on well with Isla. While the two girls were playing, Paula asked Rhianna about her mum, how she was feeling.

'Mum's okay,' Rhianna replied innocently. 'She's sick. I can't tell you why, though, because it's supposed to be a secret. But I can tell you in three weeks!'

It didn't take much for Paula to piece together the puzzle from there. Of course, when we announced the news, everyone was so happy for us.

On 28 January I competed in my first race after Kenya, running the indoor 1500 metres at the Aviva International Match at the Kelvin Hall International Sports Arena in Glasgow. Going into that race, my biggest rival was Augustine Choge, the Kenyan who had won the Commonwealth Games in 2006 with a 1500 metres PB of 3:29, four seconds faster than my time. It was a tough race and it came down to the last couple of laps, but I held off Choge to win, with the crowd raising the decibels on the last lap to hint at the sort of noise volume and level of support I could expect in London in the summer. For me, winning was good but it was more important to beat a quality performer like Choge, who has a good record at the shorter distances and on paper was better than me at the 1500 metres. I'd had a long stint training at high altitude that winter and beating Choge in that race helped me to gauge my fitness and figure out exactly what sort of shape I was in, where my training needed to be. It was the ideal start to what would be the biggest year of my career.

Seven days later I competed in a mile race in Boston. Although I wasn't expected to win, as the mile isn't my specialist event, observers still predicted that I would finish quite high up. Things went wrong for me on the first lap. Someone clipped my heel 150 metres into the race. I took a big tumble, went head over heels and did a roly-poly on the track. Undeterred, I immediately shot to my feet and carried on running. But my fall had cost me dearly. By now the pack had surged ahead and I was almost a second behind the rest of the guys. I put my foot down and managed to claw my way back to the lead pack, staying with them throughout the race, but catching them had taken a lot out of me: I was having to work harder than everyone else on the track. I came home in fourth place. Not good. Still, had I not fallen I'm confident that I would've won that race. It was my first defeat of the year.

One defeat quickly followed another. On 18 February I competed in a 2 mile indoor race in Birmingham. Everyone expected me to breeze the 3000 metres. Instead I finished second behind Eliud Kipchoge. At one point it looked as if

bove: Alberto Salazar, a coach onsidered something of a enius, and the guy who got me ver the line.

ight: My victory at the Pre Classic 0,000 metres in Eugene was the urning point of my career on the orld stage. All of a sudden, I was threat.

elow: With Galen Rupp at the ccidental High Performance meet Eagle Rock, LA.

Daegu, 2011: Out of nowhere, this guy just tore past me... Ibrahim Jeilan.

4 August, 2012. I look over my shoulder and see Galen right behind me, hardly able to believe that I've just won the race and my training partner has finished second.

Having my family with me in Daegu helped me to overcome the pain of losing in the 10,000 metres – and come back to win the 5000 metres gold.

With Usain Bolt after receiving my 5000 metres Olympic gold. I know Usain from way back.

Doing the Mobot in front of a packed Trafalgar Square. Everywhere I went after the Olympics there were huge crowds.

With two laps to go, I pull clear of Gebrhiwet... the stadium erupts.

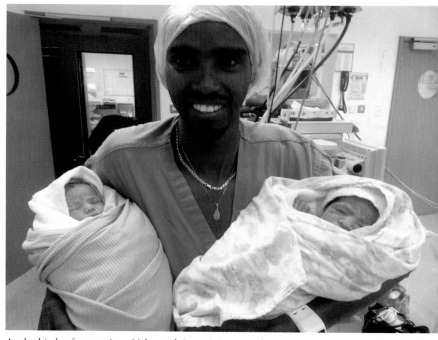

At the birth of our twins, Aisha and Amani. I was so happy I was bouncing off the walls.

Me and Hassan in front of the flag of Somaliland, the country of our birth.

It was lovely to spend time with mum and Hassan when they came over to London after the Olympics – and I got to take them around Bushy Park (*above*).

At a summit meeting at 10 Downing Street to discuss world hunger with the Prime Minister, Pele and Haile Gebrselassie.

At the 2013 Anniversary Games where I won the 3000 metres. Being there brought back some great memories.

Above: Neil Black has been my physio from day one. He's the best physio an athlete could ask for.

Left: At Nike HQ with my main training partner, Galen Rupp.

bove: At our first fundraising ball for the Mo arah Foundation. Interest in tickets exploded fter the Olympics – we ended up raising over 200,000 for the Foundation.

ight: Receiving my CBE from the Prince of Vales in June 2013. A memorable occasion.

Above: The 5000 metres was my fifth global outdoor title – making me the most decorated athlete in British history.

Above left: The 2013 World Championshi[?] in Moscow. The 10,000 metres final, two years on from Daegu. Everything about th[?] race was the same... But this time, I won.

Below left: At the Great North Run with two legends of the track, Kenenisa Bekele and Haile Gebrselassie. Next year it's the marathon.

Below: We brought the twins to watch Arsenal two weeks after they were born. Arsène Wenger ended up cradling Aisha in his arms. That made my day.

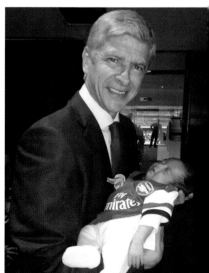

I might even finish in third. I dug deep and just about scraped home in second. Four of us crossed the finish line within about three-hundredths of a second of each other, so it was a close-run thing. But I had to work very, very hard in that race. Harder than I should have done. At that point it was starting to look like my form wasn't perhaps where it should have been, or where I'd hoped for it to be after training in Kenya. That being said, typically I'll ease off training a week before a big race so that I can go into it with fresher legs. That hadn't been the case in Boston and Birmingham, because my eyes were on the big prize that summer and the plan was to train right the way through the season up until the Olympics, doing races along the way. There would be no extended rest periods. That still doesn't excuse the fact that I came second in Birmingham. My defeat led to some people doubting whether I was capable of winning gold at the Olympics. That race showed that I was human after all – that I was beatable. I lost that aura of invincibility, and as Steve Cram has said, that's extremely important as an athlete, because the longer you're unbeaten, the more of a psychological edge you have over your opponents on the start line – they're worrying about how to beat you, rather than concentrating on running their own race.

First Boston, then Birmingham. I was on a losing streak. Worse was to follow at the World Indoor Championships in early March. Psychologically I wasn't feeling great in the build-up to Istanbul. My legs felt heavy from training and I wasn't in the best shape. I came second in the 3000 metres heats behind Choge and finished fourth in the final behind

Bernard Lagat, Choge and Edwin Soi, another Kenyan who had won gold twice in the 5000 metres and once in the 3000 metres at the IAAF World Athletics Finals in Stuttgart. In the last bend, coming into the home straight, there was a big tussle between me and Soi, some pushing and shoving, and I felt that Soi blocked me from coming around him. After the race I notified the GB team staff and they contested the result on the grounds of foul play. Soi was subsequently disqualified and I was moved up to the bronze medal position. But on my way to the medal ceremony the Kenyan team successfully appealed the decision. Soi was reinstated to third place, pushing me back down to fourth. That was a real punch in the guts. Third wouldn't have been a great result but it would still have meant a medal, and it was better than finishing fourth. To be told on my way to the ceremony that the other guy had been put back up to third and I wouldn't be getting a medal after all was disappointing. From having gone a year unbeaten previously, I had now suffered four consecutive defeats: Boston, Birmingham, the heats and the finals in Istanbul. The media had a field day. Some people wrote me off. I got pasted by the media, there was a lot of negative stuff in the press. I don't think anyone really would have backed me as a gold medal prospect after Istanbul. I flew back to London to join Tania and Rhianna for a couple of weeks, feeling depressed. The biggest year of my career, and things were not exactly looking good.

At the same time, I did feel that a lot of the coverage was unfair. I'm human, the same as everyone else, and I think people tend to forget that. They expect me to win every race and that's just not how athletics works. In the wake of Istanbul the media suddenly chose to forget about my World Championship gold and my long run of victories in 2011. Now the knives came out. 'He's done too much travelling,' they said. 'This guy is finished.' 'He's not going to win gold at the Olympics.' These are the same people who had been writing about how well I'd been doing. In my view, the fact that I lost a couple of races didn't make me a bad athlete all of a sudden. I underperformed in those races, but we all do it from time to time. In certain races things don't quite go as you've planned, you take a fall or don't feel 100 per cent. For sure, I was disappointed with myself after Istanbul, but the way the media painted it, I was being written off for London.

In the build-up to the Olympics I took part in a couple of TV shows. In January I filmed a celebrity edition of *The Cube*, a game show hosted by Phillip Schofield, where you have to complete increasingly tricky challenges while you're encased inside a 4 x 4 metre Perspex cube. Each time you successfully complete a challenge you move up the money ladder, which brings you closer to the top prize. In order to defeat the Cube you have to complete seven challenges and then you win the £250,000 jackpot. As this was a celebrity edition, I was competing for charity – in my case, the Mo Farah Foundation. At the time I appeared on the show, no one had managed to win the jackpot. The closest anyone had come was £100,000. It's not easy: you need a lot of mental strength and the ability to hold your nerve in each challenge. To everyone's surprise, I managed to defeat the

Cube with six lives to spare, making me the first (and to this day, only) person to have achieved that feat. The show wasn't due to air until the summer, but news of my performance quickly leaked. Phillip Schofield tweeted a picture from inside the Cube, having earlier claimed that he'd only set foot inside the Cube when someone had beaten it. It was a great end to a brilliant day. That morning, I'd hung out with my heroes at Arsenal.

Ivan Gazidis had invited me down to the Arsenal training ground at London Colney near St Albans. I'd got to know Ivan and his family quite well by this point and we became personal friends. I've had a great relationship with the club going all the way back to Barcelona in 2010. From time to time I'll get emails or texts from Ivan or his PA, asking how training is going, wishing me luck in a race, that sort of thing. Of course, I jumped at the chance to spend the morning training with some of the club. Thierry Henry was there at the time, on loan from New York Red Bulls. I was so excited at the chance to finally meet Henry, for me one of the greatest players of all time. And the rest of the guys too: Bacary Sagna, Jack Wilshere, Theo Walcott. I took part in all the training drills with the rest of the guys. The only thing I had to sit out was the practice game – my legs being as valuable as they are, I didn't want to risk getting on the wrong end of a meaty challenge. Combined with beating the Cube and winning a quarter of a million pounds for my Foundation, it was a dream day for me.

I also guest-starred with Clare Balding and David Walliams on *A League of Their Own* on Sky. Midway through the show the host, James Corden, turned to the audience and said, 'I was thinking . . . wouldn't it be amazing if we could come up with something that Mo could do when he wins at the Olympics?' I smiled and mumbled something like, 'That sounds like a great idea.' But inside I was thinking, 'I'm not too sure about this.' I was slightly worried that if they chose a celebration for me that was a bit weird, and I had to do it in front of that huge crowd at the Olympics, people would be ribbing me about it for the rest of my life.

'What do you think, Mo?' James asked me. 'If we come up with something . . .'

'I'll definitely do it!' I replied. The crowd started cheering as all the other panellists racked their brains to think up a celebration. That's when Clare Balding said, 'I think he should do the "M" from YMCA.' She demonstrated by putting her hands above her head to form an 'M'. James had me trying it out. Then he started doing it too. David Walliams joked that my hairy armpits might put people off when I did the 'M'.

'I can draw a smiley face on them,' I joked back.

'I've just named it,' James piped up. 'It's the Mobot!'

This was all well and good, but the most important thing for me was to get back to winning ways on the track. On 18 May I ran a low-key college race called the Oxy High Performance Meet. It's held the third week of May each year at Occidental College in the historic Eagle Rock neighbourhood of Los Angeles. The Oxy HP Meet is a sort of mini-race. That said, there are still some very good athletes competing there. It marked my first race of the outdoor season and I went into it badly needing to bury the demons of Birmingham and Istanbul. Those defeats had been in my system for two months and this was my first opportunity to make up for them. The Olympics were very close now – just seventy days away. It was crunch time.

I was scheduled to run the 1500 metres in order to work on my speed. I came through that race and won in a good time of 3:34.66. Considering that I was up against some experienced runners, to not only win but clock a fast time showed that my speed was there. Fifty minutes later, to the surprise of many including my wife, I reappeared on the track to take my place on the start line for the 5000 metres race. Although this hadn't been part of the original plan, Alberto had asked me and Galen to act as pacemakers for Dathan Ritzenhein in order to help him qualify for the Olympic standard for the US Track & Field team. The idea was, me and Galen would help Dathan go through, then we'd both drop out at the halfway mark. But then a funny thing happened. There was a guy in the pack using me as a pacemaker, sitting on my shoulder throughout the first half of the race. As we approached halfway, Galen dropped out. I still felt good, despite having had less than an hour to recover from the 1500 metres, and having done all the hard work for this guy on my shoulder and leading the race. I didn't want to drop out and let him go on to take the glory. That didn't seem fair to me. So I decided to continue – and held my position to go on and win the race. This was a great result for me, and one that had my critics frantically revising their predictions for 2012. I had done two races back-to-back within an hour of each other and won them both. That's unheard of. I'd turned the corner. I was back to winning – just in time for the Olympics.

On 27 May I returned to London and ran the Bupa 10 kilometre road race, retaining my title. I pulled the Mobot for the very first time as I crossed the line. Five days later I was back on the West Coast, in Eugene, to compete in the Pre Classic – the scene of my breakthrough in 2011. I competed in the 5000 metres instead of the 10,000 metres this time. I won that race too, in a strong field including Isiah Koech, Galen, Kenenisa Bekele, Thomas Longosiwa and Yenew Alamirew. Having endured a miserable run at the start of the year, I was now on a roll.

There were just a few races left before the Olympics. On 27 June, exactly one month before it all kicked off in Stratford, I travelled to Helsinki and competed in the European Championships. I was already reigning European Champion from Barcelona and I wanted to defend my title. It was the chance to win another gold medal and I seized it with both hands, winning by a healthy margin, a full two seconds ahead of Arne Gabius, a German athlete.

In the final few weeks before the Olympics, I retreated to the camp in Font-Romeu to begin my final preparations for London. The plan was to fly back to London on 2 August, two days before my first event, the 10,000 metres final. Tania and Rhianna joined me in Font-Romeu for ten days. That was good. They helped take my mind off training.

There were a lot of athletes hanging around the camp who were, like me, waiting to fly out to the Olympics. Being able to spend time with my family allowed me to switch off from all that and take my mind off the Games. When they left, I wouldn't see them again until I went to the Olympic village – almost a month later.

I did return to the UK briefly in mid-July for the Grand Prix at Crystal Palace. This was my last race before the Olympics and the place was buzzing. You could feel the mood of the whole country, this sense of excitement building up. Everybody was talking about the Games. The torch relay was going through towns and villages. Every time you turned on the TV it was about the Olympics. I tried not to think about any of this going into the Grand Prix. 'Just focus on doing well here,' I told myself. I knew that if I didn't do well in the 5000 metres, there'd be another round of negative stories in the press. 'Mo isn't going to do well at the Olympics,' 'Farah out of form,' that kind of thing. I was on a winning streak and I wanted to keep it going. Tania and Rhianna weren't there – the doctors had advised Tania that she was dangerously close to going into labour with the twins, so she was ordered to rest up in Teddington and not go anywhere.

The track was slick with rain that day in London but I was the strong favourite and I came through to win ahead of Moses Kipsiro and Collis Birmingham, breaking clear of the competition on the last two laps. My speed was something that I'd been working on with Alberto in training. Finally, everything was looking good. I had put in the hard hours on the track in Portland. I'd done my high-altitude work in Iten. I was in the shape of my life. I was ready for London.

In the back of my mind there was the realization that if I didn't run well in London 2012, people would say that Daegu was a fluke, that I was a flash in the pan. I tried not to think about that. I went into London with my confidence high after the Worlds, knowing that if I performed to the same level as I'd done in 2011, I had a great chance of finishing up there on the podium, a gold medal around my neck.

In between training sessions in Font-Romeu I watched the Olympics on TV. I saw Danny Boyle's breathtaking opening ceremony. I watched the other guys on Team GB competing for medals in the first week of the Games. It was a strange feeling, sitting in a room high up in the Pyrenees, watching Tom Daley and Peter Waterfield compete in the synchronized diving, Rebecca Adlington taking bronze in the 400 metres freestyle. Knowing that, in a few days' time, the attention would switch to athletics and those same cameras would be focusing on me.

On 2 August I flew back to London and headed straight to the Olympic village. Tania and Rhianna were in Teddington. Tania's due date was September, but we were told that twins are born on average a month early and sometimes two. It's very rare that twins go to full term, which meant that Tania might be going into labour during the Olympics. I wanted to be with her, but we had agreed, along with Ricky, that I needed to focus purely on the

Olympics. Any distractions could undo all the hard work of the last few years. It got to the point where we decided that if Tania did give birth while I was in training or at the village, she wouldn't let me know. This was an agonizing time for me. There I was, preparing to run the biggest race of my life in front of billions of people, and I kept thinking, 'The twins might already have been born . . .'

Once I arrived in the village I went through the usual routine of collecting my accreditation and doing all my blood tests. On the second day I rested. Even if I wanted to, going outside the village wasn't an option for me. British athletes were getting mobbed everywhere they went. If you were wearing a Team GB vest, you were getting loads of attention, didn't matter who you were. On top of that, you had to go through a ton of checkpoints to get in and out of the village. Instead I stuck around the village and watched as many Olympic events as possible. More and more Brits were winning medals and I was really getting into it. I caught some of the boxing matches. I watched Andy Murray beat Novak Djokovic in the Olympic tennis semis at Wimbledon to set up a final against Roger Federer. I felt the excitement building as I counted down the hours to my first race.

The following morning is Saturday 4 August.

I wake up early and go for a light jog around the village. I do 3 miles. I don't see much of Alberto today. Normally he's the calmest guy on the planet – so laid back he's almost horizontal – but you don't want to be around Alberto on race day. He gets so nervous that he makes everyone else nervous too.

The race doesn't start until 9.15 p.m., so I have a lot of time to burn. For the hours leading up to the race I try to keep things as normal as possible. Every athlete has a pre-race routine they like to stick to. Galen, he has his pre-race pancakes. Me, I like to shave my head – to feel my scalp smooth, the refreshing sense of slapping cold water over it. It's sort of a ritual, I guess. Then I'll listen to some tunes. Depending on my mood, it'll be some Tupac or maybe Dizzee Rascal. If I want something a bit more chilled, I'll put on some Somali music. The older stuff from the 1970s and '80s has a really good beat to it. People sing about the country, about the history and the culture. I have a few favourites: Walaalaha Sweden (Brothers of Sweden), which is where the duo, Sir Mohamud Omar and his brother, used to live. Then there's Hibo Nuura, and K'naan, the rapper and poet who recorded 'Wavin' Flag', the official song used for the FIFA World Cup in South Africa. I've met K'naan a few times. Nice guy.

All morning long I'll be drinking water to keep myself hydrated. The rest of the morning is spent chilling out and talking to one or two of the other athletes. After lunch I grab a couple of hours' sleep. Then I wait.

Three hours before the start of the 10,000 metres race, I head down to the stadium and make my way to the warm-up area. The atmosphere around here is tense. Everyone is stretching, jogging, watching the races unfold live on TV. Waiting for the call to head out to the track. Some people share a few jokes or comment on the race times, wishing each other good luck. Others are wearing their headphones and listening to music, trying to shut out everything else. Alberto is hanging somewhere in the background. He's got a second pair of spikes with him – ever the man who's prepared – just in case there's something wrong with my regular ones. Neil Black is waiting for me in the warm-up area. I lie down on the massage table and say, 'Make me feel good, Blackie.'

Neil just laughs. He knows what I'm like. He understands my body and the sheer hell I am about to put it through. At the end he claps his hands and says, 'You're good to go. Now get off my bed.'

Barry Fudge is there too. I met Barry a couple of years before the Olympics through Ian Stewart, the Head of Endurance for UK Athletics at the time. Barry is the physiologist for the English Institute of Sport (EIS) at UK Athletics. For the duration of the Olympics, Barry is my go-to guy. Whatever I need, Barry is there for me. While I was in the training camp, he would periodically check up on me and make sure that everything was going okay. When I had my blood tests done, he'd look at the samples to make sure my levels were good. If I need to be driven somewhere, Barry is the man. If something bad has happened or if something is bothering me, Barry is the guy I talk to, the guy who gets it sorted. Barry has allowed me to focus solely on the race.

As I wait for the race to begin, I watch Jessica Ennis beat Lilli Schwarzkopf and Tatyana Chernova to win the 800 metres and take the gold medal in the women's heptathlon. 'Jess has just got a gold,' I think.

Now it's my turn.

Twenty minutes before a race, I'll normally drink some coffee to wake me up. So now I have a shot of espresso – only nothing happens. I want to be pumped up for this race, so I take a second espresso. As I make my way out to the stadium track, I feel this massive caffeine high come on. I'm buzzing. My hands, my legs – everything is shaking. Then I stick my head out through the tunnel leading from the warm-up area to the track and the crowd goes mental. People are screaming and waving Union Jacks and shouting, 'Come on, Mo!' There are banners with the words 'GO MO!!!!' written in big letters. Each person shouting out pumps me up even more. And I'm already pumped up to my eyeballs from the caffeine. At that moment, I am more pumped than ever before in my life. My hands are trembling. My eyes feel as though they're about to burst out of their sockets. As I approach the track, I do a couple of strides and put my hands up to wave to the crowd. The whole stadium just erupts. The crowd is unbelievable. The noise is deafening – like nothing I've ever heard before. I try to search out Tania in the crowd but I can't see her. Too many people. Everywhere I look is this mass of noise and colour. It's the biggest day, the biggest moment of my life. Everything has been leading to this.

I'm looking around and telling myself, 'This is my moment. This is it.'

I am ready to race.

There's a lot of expectation on my shoulders going into the 10,000 metres. I'd done well in the Worlds. I'm in great form. Now I have to do it all over again. I have to bring that gold medal home, no matter what. All the big names are there for this race: the Bekele brothers, the usual mix of Kenyans, Ethiopians and Eritreans: Zersenay Tadese, Moses Kipsiro, Moses Masai, Bedan Karoki. Then there's my Oregon training partner, Galen Rupp. He's a threat. Everything has been going well for him in training, and I know what he's capable of. We are called to our marks. The crowd waits.

The gun CA-RACKS.

'Shit!' I think. 'The gun's gone. It's started.'

Early on the going is slow. I just focus on doing my thing, starting from behind and taking it as easy as possible. Telling myself, 'Work your way through the pack. Don't make any mistakes.' All I've got to do is hold level with the lead group of runners and put myself in a strong position heading into the last few laps. Then I can kick on for the big finish.

The pace is going backwards and forwards. In the corner of my eye I can see that Greg Rutherford is doing well in the long jump. He wins the gold as I pass by on another lap. The crowd is whooping and cheering. Greg has just jumped 8.31 metres. It's enough to win the gold. It's a one-two for Jess and Greg. Eighty thousand pairs of eyes turn to watch the climax of my race. At the 5000 metres point, Tadese, the half-marathon world record holder, suddenly puts a big surge in, upping the pace. Then Kipsiro goes down. The field scatters. I slip back alongside Galen. He tries to go with the pace.

'Don't worry about it,' I tell Galen. 'Don't go with them. Chill.'

Galen eases off. He settles alongside me towards the back of the pack. Gradually the two of us start picking off the other guys, working our way through the group. Just like we've trained to do under Alberto. With four laps to go, we close in on the front runners. We're still working our way through. Every lap, we're gaining a little more. The leader of the race is changing all the time. One minute it's Tadese. The next it's Tariku Bekele. Then it's Gebremariam.

'Yeah, yeah,' I tell myself. 'This is good, I'm where I need to be.'

Now the other guys start trying to get rid of Galen and me by pushing the pace. The race gets faster. But I'm calm. I know I've got my sprint finish. As long as I'm near the front with two laps to go, I'm golden. This is my race. My time. I'm not going to lose to anyone. Not here. Not in front of my home crowd, with everyone in the country cheering me on.

As we hit the two-lap mark, Tariku Bekele takes the lead again. I am right behind him with Galen on my shoulder along with Masai and Karoki. I wait for my moment to kick on. The last lap rings out.

Now I kick as hard as I possibly can. I surge past Bekele and take the lead. The crowd goes ballistic. I didn't think it could get any louder than before. But I try not to get carried away. I still have a job to do, there are still guys to take care of. Instead, I try to use the energy of the crowd, digging deeper and deeper as I veer into the final turn. I'm in a lot of pain. I'm running flat out. It hurts. At last, with 200 metres to go I manage to open up a gap between me,

Tariku Bekele and the rest of the chasing pack. The crowd is roaring and driving me on. I'm not looking behind. I'm not looking at the clock or the screen. I don't know where Bekele is or where Galen is. I focus everything on the finish line.

'Keep going,' I tell myself. 'Keep going.'

It's only once I cross the line that it hits me.

I've won.

My immediate reaction is, 'What?!? I've won!'

I look across my shoulder and see Galen coming through. On the home straight he pulls ahead of Tariku Bekele to take silver. I don't know what I'm doing at that point. It's a mad, crazy blur. All I can think is, 'I've just won the race and my training partner has finished second. What is going on?' I think back to training with Galen in the mountains in Albuquerque. Alberto had predicted that we would finish first and second in the Olympics, but he wasn't sure in which order. Somehow, standing here now, watching everything unfold, it doesn't seem real.

I see Alberto in the crowd. I run over to him and give him a hug.

'Go and enjoy it!' he shouts above the electric noise of the crowd. There are almost tears coming out of my eyes. It's an emotional moment for me – for all three of us. I'm still struggling to believe what I've just achieved. The crowd is shouting my name. Someone chucks me a Union Jack. I wrap it around my shoulders like a cape and pose for some pictures. I do the Mobot, but honestly I've got no idea what I'm doing any more. I'm just like, 'Oh my days! I'm the

Olympic champion. Have I really won? Did that really just happen?' Winning gold at the Olympic Games, in the city I call home, is one of those things that takes a long time to come to terms with.

Rhianna comes running onto the track. Then Tania joins her. The three of us together, after a month away. Tania's stomach is huge. Her doctor didn't want her to be here. I give both of them a big hug. Sharing this moment with them both is the best thing ever. The sacrifices they have made too . . . Tania is telling me, 'Go and enjoy it!'

I'm telling Rhianna, 'Come jog with me, one lap around the track.'

And Rhianna's plugging her fingers in her ears and shaking her head and saying, 'No, no! I'm scared, Dad!'

It's so loud it is literally scary.

I head off on my lap of honour around the track. I wave. People wave back. I don't know where I am. I just see this huge wall of people stretching out before me. I enjoy that moment. I enjoy it like you wouldn't believe.

Super Saturday, as it was later known, would go down in history as the greatest day in British athletics. In the space of forty-six minutes Greg, Jess and myself have all won Olympic gold, making it the best performance ever on a single day for British athletics. The gold rush had begun earlier in the day at Eton Dorney, with Andy Triggs Hodge, Pete Reed, Andy Gregory and Tom James winning the men's fours in the rowing, followed by Sophie Hosking and Katherine Copeland taking gold in the women's lightweight double sculls. A few hours later, the track cycling team landed another gold with

Laura Trott, Dani King and Jo Rowsell winning the women's team pursuit, setting their sixth successive world record in the process. Then it was our turn. By the end of the night, Team GB had won six golds – the most successful day our country has enjoyed at an Olympic Games for 104 years.

People would soon be comparing 'Super Saturday' to England winning the World Cup in 1966 and Jonny Wilkinson kicking the winner against Australia in 2003. Seb Coe called it 'the greatest day of sport I have ever witnessed'. Andy Hunt, chef de mission for Team GB, said, 'It is a day our country will never forget'. For me, standing there on the track, soaking it all up, it's a simply incredible feeling, to be a part of something so special. It's something I'll remember for the rest of my life.

It's gone midnight by the time I get back to the village. I grab some food. I'm tired, but I can't sleep. I'm still buzzing from the crowd. The next day I have arranged to meet Tania and Rhianna at the Nike HQ at BMA House, this grand old building in Tavistock Square, a stone's throw from Euston Station and King's Cross. All the Nike-sponsored athletes are at BMA House, anybody's who won a medal, plus all the top Nike executives. Getting there is a mission in itself. The traffic is ridiculous and someone explains to me that I'll have to pass all these security checkpoints going by car. It sounds like a big hassle.

'I'm not doing all that,' I say. 'I'll just jump on a train instead.'

Having changed out of my Team GB kit, I am now wearing a big jacket and a hoodie and a pair of jeans. I pop my hoodie tight over my head and hop on the Overground. My disguise works. No one recognizes me. I spend some precious time with my wife and daughter at Nike HQ. My old mate Malcolm Hassan is there too. Malcolm and his dad have come down from Sunderland; I'd managed to get them tickets for the 10,000 metres. 'I can't believe how well you've done, man!' Malcolm says when I greet him, his Geordie accent thick as the day I first met him. We joke for a bit. Then it's time to head back to the village. I take the train back. This one guy recognizes me. He's about to say something when I put my finger to my lips and go, 'Shhhh!'

To his credit, the guy doesn't say a word. It's our little secret.

When I at last get back to the village, I'm knackered. Alberto and Ricky are waiting for me back at the village. I've still got one more race to go. They can both see that I need to get some rest. But it's hard sometimes, because the other guys in the village are coming up to you, saying, 'Well done, mate!' Wanting pictures of you, wanting to shake your hand. The attention is lovely, but it also saps the energy out of me at the exact moment when I most need to conserve it.

The following day I try heading down from my room in the village to grab a bite to eat. Again, there is a lot of attention on me. Usually I wouldn't mind, but I still have a race to compete in and this isn't ideal preparation, posing for pictures and shaking hands wherever I go. In the end I decide it's best not to leave my room, but how am I going to get food? Barry Fudge steps in to save the day, making food runs back and forth from the restaurants. I also get rid of my SIM card in my phone so that no one can get hold of me. The only person who has my new number is Tania. Anyone else that I needed to speak to on a regular basis, like Alberto, is already in the village. It's a case of cutting off the outside world. Even my brother and mum don't have this number. (Later I'll find out that some random guy ended up with my old phone number. Every time I do well in a race or I'm in the spotlight, this poor guy's phone explodes with phone calls and text messages from people looking for me.) Today I do nothing but sleep and chill. Rest is the most important thing. The 5000 metre heats are set for the following Wednesday. I have to recover in time, because if there's one lesson I learned from Beijing it's that you can't take your place in the final for granted.

It's very nearly not enough. On the morning of 8 August I limber onto the track feeling tired and drained. Despite putting everything into my recovery, that 10,000 metres race has taken a lot out of me. Somehow I've got to make it through this heat and hope I can recover a bit more ahead of the final. I tell myself, 'Just get the job done. Because if you don't make it through qualifying, you have no final.' There's no way I am going to suffer a repeat of Beijing. Today, this heat is my final.

I struggle in the heats. It's hard. My whole body is aching. I scrape through in third place behind Hayle Ibrahimov and Isiah Koech. Massive relief. If that heat had been the final, I would've struggled. Big time.

Galen makes it through in the second heat as one of the

five-fastest times. I'm just glad that we've both qualified. I watch the replay of my heat on TV. I look visibly tired. I spend the next two days resting. Only now, with the heats safely negotiated, do I start thinking ahead to the final. I turn over the race in my head, asking myself what I have to do in order to win. Telling myself, 'Damn, I want the same feeling I had in the 10,000 metres. I want to feel like that again. I want to make history.'

Only a select few athletes have ever done the 10,000 and 5000 metres Olympic double. Kenenisa Bekele did it in Beijing in 2008. Lasse Viren did it in Munich in 1972 and again four years later in Montreal. Emil Zátopek, he did it in Helsinki in 1952. I want to put my name up there among the greats. For the next two days I don't venture outside at all. Barry Fudge is busy making his by now regular food runs, bringing my meals up to my room. So I rest. And I think. And I wait.

Three days after the heats, it's the 5000 metres final.

There are some fresh legs out there on the start line. Guys who haven't competed in the 10,000 metres: Dejen Gebremeskel, Thomas Longosiwa, Bernard Lagat, Abdalaati Iguider, plus Koech and Ibrahimov. Seven guys on that start line have run faster personal bests than me. So, a lot of fresh legs. But I feel strong. I'd shown in Daegu that I can run a tough 10,000 metres race and then a few days later recover to win a 5000 race against the best guys in the world. And I've done so many races at the shorter distance that I know what to expect. It's different with the 10,000 metres. If you think about a football match, where a game can be quite slow for the first sixty or seventy scoreless minutes, the pace suddenly picks up as the final whistle approaches and both teams are chasing a win. That's how 10,000 races are run. You don't want to go too hard at the start because you have a *looooong* way to go. The 5000 metres is nothing like that. There's no gentle tempo at the start. As soon as that start gun goes, you're off.

I emerge onto the track and – wow! Somehow the crowd is even louder than the other night, if that's possible. It's like someone has just scored a winning goal in the World Cup Final. We are called to our marks. The crowd is going crazy and we haven't even started racing yet. I look around at this sea of British flags. People bouncing up and down. The reception I get is mind-blowing. There are 80,000 people cheering me on. I feel the weight of the whole country behind me, willing me to win.

It is 7.30 p.m. on a beautiful August evening and I am about to make history.

The pressure is off for me tonight. I've already got one Olympic gold medal in the bag. Most athletes will only ever dream of winning Olympic gold and it meant so much to me. I had no intention of taking my foot off the gas, but being Olympic champion at the 10,000 metres has taken the edge off in terms of the pressure. There are no big bags of sugar weighing heavily on my shoulders this evening.

The first five laps are relatively slow – a relaxed 77 seconds a lap. Then Gebremeskel, one of my main rivals for the title, pushes to the front and begins picking up the pace, doing 60-second laps. This is a big surprise. I'd reckoned on Gebremeskel kicking on more towards the end of the race, so why has he gone now, so early? Maybe he's hoping to burn me out. Maybe he thinks that I'm still feeling the effects of the 10,000 metres. In years gone by, I might have struggled. But I've done the miles. I've given it all in training. I have spent the past year waking up each day and asking myself: 'What more do I need to do? Do I have the speed? Do I have the endurance? What about my mental preparation? What else is there?' Now, in front of massed ranks of flag-waving Brits, everything is coming together.

With 1 kilometre to go, I close in on Gebremeskel. Then I surge past him. Then the bell rings.

Then I hit hard.

That last lap is absolutely fearsome. I go for it. I don't let up. As I get to the 200 mark, the noise from the crowd swells. I can't hear a thing. The ground is trembling. It feels like I'm running into a wall of noise.

I dig. I keep going. I dig some more. And I cross the line in first place. For the second time in seven days I can't believe I've won. I have just run the most painful race of my life. And now I'm a double Olympic champion.

Suddenly, every sacrifice I've ever had to make seems worth it: being away from my family, locked up in a small room, the loneliness of training at high altitude, the tiredness – always the tiredness. Some days I'd be so exhausted that I'd have to resort to mind tricks in order to rack up the required number of miles. I'd tell myself, 'I'm only doing 6 miles today.' Then I'd run that distance in one direction, stop, think, 'Well, how am I going to get home now?' And I'd have to run the 6 miles back.

There are no short-cuts to success. I have been striving towards this moment for such a very long time. In the wake of the World Championships in Daegu some people made it sound like I'd come out of nowhere. They didn't take into account the years and years of running behind that victory, of building up that base of mileage. Winning a gold medal in a track event isn't something that takes one or two years of graft. It takes ten or even fifteen years of hard work. I have grafted and grafted to get here.

Galen comes home in seventh place, but he already has a silver medal in his pocket. He's young. He's knocking on the door. All he needs to do is get that little bit stronger and then there's no limit to what he can achieve. There's no doubt in my mind that Galen has what it takes to be a future World and Olympic champion. It's a case of when, not if. And when Galen does cross that finish line in first place, I'll be delighted for him.

The celebrations continue. After winning the 200 metres, my friend Usain Bolt celebrated by dropping to the track and busting out some press-ups. Now I lie on my back and start doing crunches. Later on the same night, Usain goes one better when Jamaica wins the 4 x 100 metres men's relay and uses the relay baton to do the Mobot. At the end of the night we're left standing on the victory rostrum with our gold medals round our necks, the entire crowd having sung 'God Save the Queen', when out of nowhere we start doing each other's moves. We hadn't planned it at all. We just did it. It was one of those spur-of-the-moment things. Me standing there in the lightning-bolt pose, Usain with his hands on top of his head forming an 'M'. I know Usain from way back. We've had fun times together. When I was getting married, he sent me a video message that was played at my wedding. 'Mo, don't do it! Don't get married!' Usain pretends to plead. Then he turns on the smile and says, 'I'm only joking, man. Congratulations!'

Alan Watkinson was there to watch me win both races. He'd put in for loads of events through the public ballot system, but the only event he secured tickets to was, co-incidentally, the 10,000 metres. A friend got him tickets for the 5000. I only had two tickets for the final – the standard allocation for athletes competing in the Olympic Games – so I wasn't able to get Alan one. Otherwise I would've sorted Alan out myself. After the Olympics he told me that he'd been screaming his head off during each lap. When the race was finally over, he sat down and cried. He didn't enjoy watching the race. At least, not until the home straight. He enjoyed it a bit more after that.

Someone asked me after the race how it felt to be a double Olympic champion.

'Those two medals are for my girls,' I said. 'They can have one each.'

15
TWIN REWARDS

Although I was drained after the emotional high of London, I still had one more track race left to compete in after the Olympics, a Diamond League meeting in Birmingham at the end of August. I was booked to travel up there on the Friday before the competition. At 1.30 on Friday morning, Tania's waters broke. It was like a water balloon erupting. I snapped out of my sleep and sat up. There was water everywhere – all over the bed. I looked quizzically at Tania.

'What does this mean?' I asked.

Tania said, 'I'm going into labour.'

'Are you sure?'

Tania nodded. 'One hundred per cent.'

That was the trigger. As soon as Tania said those words, I bolted out of bed and leapt into action, rushing into Rhianna's bedroom to wake her up. She didn't want to get out of bed at first. 'Babies are on the way!' I said. Then Rhianna leapt out of bed and the three of us rushed madly about the house, throwing stuff into bags. It was pandemonium. I got Tania into the car and hammered it down to Queen Charlotte's & Chelsea Hospital on Du Cane Road in Hammersmith. At any other time of the day it takes thirty minutes to drive from our home in Teddington to the hospital due to traffic, but at that early hour the roads were dead and I managed to get us to the hospital in fifteen minutes flat. Dr Kumar, who had looked after Tania throughout the Olympics, took one look at Tania and said, 'You're already 9 centimetres. These babies are coming out *now*.'

Both babies were in the breech position, which meant their heads were facing upwards. It's too dangerous to deliver twins that way, so the doctor had to perform an emergency C-section. Tania had wanted to deliver naturally, but with the babies in the breech position we had no choice. As the father, I wanted to be there with Tania for the birth. I cleaned up and put on some hospital scrubs. Then we rushed into the operating theatre. Tania was given gas and air to lessen the pain from the contractions. I was nervous and excited at the same time. I'd never been through anything like this before. It was nerve-racking, being there for the birth. It's something that you don't have any control over. I was probably more nervous at that moment than I've ever been in my life. Meanwhile Rhianna was waiting in the room next door, since only one person was allowed in the operating theatre at any time. Before the epidural we asked the doctor, 'Where's Rhianna?'

'She's pacing up and down the corridor like an anxious father,' Dr Kumar replied.

I could see that Tania was in a lot of pain and I did my best to keep her calm, talking to her and holding her hand. They gave Tania an epidural. I think she was more scared of the epidural than anything else, because of all the horror stories you hear about it.

I wanted to know what was going on all the time. I was

asking Dr Kumar lots of questions about this and that. Once Tania confirmed she had no feeling left in her stomach, Dr Kumar looked up at me and said, 'Are you ready to see some babies, Mo?'

'Yeah, yeah, yeah!' I replied excitedly. 'I'm ready!'

I looked on as they performed the C-section. It was totally gross but fascinating at the same time, watching them cut Tania's stomach open and fold it back. Dr Kumar reached in with both hands and pulled the first baby out. When I saw my daughter I almost fell to bits. We'd already decided as parents that the first baby to come out would be named Aisha, after my mum. As they took Aisha over to get weighed, I kept repeating, 'My daughter, my daughter, my daughter!' I started taking pictures of Aisha. I was using a camera even though typically you're not allowed to take pictures in the operating theatre. This is something I do a lot of: taking pictures of my family, for the simple reason that there are so few shots from my own childhood. I want to be able to look back when I'm older and remember all those moments we've shared as a family.

I was still coming to terms with seeing Aisha for the first time when, two minutes after Aisha had been born, Dr Kumar said, 'Mo, come back over here! The second baby's about to come out.'

I quickly rushed back over to Tania and watched Amani being pulled out. I was falling to bits by this point. I cradled the twins and talked to them. I thanked Dr Kumar. He'd looked after Tania while I was competing in London, which meant I didn't have to worry about her. I knew Tania was in safe hands. Although Aisha and Amani had been born six weeks early, they were both healthy babies. One by one I brought them over to Tania so they could see their mum. I was bouncing off the walls. In all my life, I'd never been that happy. Everything came together for me in that one moment. Within minutes of the babies being born we were carted back into the waiting room. Rhianna was there. When she set eyes on her sisters, she almost burst into tears with happiness. She held the babies. That was an emotional time for me. The whole family together for the very first time. It was beautiful. We felt such a unit, the five of us.

Looking back, I was lucky to be there at all. If the twins had been born a day earlier, I would have been stuck in traffic in central London doing media appearances. A day later, I would have been up in Birmingham.

At the end of it all, I returned home with Rhianna. Tania had to stay at the hospital to get some sleep and recover. I'd been up all night. We all had – none of us had slept for twenty-four hours. But I didn't feel tired at all. I was on the biggest high, thinking about the girls. I tried to get some sleep but I simply couldn't switch off. Every half hour I called and texted Tania, asking her to send me pictures of the girls, checking on how she and the twins were doing, were they sleeping, and so on. Later on in the day I finally got some sleep. That evening I travelled up to Birmingham for the race. No one in the media knew about the twins at that point. Before competing I always take part in a press conference. So there I was, sitting in this room, fielding the usual questions about my performances, the Olympic medals and my expectations for the race, when about halfway through the conference one reporter, knowing that the twins were due imminently, asked how Tania was doing.

'Yeah, she's fine,' I replied casually. 'She had the twins last night, actually.'

I hadn't planned on mentioning it; it just sort of slipped out. For the rest of the conference, every question was about the twins. They were a day old and they were already big news!

As every loyal fan should, I took the girls along to their first football match about two weeks after they were born, following an invitation from Ivan Gazidis. I didn't want to miss the opportunity, as I so rarely have the chance to attend a live match at the Emirates. We ended up bringing the twins along with us. Arsène Wenger came up to the director's box before the match. He immediately warmed to Aisha and Amani. In fact he ended up cradling one of the twins in his arms. Seeing Arsène Wenger cradling my daughter made my day. What else do you need to say about that? It's Wenger.

Three weeks after the Olympics we had another big milestone: our first fundraising ball for the Foundation. It was great timing for us. Interest in the Foundation and the fundraiser exploded after the Olympics, after I mentioned in my interview after the 5000 metres final that we were holding a Foundation ball and tables were still on sale to the general public. At that moment in time the venue we'd chosen, the Grosvenor House Hotel in central London, had a capacity of up to a thousand people. Before mentioning the fundraiser live on air, we had about four hundred tickets still up for grabs. After the post-race interview, the website crashed – there were so many people trying to buy tickets. We probably could have sold that room three times over. Everyone made it a truly special evening. Usain Bolt came along, which was a huge boost for the Foundation's profile. Sir Steve Redgrave attended. Phillip Schofield was there, along with Jamie and Louise Redknapp, Ugo Monye, the England rugby player, Colin Jackson and Christine Ohuruogu. We held an auction and ended up raising over £200,000 for the Foundation. The biggest lot of the night was Usain's running spikes. To begin with they were on silent auction and the highest bidder was £11,000. Then someone suggested putting the spikes on live auction, with Usain himself acting as the auctioneer. Brilliant. Usain did a great job, really getting into the role and bringing the value up to £36,000. It was a great night for the Foundation. The money that we raised that night has gone towards building a brand-new orphanage in Hargeisa – the same city where we'd originally visited the orphanage and seen the appalling conditions that kids were living in, and which had inspired us to set up the charity in the first place.

We stayed in Teddington for a couple of months after the Games. The last race of my season was a two-mile road race at the Great North CityGames. It's a sort of tradition for me to end my season here. Going into that race I was not in the best shape, having been busy with the twins and having hardly trained post-Olympics. Throughout the whole race my chest was burning. Like a lifetime smoker going for a run. That's what it felt like. I could have eased off the gas and settled for second or third, but having just had the season I'd had, and being a double Olympic champion, I wanted to end my season on a high and make the crowd happy. Somehow I managed to dig deep. I pulled out all the stops and came home with a win. The following day five of Team GB's Olympic and Paralympic champions fired the starting pistol for the Great North Run: me, Greg Rutherford, boxer Nicola Adams, rower Kat Copeland and swimmer Ellie Simmonds, who won gold in the 400 metres freestyle and the 200 metres individual medley at the Paralympics. We were high-fiving forty thousand-odd people as they crossed the start line. That was it for me: the curtain call for my season.

'At last,' I thought, 'I can start putting my feet up.'

If I was hoping for peace and quiet, it didn't work out that way. The media attention surrounding me and my family was ridiculous. I remember Paula's husband, Gary, saying to me after I'd won gold, 'You know what? Your life is going to change now.' At the time I didn't believe him. I just laughed and said, 'No way, how are things gonna change? I'm still me.' But Gary was right. Things went nuts. My phone was going off constantly. If someone couldn't get hold of me, then they were trying to get hold of my family.

The experiences I'd had with the media before paled in comparison to London 2012. The interest in me exploded after Super Saturday. To a large degree I was shielded from it, but during the week between my first and second golds, things went crazy. Somehow the paparazzi had discovered where Tania and Rhianna were staying. The media turned up in force and camped outside our home. Then the media somehow caught wind of the story of my twin. When that story broke, the media frenzy went into overdrive. One guy in particular hounded Tania day and night with emails and texts and voicemails. When he eventually got through and asked about Hassan, Tania denied everything, hoping to delay the story for just a few more days so I'd be free to concentrate on the 5000 metres. Her only concern was trying to protect me from any distractions. If anyone had asked about my brother after the Olympics, there would've been no problem. But there was still a gold medal at stake and any distractions could have proved fatal to my medal hopes.

When the story about Hassan broke in the *Mail on Sunday* all the papers were eager to find out more. The *Daily Mail* went a few steps too far as far as I was concerned. I was worried that they were trying to take advantage of Hassan when they tried to sign him up to a contract that would have involved him handing over stories and pictures of our childhood. I had nothing to hide but I felt they were trying to create a rift between me and Hassan in their efforts to get their story. Paying one brother to talk about the other didn't seem right to me. The contract would have made him a rich man by Somali standards and there were plenty of people in Somaliland whose eyes would have lit up at the thought of trying to get a share. A local man even pretended to be Hassan and signed the contract in the hope of getting the money. I don't think the *Daily Mail* realised what they might be letting Hassan in for, but I was really upset that my family were being hounded by the British press, just because of their connection with me.

For a while after the Olympics, we couldn't do anything. People were coming up to me in the street and congratulating me, asking for their picture to be taken with me on their mobile. Others would just start doing the Mobot. They weren't being rude or anything. I just found it a bit overwhelming. And it wasn't just me: my family were the centre of attention too. People had seen Tania and Rhianna on TV, hugging me at the side of the track, and Tania was especially recognizable given that she was heavily pregnant at the time. One day she and Rhianna went out to Tesco to do a bit of shopping and found this guy waiting outside taking pictures of them both.

This one photographer followed us everywhere. All day, every day. He'd park his car outside our house at the crack of dawn, sit there and wait for one of us to emerge. Then he'd follow us. It got to the point where we could recognize him. Tania once tried to evade the guy and almost ended up causing an accident as a result. Obviously, the photographer was just doing his job, but it doesn't make it any more pleasant to be hounded like that. In the end it was simpler for us to stay indoors all day with the curtains drawn. This was during a really hot time of year, but we couldn't even open our doors or windows for fear that someone would catch a glimpse of us or the twins and take a picture.

We worked around the attention as best we could. There's a curry house in Teddington that I love eating at and I've been going there for years. They don't usually do deliveries, but they knew me, so I'd ring up and ask them if they'd mind delivering the food to our house rather than us having to go outside. We were only down the road from them and the guys were happy to help. When I needed formal wear for media appearances, Tania would go out and do my shopping for me, braving the photographer outside. If I went to do my own shopping, I'd never have made it to the shops – everywhere I went this huge crowd of people instantly swarmed over me. Normal life went out of the window. I was still Mo, but I was no longer the Mo who could walk down the street and buy a pint of milk without being mobbed. Obviously, I'm grateful for all the success I've had and I wouldn't change it for the world, but it was hard to adjust to.

Photographers were also responsible for reports that Tania supposedly had a go at me after I won the 5000 metres, but the situation was completely misconstrued. After she had come on to the track after Rhianna at the end of the 10,000 metres, it turned out that the organizers frowned on that sort of thing because of security concerns. My family didn't know this at the time, of course. In fact, one or two officials had actually waved Tania onto the track after Rhianna had rushed ahead to hug me on Super Saturday. It wasn't exactly a case of my wife and daughter breaching security, but their spontaneous reaction had unpleasant repercussions.

Come the evening of the 5000 metres, they took their seats halfway up the home straight and watched the race. As I started doing my victory lap, they made their way down to the front row so that I'd see them both as I came around the home straight. As soon as they reached the front row, Tania noticed three officials glancing in her direction, talking into their radios. At this point I was about 100 metres away from my family, stopping every few strides to sign autographs and have my picture taken. Tania overheard this one security official talking into his radio. Quick as a flash, the official ran towards me. As soon as I got to Tania and Rhianna, I started to say a couple of words when the official cut in, 'Keep moving, Mo! Keep moving! You can't talk to them now!'

I looked at the guy. 'I just want a minute with my family.' It was supposed to be a family celebratory moment for the three of us, and it was ruined by one track official.

'No, you can't,' the official snapped. 'Keep moving.'

Tania gave the official a look. When the photographs were printed in the papers the next day, they'd been taken at such an angle that Tania appeared to be having a go at me rather than arguing with the official at my side.

In the middle of all this media attention, I'd arranged for Hassan and my mum to come over to the UK. We kept their arrival very quiet. If word got out that my family was over from Hargeisa, I worried that reporters would start hassling us for an interview, and follow us around. Thankfully, no one found out. We had a great laugh. It was the first time my brother had visited England and I took Hassan up to central London with my mum to see all the main tourist attractions: Big Ben, Buckingham Palace, the River Thames. Back at my home Hassan and me had these epic sessions on FIFA. I was like, 'For real, you play FIFA back home?' Hassan grinned. 'Of course.' Turns out there's a café in Hargeisa where all the kids go to rent a PlayStation or an Xbox for an hour or two.

While he was in England, Hassan was soon up to his mischievous tricks again. On a trip up to central London we went into Nike Town on Oxford Street. Suddenly loads of people started flocking over to me. Tania and Hassan were in another part of the store when my brother decided to play a joke. Hassan sauntered up to this woman, pretending to be me and offering to have a picture taken with her son. Hassan still looks a lot like me from a distance, but up close you can sort of tell the difference – especially around the waist! The mum and her son fell for it at first. It was only as the pair of them walked away from Hassan and they looked at the picture on their phone that they realized it wasn't me.

Hassan was also there the day Boris Johnson, the Mayor of London, came over to my house for a cup of tea. Outside of my immediate family, no one knew that my mum and twin brother were staying with me in London, so Hassan was hiding in the next room while I chatted with the Mayor. I'm sure Boris can keep a secret, but I didn't want to take any chances.

As a double Olympic champion, new doors opened up to me. I was showered with gifts: phones, kit, baby clothes for the twins. I was loving it. We had exposure that most athletes can only dream of. I got to attend the GQ Awards at the Royal Opera House in Covent Garden along with Sir Chris Hoy, Louis Smith, Jo Cundy and the rest of Team GB to accept the Team of the Year award from Seb Coe. I also presented Robbie Williams with the Icon award at the same ceremony, and got to meet him afterwards.

On a more serious note, I was invited to a summit meeting

at 10 Downing Street to discuss world hunger with the Prime Minister, David Cameron, along with the football legend Pele and my running hero Haile Gebrselassie. It was a valuable opportunity to highlight the importance of tackling starvation and malnutrition, and the good work we were doing through my Foundation. Following the Olympics, the Mo Farah Foundation has continued to grow. The Olympics gave us a huge boost in terms of profile and donations, which in turn enabled us to expand. Thanks to everyone's generosity, by the end of 2012 we had built fifty water wells in Somalia, supplied food to more than 20,000 people, set up medical clinics, built water canals and much more. We now have six full-time members of staff at the Foundation's office in Twickenham. It is very close to my heart and I'm looking forward to dedicating more time and energy to it once I hang up my spikes.

In 2013, in conjunction with the elite sports training programmes at my old uni, St Mary's, and also at Brunel University in Uxbridge, the Foundation launched the Mo Farah Academy, which will provide scholarships for promising young athletes who have the potential to compete internationally. Both universities have a great track record of sporting success, and the Academy will provide financial and practical support for talented young athletes, especially those who come from disadvantaged backgrounds. It will also give them access to world-class coaching and advice in order to help them fulfil their potential on the track. I was lucky enough to be given a scholarship through London Marathon, and now through my Foundation I'm in a position where I can help other young athletes who are at the start of their careers in athletics. Through the Academy, I hope to be able to play a part in bringing on the next generation of British sporting talent. It's another way of me giving something back.

My training suffered a bit in the wake of London 2012. To run 100-plus miles a week *and* do all this extra stuff on top – TV, newspaper and magazine interviews, signing autographs and having my picture taken all the time – I couldn't juggle it all. I know what my body needs, and in order to be at my best, I have to recover properly after training – eating well and getting plenty of rest. This simply wasn't possible after the Olympics. I ate a lot of takeaways and Nandos, and I ended up putting on several kilograms. Once the twins were born, our sleep patterns just went out the window. For the first few weeks, I couldn't get a decent night's sleep. But once we got back to Portland, it was business as usual. We moved into a new home and got a part-time nanny to help look after Aisha and Amani. It was a relief to be back in the US. No one in the city knew who I was. There was no media circus, no photographers following our every move. Here I was just another guy. I was like, 'Wow! This is brilliant. Not one person recognizes me!' I don't expect anyone to know who I am over there. It's not like the US is short of its own track-and-field heroes.

Coming back to the UK can be difficult, especially if I'm having to spend a large amount of time in training. As an athlete, it's easy for people to forget the fact that if I didn't do what I do – running 120 miles week in, week out, getting the right amount of rest – I couldn't be at the level that I am. It's almost impossible for me to spend a lot of time in England and train properly, because of the attention on me. I'll go for a coffee and get stopped and asked to have a picture taken. I'll go to a restaurant, same thing. Not in a bad way, and I'll never turn down a request from a fan, but it just means it takes a lot more time and effort on my part to get anything done. Being able to get away from that is important. In Portland, I could walk around naked if I wanted to and no one would care.

Looking after twins is harder than I thought it would be. You have to change twice as many nappies, buy twice as many clothes. The girls would cry at the same time, or I'd comfort a wailing Aisha and then Amani would start crying. Fitting my runs in was difficult. I made a big effort to spend as much time as possible with the twins in those first couple of months, knowing that before the year was out I'd have to fly to the training camp in Iten. I'd get my long run out of the way nice and early so I could help out more around the house and spend more time with the girls.

I insisted on having the twins sleep on my chest. You can blame Bono for that one. I met him shortly after the Olympics. Bono has two girls and he told me that it's really good to have your daughters sleep on your chest. Apparently, it helps strengthen the bond between father and daughters. When I heard this I thought, 'I'm gonna give it a try.' I had the twins sleeping on my bare chest throughout the day. It got to the stage where they wouldn't sleep in their cribs because they were so used to napping on their dad's chest.

Leaving for Kenya that winter was hard. I missed the girls in the camp. Big time. Tania would message me pictures and videos of them every day. Just a couple of simple snaps of the twins sitting down and eating gave me a huge lift. It's important for me to have that relationship with my kids that I never had with my dad. But it's hard when you have to spend a long time away from your family. It's hard when you miss your kid's first steps because you're in camp, and your wife sends you a video clip of your little girl walking for the first time and you think, 'I wish I'd been there.' Only parents can understand that feeling.

It's not just about finding time for my twins. It's about finding time for Rhianna too. Whenever I'm back home with the family, whether we're in Oregon or London or wherever, we'll have a father–daughter day, just Rhianna and me. We'll go out and ride bikes or run around the track, just doing stuff and spending time together. From an early age Rhianna started calling me 'Dad'. I've looked after her and been there for her since she was three years old, raising her as one of my own. That's how I see Rhianna. There's never been even the slightest element of doubt in my mind about that. I don't like it when people refer to Rhianna as my stepdaughter. That's not how I see it, or Rhianna or Tania for that matter. As far as I'm concerned, Rhianna is my first child. It's just a technicality that she isn't my biological daughter. She carries the Farah name, she's as good as my own blood, and I love her just the same.

The truth is that I want to be there at the crucial times for all my girls, but my job makes that very difficult.

It's taken a phenomenal amount of dedication to get to where I am today. For the last eight years I've been running on average 100 miles a week. Latterly, it's been more like 120 miles a week. Every week. No excuses. That's how much training I've had to put in to become an elite runner. That's what it takes to go from being the fastest kid in Year Nine at school to winning gold. The guy you see on TV, smiling and joking around, that's only half the story.

Tania tells me that I have this ability to switch off rather than let something bother me. She'll look at me and say, 'How do you do that?' I try not to let things get to me. I don't stay awake at night, staring at the ceiling and thinking about what I did wrong or if I should have done this instead of that. It's the same when I'm running. I block out every distraction. I forget everything else. I am no longer the chilled-out, smiling father. I'm the guy who wants to win.

One of my favourite quotes is from the basketball coach Taras Brown: 'Hard work beats talent when talent fails to work hard.' He used to make the young Kevin Durant (now a star player in the NBA) repeatedly write down this quote on a piece of paper before he was allowed to play a game. The first time I set eyes on that quote I instantly felt it summed up my own attitude to running. I believe that talent can get you a certain distance – maybe halfway to where you want to be. Then you start thinking, 'Hey, I don't need to put in that much effort.' Wrong. Unless you work hard, your talent will slowly start to slide away. You might not see it at first, but one day you'll be doing a race when someone with less talent suddenly shoots past you on the home straight.

Winning double gold at the Olympics has been the defining moment of my career. But as soon as London was over, I looked in the mirror and told myself, 'I want more.' That's just how I am. When I win a race, I'm happy for a little bit. Then I forget about it and focus on the next thing. In 2012 it was all about the Olympics. And in 2013 I had my sights set on the World Championships in Moscow – and the chance to avenge my silver in the 10,000 metres final in Daegu.

16
ONLY THE ENDING IS
DIFFERENT

2012 had been such a massive high for me that I found it hard to motivate myself at the start of the following year – at least to begin with. As an athlete, one of the hardest things is letting go of a win. When you win a title or a medal, you celebrate, but then you have to let go and move on. That's hard when you've spent years training for it. And in the wake of the Olympics I found that my motivation wasn't quite there in terms of winning further championships. As usual, I took myself off to Kenya for my high-altitude training, a time I always regard as the beginning of my season. As soon as I arrived in Iten, I said to myself, 'Right, that's it. I'm not doing any more media appearances now.' I stopped doing any TV and press interviews. I threw all my energy into preparing for 2013. I had one eye on the World Championships in Moscow that August. It was critical for me to get off to a good start – beginning with the 3000 metres indoors at the British Grand Prix on 16 February. I eased ahead of Florian Carvalho to win the race in 7:42.00. A good, solid start.

I flew back to the US to compete in the New Orleans half-marathon on 24 February. Training had gone well. I'd worked hard in Kenya, had my motivation back and was in good shape heading into the race. The time wasn't ridiculously fast, but I won, beating Gebre Gebremariam, the same guy I had beaten in the New York half-marathon in 2011, and setting a new course record in the process, with a time of 60:59 on only my second-ever half-marathon. I suffered a severe stitch around the 8-mile mark. Alberto was following me in the lead truck and could see the pain etched across my face. I pushed through it and officially broke the record this time, unlike New York. As I warmed down, one of the officials strolled over and told me that WDSU, a local news channel, wanted to do a live interview with me. Fair enough. I agreed to do it and inserted my earpiece ready for the interview. But as the presenter, LaTonya Norton, started asking me questions, it became clear that she didn't know who I was. That's not her fault. The interview had been set up in a rush and she hadn't been properly briefed about me.

At one point she asked me, 'Now, haven't you run before?'

At first I thought I'd heard it wrong. 'Sorry?' I asked.

There was a pause. 'This isn't your first time?'

There was another pause as I tried to think about how to reply without embarrassing this woman. Someone had put her on the spot and I felt bad for her, so I tried to change things around with my answer. 'No, no, it's not my first time,' I said. 'I've done half-marathons before but not in New Orleans . . . this is my first time in New Orleans.'

One of the UK newspapers picked up on this interview and posted a link to it online. From there it went viral. Before you knew it, the link was all over Facebook and

Twitter. The phones were ringing like crazy with journalists wanting to talk to me about it. Norton came in for a ton of criticism. A lot of it was unfair, I thought. She's a TV presenter. It's not her job to keep up to date with who's who in British athletics. Besides, in the US *no one* knows who I am. I rather like it that way. In Portland I can live like a normal person. I can do regular stuff, like go to Starbucks, buy nappies, do the grocery shopping. Sometimes people back home don't get that.

In April I flew back to the UK and ran half the course at the London Marathon. A few people openly criticized my decision not to run the full race. I felt some of their comments were ridiculous and frankly quite bizarre. Some sections of the media made it seem as if I was putting in the bare minimum of effort just to cash a cheque, and insinuating that this was an affront to the many thousands of people who participate in the London Marathon each year. This upset me. I'm not the first person to have run a part of a marathon – in fact, it's not unheard of for athletes to run up to twenty miles, as a pace setter or simply on a practice run, and return to race, and win, the full marathon the following year. I had a very good reason for running half the distance: I wanted to learn the course and understand it before competing at the full mileage in 2014. I'd never run a marathon before, so it made no sense for me to run the full distance at my very first attempt. Besides, why wouldn't I practise for the world's biggest road race? Preparation is everything in athletics, and that race was a big learning curve for me. Maybe that's not so obvious from the outside, but running a marathon is completely different from running 10,000 or 5000 metres on a track. Unlike track events, which often take place late in the afternoon or early in the evening, the marathon starts in the morning. That means you have to eat well the night before and get up five or six hours before the race to get a good meal in. For the London Marathon, this involves getting up at 5 a.m., and I'm not used to that. Then you have to learn the course: where to go fast, where to push it. And there are all the little details, such as making sure you pick up the right drink at each water station. In the professional race, each athlete has their own bottle specifically tailored to their needs. The bottles are labelled at each water station, but I didn't realize this. I just saw a red bottle and thought, 'That must be mine.' Then I took a sip. It was horrid! I'd picked up someone else's bottle by mistake. There was no way I could drink any more of it and it was too late to run back to the water station and leave it there, so I just chucked it over my shoulder. I missed the next drinks station. It was to the left of the road, and I was on the right. I didn't see it. I basically ran that half distance without any fluid intake, and we were running at a serious pace. By the end of the route I was gasping. So I learnt a lot at the race, from the big stuff right down to the details. And when it comes to running the full race, I'll have a much better idea of what to expect.

After London I went back into training, and in mid-May I took part again in the Oxy HP Meet at Eagle Rock, competing in the 5000 metres. On the morning of the meet I had my usual pre-race meal of pancakes and syrup. A short while later, my stomach started playing up. Then I was violently sick. Two or three hours until the race, I was feeling terrible. Somehow I managed to get through the race and actually win, but it took a lot out of me. As soon as I crossed the line, I dashed for the toilets and threw up. That night I alternated between lying in bed and emptying my stomach in the bathroom. Galen was sharing a room with me and the poor guy had basically to look after me all night. The next day I felt a little less rough, so I flew back to the high-altitude training camp at Park City in Utah to spend time with my family. They had travelled down from Portland, but soon they were sick too: Tania, Rhianna, the twins, Tania's mum Nadia – the whole family was throwing up. Even the nanny fell ill. It was obvious that we'd all picked up some kind of virus. It was the worst possible timing because I had the 10 kilometre Bupa road race coming up in London at the end of May, and the Pre Classic was scheduled for five days later in Eugene. I talked it over with Alberto and stopped training for a few days. I then did one light session and flew to London for the Bupa race. I won it and flew back to Utah the same day. I still wasn't feeling great, and told Alberto.

'All right,' he said. 'Here's what we're going to do. The Pre Classic is coming up in a few days. Personally, I don't think you should be doing the 10,000 metres. The field is loaded, it's the longer distance, it'll be a hard race.'

I nodded. It made sense not to run. 'So what am I gonna do instead?'

'Well, why don't you go in for the 1500 metres?' Alberto suggested.

That didn't appeal to me. There were some strong guys competing in the 1500 metres, and the best I could hope for would be sixth or seventh place. I didn't see the point in running a race I couldn't win. I reached a compromise with Alberto and we agreed that I'd run the 5000 metres. It would be less arduous than the 10,000 metres and I still had a good chance of winning, no matter what. But my fitness was off because of the lingering effects of that stomach virus, and on the last lap Edwin Soi, the Kenyan who won bronze at the same distance at the Beijing Olympics, kicked on and pulled away from me over the last 200 metres. I finished nearly a second behind him, on 13:05.88, but I was still working much harder than normal because of the effects of that virus. It was my first defeat on an outdoor track since 2011. I was gutted that my long-unbeaten run was over – I'd wanted to keep that record going for much, much longer. I just had to look back and accept that in terms of my condition at the time, second was where I was at. I'd tried my hardest in that race and there was nothing else I could have done, but I was hurting on the inside.

I travelled home to Portland, spent a day with my family, then returned to the training camp at Park City, determined to get myself back in shape for the World Championships. That first session on the track, I nearly killed myself. Hands down, it was the hardest session ever. By the end of it I was lying on the ground, absolutely spent, having pushed myself to breaking point. My defeat to Soi at the Pre Classic burned inside me, and sometimes the only way I can get over a result like that is to take it out in training. Alberto was by the track at the time and he told me he'd never seen anything like it – he'd never seen someone go so hard in training. For me, it was a great session. I wanted to feel better after Eugene, and the only way I could do that was to go as hard as possible in training.

In late June 2013 I flew back to the UK and took part in the European Team Championships in Gateshead. I won the 5000 metres in a time of 14:10.00, running a last lap of 50:89 and finishing more than 3 seconds ahead of France's Bouabdellah Tahri. I was feeling sharper. I felt like I was getting back on track after the Pre Classic. A week later I travelled down to Birmingham for the British Grand Prix and won the 5000 metres again at the Diamond League meeting. Everybody was there for that race: the Ethiopian Hagos Gebrhiwet, the current World Cross Country champion, and his compatriot Yenew Alamirew; Mark Kiptoo of Kenya and Moses Kipsiro of Uganda; and my nemesis from the 10,000 metres in Daegu, Ibrahim Jeilan. No one was missing. That's the way I like it. A loaded field: that's what you need when you want to purge your system of a defeat. Gebrhiwet and Alamirew were in great form and had posted the fastest times in the world going into the race. They both looked like they would take some beating going in to Moscow. Prior to this, I'd not faced any serious threats to my crown. This was different. I pulled ahead of both Alamirew and Gebrhiwet to win. Now I was on a roll – and the Pre Classic result was ancient history.

The following day I retreated to my training camp in St Moritz, Switzerland. I spent the best part of three weeks working on the speed I needed to produce that sprint finish in the distance events. In the third week of July I competed in the 1500 metres at the Diamond League meeting in Monaco. I wanted to compete at Monaco because I saw it was a valuable opportunity to test out my speed in a race where I knew I'd be up against some very quick guys: Asbel Kiprop, Caleb Ndiku and Bethwell Birgen, all from Kenya. And although the 1500 metres isn't my usual event, I felt confident going into Monaco. In St Moritz one week earlier, I'd had a stunning session on the track. Alberto came up to me afterwards and said, 'You're ready to run 3:30.'

Monaco is always a fast race. The track is dead – there's no wind, nothing. It's just fast. Pure speed. I love that track. In 2010, I'd run 12:53 there in the 5000 metres, and the year before that I'd clocked 3:33 in the 1500 metres. I knew if I got into the right place and ran a good race, I'd do well and clock around or just under 3:30. My aim was to follow the leader, Asbel Kiprop. I knew that it was important for me to get to the front as quickly as I could and then follow Kiprop, who was the hot favourite. That was my plan. At the same time, I went into that race with no fear. My mentality was very much, 'Whatever happens, happens.' As far as I was concerned, Monaco was just another race, another event. It didn't have my name on it, unlike, say, the 5000 or 10,000 metres. If I ran a bad race, people wouldn't be on my back. I had nothing to lose.

The first 300 metres I went flat out. I managed to settle into a good pace and I was sitting in third place for almost the entire race. Towards the end I surged into second place, but I couldn't catch Kiprop. The guy was in a different league. He was always out in front. As we raced to the finish line, I began closing the gap, but it was too late. Kiprop won the race in 3:27.72. I finished second in 3:28.81, breaking Steve Cram's British record of 3:29.67, which had been set twenty-eight years earlier. Before that night in Monaco, my best time at the 1500 metres was 3:33.98. When I first saw my time on the screen I was like, 'What the f—?' I had no idea I could run that fast. I'd figured I could do 3:29 at a push. But 3:28 was a big surprise. It just shows you that if you just switch off and go with it, anything can happen. It was also the sixth-fastest time at 1500 metres of all time. I now placed higher in the all-time rankings at 1500 metres than for my normal 5000 and 10,000 metres races. When I was younger I'd done some work with Hicham El Guerrouj's coach, who said I should be a 1500 metres runner. He mentioned it again after the race. He reckons in some ways I was more suited to 1500 metres than the longer distances.

I returned to London for the Anniversary Games, held on 27 July, to celebrate a year since the city had hosted the Olympics. I was running a shorter distance than the previous year, but won the 3000 metres to continue my winning streak at the Olympic Stadium, and the crowd did their bit to recreate the wonderful atmosphere. Being there brought back some great memories of the Olympics. And on a personal level, it was the first time my twin girls had come to watch Daddy race at a meet. Seeing my family after the race was a bittersweet moment. Amani started crying because she didn't recognize me. That upset me, obviously. You want your kids to be smiling when they see you, especially after you've been away for a long time, as I had been in Kenya and then Park City and St Moritz. At times like these I have to remind myself that I'm working hard not just for myself, but for my family too – I want them to have a good start in life. Don't get me wrong – I love what I do, and the rewards my success has brought. But at the same time I'm looking forward to life after running, in terms of spending more time with my family. I want to see my kids grow up, take them to the park, play with them – do the stuff normal parents do.

Two weeks later, I competed at the World Championships in Moscow. Revenge was on my mind. Before competing in the 10,000 metres, I sat down and watched the video of my defeat to Jeilan. It served as a powerful motivation – a reminder of what I had come here to achieve. I watched that video several times, kept playing it back. Watching as I went too early. Watching Jeilan streak past me to win the race and leave me in the silver medal position. Two years. That's how long I had been carrying that defeat inside me. Now I had the chance to put things right. I had my Olympic golds, but the 10,000 metres world title was missing. More than anything else, I wanted to win that race.

If you watch a recording of that 10,000 metres final, the set-up looks so similar to Daegu it's almost scary. The same blue track. The same faces on the start line: Imane Merga, Paul Tanui of Kenya, my training partner, Galen. And, of course, the guy who had beaten me last time out: Jeilan. There were some new faces in the mix, top runners like Abera Kuma of Ethiopia and Bedan Karoki of Kenya. Dejen

Gebremeskel was there too, and Dathan Ritzenhein, another of Alberto's runners from the Oregon Project. The race played out very similarly to 2011 as well. In the first half the pace was quite slow: I started at the back with Galen and worked my way through. I took the lead with 400 metres to go. Then the pace became much faster. It was almost like a replay of Daegu. Going into the final 150 metres, Jeilan and me were neck and neck, exactly as we had been in 2011. Back then, Jeilan had surged past me to win the race. This time, as we sprinted towards the finish line, I was thinking, 'Oh God, not again. Please not again.' I didn't want it to be a case of déjà vu. I was determined not to get beaten, so I dug deep and told myself: 'No way. Not this time. I'm not gonna let it happen again.' I'd trained for this. Prepared for it. I knew what was coming. What I had to do. In Daegu I'd kicked on too early and left myself with no more gears to shift up into when Jeilan had ghosted past me. This time, I had something left in the tank. Jeilan didn't. Right at the end I moved up into another gear. I had that little bit of extra speed to hold him. Everything about that 10,000 metres was the same. Only the ending was different. This time, I won.

I was the first British man to win a 10,000 metres World Championship title. I'd created another piece of history. When I crossed that line it was a special feeling for me. I'd waited two years for that moment – that chance to avenge Daegu. Now I had a few days to rest and recover for the 5000 metres, and my opportunity to make history as only the second man after Kenenisa Bekele to do the 'double-double' – to win both Olympic and World gold at the two distance events. I felt good about my chances of joining Bekele in the history books. In the twelve months since the London Olympics I had put even more effort into training. I remember feeling tired going into the 5000 metres heats in 2012, having to somehow just get through it. Now my body was responding much better. I was ready for this. I wanted to win.

I came through fifth in the second heat, trying to conserve as much energy as possible for the final. Three days later, on 16 August, I walked out onto the track, determined to make history.

The pace was slow at the start of the race. There had been a lot of talk beforehand about some of the African guys using team tactics against me, but, as usual, this talk didn't translate into action. Having done the 10,000 metres, I thought that maybe the guys with fresh legs on the start line of the 5000 metres – guys like Edwin Soi and Bernard Lagat – would have pushed the pace harder early on to try and burn me out. But it didn't work out like that. To my surprise, the guys sat back. Nobody wanted to make a break for it. Hagos Gebrhiwet sat on my shoulder near the back of the pack. Galen and me had talked beforehand and agreed on our plan: sit back rather than go hard, don't take any risks, do our thing of working our way through the pack, then put the foot to the pedal at the end. With 1 kilometre left, my rivals finally made their move. First to take the lead was Isiah Koech, the Kenyan 5000 metres specialist, who had won gold as a junior at the World Youth Championships in 2009. The pace quickened to 62 seconds a lap. Then Yenew Alamirew moved out in front. The pace got ridiculously fast. That last kilometre was 2:26. In any major championship, if you run close to 2:26, you're going to win the race. At that speed we were going faster than at the Olympics. With just over 600 metres to go, I went out in front, moving past Alamirew. Koech tried attacking me on the last lap, but I just pushed and pushed and pushed. With 40 metres to go, I pulled away from Koech. And that was enough. I came home in first place with a time of 13:26.98. Gebrhiwet finished less than three-hundredths of a second behind me and one-thousandth of a second ahead of Koech. That's how close we all were.

It was my fifth global outdoor title, making me the most decorated athlete in British history. At the end of it all – at the end of a crazy, crazy twelve months – I was overwhelmed with this feeling of indescribable joy. To have gone into a major competition a year after the Olympics and done it all over again, winning gold at both distances, now decisively proved that London wasn't just a one-off. For my family, for the people who had supported me and stuck by me through the years, good times and bad, to add the World Championship golds to the Olympic medals meant a lot. I could rightfully claim my place on the list of all-time greats. I couldn't have done it without my family. My friends. My support team. And the public. To have the entire country behind you at home and in the stadium is such a fantastic feeling. In my career, I never thought I would achieve everything that I have. It just goes to show that anything is possible.

Surprisingly, there were a few critical voices in the media after my double. Some observers claimed that I couldn't consider myself one of the greatest athletes ever until I had broken world records. Everyone's entitled to their opinion, but you can't have it both ways. My target has always been to win as many medals as I can, both on a personal level and for my country. Records are different. They don't last. They're there to be broken. Let's say you train hard and throw all your effort into breaking a world record. What's going to happen to it? Your record might stand for one year, or maybe even ten, but sooner or later, someone else is going to come along and beat it. Then you're a footnote. But no one can ever take an Olympic medal or a world title away from you.

Some people fail to understand that training to win medals involves a different strategy from training to run a faster time. In a championship race you have to combine speed and endurance, you have to work out your tactics and what your rivals are going to do. You have to have every angle covered because you don't know what others are capable of. When it comes to posting a fast time, though, you can simply say, 'I'm going to go for it,' and you don't have to worry about tactics or rivals or anything else. You can focus purely on teaching your body to run at a particular pace.

Now the 2013 World Championships are out of the way, there are no major track championships for me until 2015.

For the next year I'll be able to focus on running faster times. Then let's see how fast I can push it. But if it comes down to a choice, I'll always choose medals over records. I want titles. I want to be up there on the podium, gold medal hanging around my neck, draped in a Union Jack, the national anthem playing, doing my country proud. As long as I can do that, I'll be happy.

Looking ahead, my target is the marathon. The plan with Alberto has always been for me to step up to the 26.2 mile distance in 2014, working my way up by running half-marathons. The type of person I am, I don't like standing still. I like to try different things. The marathon is something new, and I want to know what it feels like to run it. It'll be a different type of pain. I've tasted the pain of running at 5000 and 10,000 metres on the track – now I want to taste the pain of running a marathon. Running it is all about testing my limits, pushing myself while I still have the chance. The motivation to do that doesn't come in the form of a cheque. It doesn't come from your agent or your coach or your sponsors. It comes from you and you alone. I want to be able to do things that I feel good about. All the miles I do, all the training and recovery, pushing my body week in, week out: it all comes down to me. I'm the one who has to make that effort, that sacrifice.

The London Marathon is the biggest challenge for me in 2014. I'm looking forward to running through the streets of London, soaking up the love of the crowd. Dave Bedford, together with Hugh Brasher, his successor as Race Director, and the rest of the team at London Marathon always put on a great show. Best of all, I know it's going to be really tough. I won't be running against a few easy guys. The race is going to be loaded. The pressure is on for me to get my training right. To tell you the truth, I can't wait.

And beyond that – who knows? I try not to think that far ahead. Sure, there are things I'm looking forward to when the time comes for me to finally call it a day. I'll catch up with friends I haven't seen for too long. I'll chill out. Maybe do some travelling. I've been to loads of countries, but all I've seen of most of them is a running track and a hotel. I get on a plane. Fly some place. Get off. Check in at the hotel. Sleep. Rest. Eat. Run. Recover. Back to the hotel. Sleep. Get on another plane. Different countries for me just mean different hotel rooms. They all start to seem kind of the same, apart from the language of the sitcoms on the TV. If you ask me what China is like, I couldn't tell you. I haven't seen the Great Wall or the Forbidden City. At least I've got my laptop, so I can Skype my family while I'm away from home. Otherwise I'd be lost.

There's one other thing I'm looking forward to doing once I retire: playing football. I love the game, yet I haven't been able to play for years. I wouldn't change anything for what I've achieved as an athlete, but at the same time, I have missed kicking a ball around a pitch, putting tackles in, running down the flanks. When I'm done, I'll put on a bit of weight and just enjoy life. I like the idea of getting back into Sunday League.

One thing I won't do when I retire is run. When that day comes, I'm done. I've run so many thousands of miles. That's it. No more running. Just the football, and maybe the odd bit of boxing. Having said that, retirement is a *looooooong* way away for me. I try not to think that far ahead. There's still so much I want to do in my career. There are more championships to compete in, more races to run, more medals to be won for my country. There's the World Championships in Beijing in 2015; the Olympics in Rio de Janeiro in 2016; the marathon. I just want to keep pushing it and do well because, as an athlete, you know this moment isn't going to last for ever.

My faith helps to keep me grounded. Take Ramadan, for example. I'm not about to adopt the attitude of, 'I'm an Olympic champion, I'm not doing that now.' I have never looked at myself as better than other people. I expect to be judged just the same as anyone else. Islam teaches you to be thankful for the things you have, to be charitable and kind, not to be resentful over the things you don't have. Whether something good or bad happens, you still thank Allah for everything he has given you. At the same time, I would never wish to impose my religion on someone else. In my view, religion is a private, personal thing. What you believe is what you believe. It's not for me to decide what someone else should believe in and, as much as possible, I keep my beliefs to myself. I hate the idea of imposing my views on someone else. It's important to respect everyone's beliefs, even if you don't agree with them.

A lot of it comes down to education. At school I was in a minority and marked out for treatment by some of the other kids. Because I was known as the athlete, I escaped the worst of it. I imagine it was worse for some of the other kids. Thankfully, things have improved dramatically since those days, although it'd be a lie to say that racism has completely disappeared. I'm regularly stopped and interrogated by customs in the US, and as a general rule of thumb, I need two hours when catching a flight connection because that's how long it takes me to get through immigration. As soon as the name 'Farah' flashes up on the screen, everyone's on alert. Tania gets stopped even when she's travelling without me, purely because she now has a Somali-sounding surname.

Changing perceptions takes time. Parents can do their bit by encouraging their kids to make friends with people from other cultures and backgrounds. That way they're less likely to be prejudiced. For me, speaking as a kid who moved from one culture to another, when I'm walking down the street, I don't see myself as black, I'm just Mo. I don't judge people by the colour of their skin. I just see people. At the end of the day, everyone bleeds the same.

I'm trying to do my bit to change perceptions. In the past few years there's been a lot of negative coverage of Somalia and Somali people: the gangs, the civil war. That's started to change thanks to the success stories of people from Somali backgrounds, such as the writer and journalist Rageh Omaar and the singer K'Naan. I'd like to think that my achievements have played a part too. The country has a transitional government now and is starting to rebuild, but that will take time. In early 2013 the new Somali president, Hassan Sheikh Mohamoud, called me to ask me to move back there as part of a drive to get Somali people living elsewhere to return home and help rebuild the country after decades of war and devastation. For now, my life is in Britain and the US. My family is here. My friends, my career. And whenever I run, I'm doing both Britain and Somalia proud. Even though I represent another country, Somali people still take great joy in seeing me win. The country has never had someone achieve what I've achieved in my lifetime. I hope that, in my own small way, I can help create a more positive image of the country of my birth.

One of the reasons that I decided to write this book was so that I could open people's eyes and make them see that if you set your mind to a task and graft at it really, really hard, then you can go a long way. When I was new to Britain I was distracted; I didn't know how things worked and I got into trouble. I did things that, looking back now, I can say, 'I shouldn't have done this or that.' But at the time, you're just a kid. You don't know any better. I had to make those mistakes and learn from them because no one else was going to teach me.

Most importantly, I have my three girls. I have my wife. I have my family. That matters even more to me than being double Olympic champion or double World Champion. When this is all over, when the races are done, I'm looking forward to spending more time with my family. I have this dream that when I stop running, Hassan will be there. His family living next to my family. His kids playing with my kids. Tania and Hoda joking around. My mum will be there too. Me and Hassan causing trouble. All of us together. I'm looking forward to that day already.

CAREER STATISTICS

Prepared by Peter Matthews

Mohamed Farah

Born: 23 March 1983, Somalia

Height: 175 cm

Weight: 65 kg

Club: Nike Oregon Project

UK Clubs: Borough of Hounslow 1995–2000; Windsor, Slough, Eton & Hounslow 2001–4; Newham & Essex Beagles 2005–

Coach: Alberto Salazar

Management: PACE Sports Management

Key to abbreviations:
+ = intermediate time in longer race
A = Altitude over 1000 metres
AAA = Amateur Athletics Association
AUS = Australia
BEL = Belgium
BL(P) = British Athletics League (Premiership)
BMC = British Milers Club
CAU = Counties Athletic Union
CC = Cross country
CHN = China
CP = Crystal Palace
CRO = Croatia
CZE = Czech Republic
dnf = did not finish
er = en route
ESP = Spain
ETH = Ethiopia

FIN = Finland
FP = Finsbury Park
FRA = France
GER = Germany
h = heat
Ha = Haringey
He = Hendon
i = indoors
IAAF = International Association of Athletics Federations
Int = Intermediates
IRL = Ireland
ITA = Italy
J = Juniors or Junior race
JPN = Japan
KEN = Kenya
KOR = Korea
m = metres
MON = Monaco
N&EB = Newham & Essex Beagles
NED = Netherlands
NJL = National Junior League
NOR = Norway
NZL = New Zealand
OS = Olympic Stadium
PH = Parliament Hill
POL = Poland
POR = Portugal
Rd = Road
RR = Road Relay
SLO = Slovakia
SP = Southwark Park
St = Steeplechase
SUI = Switzerland
SWE = Sweden
TUR = Turkey
U = Under
WL = West London
WSEH = Windsor Slough Eton & Hounslow Athletics Club
YAL = Young Athletes League

Personal Bests

Distance	Time	Position	Venue	Date
800m	1:48.69	3	Eton	3 Aug 2003
1500m	3:28.81	10	Monaco, MON	19 Jul 2013
1 mile	3:56.49	1	London	6 Aug 2005
2000m	5:06.34	4	Melbourne, AUS	9 Mar 2006
Indoors	5:04.68+	2	Boston, USA	5 Feb 2011
3000m	7:36.85	1	London	27 Jul 2013
Indoors	7:34.47	1	Birmingham	21 Feb 2009
2 miles	8:20.47	2	London	3 Aug 2007
Indoors	8:08.07	2	Birmingham	18 Feb 2012
5000m	12:53.11	1	Monaco, MON	22 Jul 2011
10,000m	26:46.57	1	Eugene, USA	3 Jun 2011

Road race bests

5km	13:30	1	Stranorlar, IRL	26 Dec 2006
10km	27:44	1	London	31 May 2010
10 miles	46:25	1	Portsmouth	25 Oct 2009
Half-marathon	60:10	2	South Shields	15 Sep 2013

Annual Progression

	1500m	1 mile	3000m	5000m	10,000m	10k Rd
1996	4:43.9					
1997	4:06.41	–	8:47.48			
1998	3:57.67	–	8:33.51			
1999	3:55.78	4:12.21	8:21.25			
2000	3:49.60	–	8:12.53	14:05.72		
2001	3:46.1	–	8:09.24	13:56.31		
2002	3:47.78	–	–	14:00.5		
2003	3:43.17	–	8:03.0+	13:38.41		
2004	3:43.4+	4:00.07	–	c.14:25	–	28:58
2005	3:38.62	3:56.49	7:54.08i	13:30.53		
2006	3:38.02	3:58.36	7:38.15	13:09.40	–	28:37
2007	3:45.2i+	4:00.46i	7:41.86	13:07.00	–	28:07

	1500m	1 mile	3000m	5000m	10,000m	10k Rd
2008	3:39.66		7:39.55	13:08.11	27:44.54	28:39
2009	3:33.98		7:34.47i	13:09.14	–	27:50
2010	–	–	7:40.75	12:57.94	27:28.86	27:44
2011	–	–	7:35.81i	12:53.11	26:46.57	29:15
2012	3:34.66	3:57.92i	7:37.4i+	12:56.98	27:30.42	29:21
2013	3:28.81	–	7:36.85	13:05.88	27:26.71	28:39+

Major International Championship results

	Date	Distance	Position	Time
Olympic Games	2008	5000m	6 (heat)	13:50.95
	2012	5000m	1	13:41.66
		10,000m	1	27:30.42
World Champs	2007	5000m	6	13:47.54
	2009	5000m	7	13:19.69
	2011	5000m	1	13:23.36
		10,000m	2	27:14.07
	2013	5000m	1	13:26.98
		10,000m	1	27:21.71
European Champs	2006	5000m	2	13:44.79
	2010	5000m	1	13:31.18
		10,000m	1	28:24.99
	2012	5000m	1	13:29.91
Commonwealth Games	2006	5000m	9	13:40.53
World Juniors (U20)	2000	5000m	10	14:12.21
World Youths (U18)	1999	3000m	6	8:21.25
European Juniors (U20)	2001	5000m	1	14:09.91
European (U23)	2003	5000m	2	13:58.88
	2005	5000m	2	14:10.96
World Indoors	2008	3000m	6	7:55.08
	2012	3000m	4	7:41.79
European Indoors	2005	3000m	6	7:54.08
	2007	3000m	5	8:03.50
	2009	3000m	1	7:40.17
	2011	3000m	1	7:53.00
World Cross Country	2000		25J	
	2001		59J	
	2005		37	

	Date	Position
	2007	11
	2010	20
	2003 (4k)	74
	2006	40
European Cross Country	1999	5J
	2000	7J
	2001	2J
	2002	30J
	2004	15
	2005	21
	2006	1
	2008	2
	2009	2

National titles won

AAA: U15 3000m 1997; U17 3000m 1999; U23 5000m 2003; Indoor 3000m 2003 & 2005

UK: 5000m 2007 & 2011; Indoor 3000m 2007; 1500m 2009; 10k Rd 2011; Junior CC 2001

National Cross Country: U17 1999 & 2000; U20 2003

English Schools: Junior 1500m & CC 1997; Intermediate 3000m 1998; CC & 1500m 1999

UK Records – Outdoors

(Text in **bold** indicates this is also a European record.)

1500m	**3:28.81**	2	**Monaco, MON**	**19 Jul 2013**
5000m	12:57.94	5	Zurich, SUI	19 Aug 2010
	12:53.11	1	Monaco, MON	22 Jul 2011
10,000m	**26:46.57**	1	**Eugene, USA**	**3 Jun 2011**

UK Records – Indoors

3000m	7:40.99	1	Glasgow	31 Jan 2009
	7:34.47	1	Birmingham	21 Feb 2009
2 miles	**8:08.07**	2	**Birmingham**	**18 Feb 2012**
5000m	**13:10.60**	1	**Birmingham**	**18 Feb 2011**

British Top Ten Annual Merit Rankings

Year	1500m	5000m	10,000m	HMar
2003	6	4	–	–
2005	8	1	–	–
2006	1	1	–	–
2007	–	1	–	–
2008	7	1	1	–
2009	4	1	–	1
2010	–	1	1	–
2011	–	1	1	1
2012	5	1	1	1
2013	1	1	1	1

World Merit Rankings

5000m: 1st 2011, 2012 and 2013
10,000m: 2nd 2011, 2012 and 2013

Year-by-year Race Record

Date	Event	Time	Pos	Venue	Meeting
1995					
2 April	Road	16:00	10	London	Mini-marathon 12–13
10 Dec	CC 3k	12:38	1	Ruislip	Middlesex U13
1996					
13 Jan	CC	12:30	3	Luton	CAU U13
27 Jan	CC 4k	18:48	3	London (PH)	Southern U13
8 Feb	CC	12:29	2	London (Hampstead)	Middlesex Schools (J)
2 Mar	CC	17:44	9	Weymouth	English Schools Juniors
19 Oct	CC	13:18	3	London (Lambeth)	U17 race
16 Nov	CC 2.7mi	53:03	3	Roehampton	U17 race
23 Nov	CC 3k	8:38	1	London (PH)	London Youth Games U15
15 Dec	CC 4k	13:42	2	London (WL)	Middlesex U15

1997

11 Jan	CC	15:57	3	Luton	CAU Boys (U15)
25 Jan	CC	17:27	2	London (PH)	Southern Boys
8 Feb	CC	10:56	1	London (Highgate)	Middlesex Schools (J)
22 Feb	CC	14:54	1	Coulsden	U17 race
1 Mar	CC 5k	15:47	1	Newark	English Schools (J)
13 Apr	Rd	13:58	2	London	Mini Marathon 14–15
27 Apr	800m	2:10.7	2	High Wycombe	YAL
27 Apr	1500m	4:22.8	1	High Wycombe	YAL
18 May	3000m	9:10.0	1	Bournemouth	YAL
15 Jun	1500m	4:23.3	1	Enfield	Middlesex Schools (U15)
29 Jun	1500m	4:29.45	1	Reading	YAL
5 Jul	3000m	8:47.48	1	Bedford	AAA U15
12 Jul	1500m	4:06.41	1	Sheffield	English Schools (J)
20 Jul	3000m	8:50.4	1	Feltham	YAL
21 Sep	RR	6:57	1	London (FP)	3rd leg for Hounslow U15 1st
28 Sep	RR	9:13	–	South YAL 4-stage Relay (4th 3k leg for Hounslow 5th)	
18 Oct	CC 2.5mi	14:38	1	London (Lambeth)	U17 race
15 Nov	CC	14:25	1	London (Wimbledon)	U17 race
22 Nov	CC	9:11	1	London (PH)	London Youth Games U15
6 Dec	CC 4.325k	14:33	1	Crawley	English Schools Cup
14 Dec	CC 4k	13:46	1	Uxbridge	Middlesex U15

1998

17 Jan	CC	14:35	1	West Wickham	U17 race
31 Jan	CC	17:05	1	London (PH)	Southern U15
5 Feb	CC	16:15	1	London (Highgate)	Middlesex Schools (Int)
1 Mar	CC 4k	11:39	1	Cardiff	CAU Boys (U15)
7 Mar	CC 6.4k	21:04	2	Cheltenham	English Schools (Int)
26 Apr	1500m St	4:46.2	1	St Albans	YAL
3 May	1500m	4:20.1	1	Feltham	Southern League
9 May	1500m	4:02.7	1	Enfield	Middlesex U17
9 May	1500m St	4:43.6	1	Enfield	Middlesex U17
24 May	1500m	3:58.20	1	London (Ha)	Southern U17
7 Jun	3000m	8:49.70	1	Bedford	YAL
7 Jun	1500m St	4:43.96	1	Bedford	YAL

13 Jun	3000m	8:41.0	1	Enfield	Middlesex Schools (Int)
28 Jun	1500m	4:06.6	1	London (WL)	YAL
10 Jul	3000m	8:34.90	1	Exeter	English Schools (Int)
18 Jul	3000m	8:33.51	1	Ayr	Schools International
2 Aug	1500m	3:57.67	2J	Sheffield	British Grand Prix
– Sep	800m	2:06.7	1	Feltham	Club U20 champs
– Sep	1500m	4:17.2	1	Feltham	Club U20 champs
27 Sep	RR	8:49	–	Aldershot	South YAL 4-stage Relay
				(4th 3k leg for Hounslow 2nd)	
17 Oct	CC	11:58	1	London (Lambeth)	U17 race
14 Nov	CC relay	9:08	–	Mansfield	4th leg for Hounslow U17 (2nd)
21 Nov	CC 2.5mi	13:36	1	London (Wimbledon)	U17 race
28 Nov	CC 2.5mi	14:38	1	London (PH)	London Youth Games U17

1999

13 Jan	CC 6.4k	21:35	1	Ruislip	Middlesex U17
30 Jan	CC	22:39	1	London (PH)	Southern U17
4 Feb	CC	15:25	1	London (He)	Middlesex Schools (Int)
20 Feb	CC 6k	19:16	1	Nottingham	CAU Youths (U17)
6 Mar	CC 6.5k	21:22	1	Luton	English Schools Inters
13 Mar	CC 6k	21:34	1	Newark	National Youths
20 Mar	CC 6k	18:26	1	Bundoran, IRL	Schools International
18 Apr	Rd	13:00	1	London	Mini Marathon
15 May	800m	1:58.1	1	Feltham	Southern League
30 May	1500m	4:00.44	1	London (Ha)	Southern U17s
12 Jun	1500m	4:12.0	1	Enfield	Middlesex Schools (Int)
9 Jul	1500m	4:06.85	2h2	Bury St Edmunds	English Schools (Int)
10 Jul	1500m	3:55.78	1	Bury St Edmunds	English Schools (Int)
16 Jul	3000m	8:21.25	6	Bydgoszcz, POL	World Youths
7 Aug	1 mile	4:12.21	1J	London (CP)	British Grand Prix
21 Aug	3000m	8:16.18	1	Neubrandenburg, GER	v GER, FRA, POL U20
25 Sep	RR	18:02	–	Aldershot	South YAL 6-stage relay
				(4th 6k leg for Hounslow 7th)	
26 Sep	RR	11:23	–	Aldershot	South YAL 4-stage relay
				(4th 3.851k leg for Hounslow 1st)	
30 Oct	RR	11:19	–	Sutton Park	AAA U17 3-stage relay

				(3rd 3.8k leg for Hounslow 1st)	
13 Nov	CC relay	8:57	–	Mansfield	3rd leg for Hounslow U17 (1st)
21 Nov	CC 6k	18:42	2	Margate	U20 race
27 Nov	CC 4.5k	13:55	1	London (PH)	London Youth Games U17
12 Dec	CC 6.5k	23:18	5	Velenje, SLO	European Juniors

2000

16 Jan	CC 7k	25:20	3	Cardiff	
29 Jan	CC	21:36	1	London (PH)	Southern U17
12 Feb	CC 8k	25:44	2	Nottingham	UK & CAU Juniors
26 Feb	CC 6k	19:11	1	Stowe	National Youths
4 Mar	3000m	8:32.64i	1	Neubrandenburg, GER	GB v GER, FRA U20
19 Mar	CC 8k	24:37	25	Vilamoura, POR	World Junior CC
2 Apr	RR	24:09	–	Milton Keynes	Southern 12-stage relay (1st leg for Hounslow)
29 Apr	RR	26:24	–	Sutton Park	National 12-stage relay (1st leg for Hounslow dnf)
7 May	800m	1:59.8	1	Woking	NJL
7 May	1500m	3:59.7	1	Woking	NJL
27 May	2000m St	5:55.72	1	Watford	Southern Juniors
2 Aug	3000m	8:28.57	1	Watford	
5 Aug	1500m	3:52.8	1	Woodford	
12 Aug	5000m	14:22.14	2	Mannheim, GER	
19 Aug	5000m	14:05.72	8	Solihull	BMC
27 Aug	1500m	3:49.60	2	Bedford	AAA U20
10 Sep	800m	1:53.5	2	Abingdon	NJL
10 Sep	1500m	4:08.8	1	Abingdon	NJL
16 Sep	3000m	8:14.87	1	Bath	BMC
7 Oct	3000m	8:12.53	1	Grosseto, ITA	GB U20 Int v ITA, ESP, FRA
18 Oct	5000m	14:18.82	5h2	Santiago de Chile	World Juniors
21 Oct	5000m	14:12.21	10	Santiago de Chile	World Juniors
4 Nov	CC	36:10	6	Birmingham	1st junior
11 Nov	CC relay	8:58	–	Mansfield	3rd leg for Hounslow (2nd)
19 Nov	CC 6k	18:24	1J	Margate	
10 Dec	CC 5.135k	19:12	7	Malmö, SWE	European Juniors

2001

14 Jan	CC 7k	25:08	1	Cardiff	J
10 Feb	CC 8k	26:21	1	Nottingham	UK & CAU Juniors

Date	Event	Time	Pos	Venue	Meeting
25 Mar	CC	28:06	59	Ostend, BEL	World Junior CC
28 Apr	RR	14:44	–	Sutton Park	National 12-stage relay
				(12th leg for WSEH 10th)	
12 May	1500m	3:54.9	1	London (He)	Middlesex Champs
20 May	3000m	8:09.24	7	Loughborough	Loughborough International
26 May	1500m	3:59.5	2h	Watford	South Junior
27 May	1500m	3:46.41	1	Watford	South Junior
2 Jun	800m	1:53.1	1	Watford	BL2
2 Jun	5000m	14:28.3	1	Watford	BL2
23 Jun	5000m	13:56.31	12	Solihull	BMC
1 Jul	1500m	3:52.9	3	Bedford	AAA U20
7 Jul	1500m	3:54.51	2	Exeter	English Schools
22 Jul	5000m	14:09.91	1	Grosseto, ITA	European Juniors
4 Aug	800m	1:54.9	1	Portsmouth	
18 Aug	3000m	8:20.35	1	Stoke-on-Trent	GB v USA Junior
29 Aug	1500m	3:46.1	1	Watford	BMC
29 Sep	5.999k Rd	17:28	–	Aldershot	Southern Road Relay
				(4th leg for WSEH 1st)	
20 Oct	CC	26:08	4	Liverpool	Trials, 1st junior
27 Oct	RR	16:58	–	Sutton Park	AAA 6-stage relay
				(6th leg for WSEH 2nd)	
3 Nov	CC	34:32	9	Birmingham	1st junior
11 Nov	CC relay	8:47	–	Mansfield	3rd leg for WSEH (2nd)
18 Nov	CC	17:58	1J	Margate	
9 Dec	CC 6.15k	19:38	2	Thun, SUI	European Juniors

2002

Date	Event	Time	Pos	Venue	Meeting
26 Jan	CC	30:15	1	London (Hampstead)	Southern Juniors
9 Feb	CC	25:13	1	Nottingham	UK & CAU Juniors

(Stress fracture of the hip in February)

Date	Event	Time	Pos	Venue	Meeting
29 Jun	5000m	14:48.1	2	Bedford	AAA U20
7 Jul	1500m	3:53.8	2	Wigan	BL2
21 Jul	1500m	3:48.6	1	Eton	
4 Aug	800m	1:50.2	1	Derby	BL2
4 Aug	5000m	14:39.2	1	Derby	BL2
14 Aug	5000m	14:00.5	3	Watford	BMC
17 Aug	800m	1:51.97	2	Bedford	BL Cup
28 Aug	1500m	3:47.78	9	Watford	BMC
28 Sep	5.922k Rd	17:49	–	Aldershot	Southern Road Relay
				(4th leg for WSEH 5th)	

Date	Event	Time	Pos	Venue	Meet
19 Oct	CC c.8k		dnf	Liverpool	Trials
2 Nov	CC 10k	34:32	6	Birmingham	1st junior
8 Dec	CC 6.17k	19:25	30	Medulin, CRO	European Juniors

2003

Date	Event	Time	Pos	Venue	Meet
25 Jan	CC	20:06	1	Exmouth	Southern Juniors
22 Feb	CC	33:20	1	London (PH)	National Junior CC
2 Mar	3000m	8:05.58i	1	Birmingham	AAA Indoors
8 Mar	CC 4k	11:47	5	Brighton	World 4k CC Trial
29 Mar	CC	12:13	74	Lausanne–La Broye, SUI	World Juniors
14 Jun	1500m	3:43.17	2	Eton	BMC
22 Jun	1500m	3:45.57	1	Portsmouth	Southern Champs
28 Jun	5000m	13:58.58	1	Bedford	AAA U23 Champs
5 Jul	800m	1:50.84	1	Birmingham	BL1
5 Jul	1500m	3:49.08	1	Birmingham	BL1
20 Jul	5000m	13:58.88	2	Bydgoszcz, POL	European U23 Champs
25 Jul	1500m	3:44.79	1h3	Birmingham	AAA Champs
27 Jul	1500m	3:44.31	4	Birmingham	AAA Champs
3 Aug	800m	1:48.69	3	Eton	BL1
8 Aug	5000m	13:38.41	9	London (CP)	London Grand Prix
	(3000m	8:03+ er)			
1 Nov	CC 10k	–	dnf	Birmingham	

2004

Date	Event	Time	Pos	Venue	Meet
6 May	1mi	4:00.07	2	Oxford	Bannister 50th anniversary
	(1500m	3:43.4+ er)			
8 May	5k	14:04	8	Balmoral	
12 Jun	5000m	14:25+ er	m	Watford	pacemaking in AAA 10,000m
20 Nov	CC	30:05	1	London (PH)	Trials
28 Nov	10k	28:59	3	London (SP)	Nike Run
	(5k	14:41+ er)			
12 Dec	CC 9.64k	28:26	15	Heringsdorf, GER	European CC
19 Dec	CC 10k	34:46	15	Brussels, BEL	

2005

Date	Event	Time	Pos	Venue	Meet
8 Jan	CC 9k	30:04	6	Belfast	
13 Feb	3000m	7:56.86i	1	Sheffield	AAA Indoors
4 Mar	3000m	7:54.99i	2h1	Madrid, ESP	European Indoors
5 Mar	3000m	7:54.08i	6	Madrid, ESP	European Indoors

20 Mar	CC	37:50	37	Saint-Galmier, FRA	World CC
1 Jun	5000m	14:02.42	10	Milan, ITA	
4 Jun	800m	1:50.07	3	Eton	BL1
11 Jun	1500m	3:42.73	11	Watford	BMC
19 Jun	3000m	8:17.28	2	Florence, ITA	European Cup
25 Jun	5000m	13:30.53	3	Solihull	BMC
9 Jul	1500m St	3:46.06	5h1	Manchester	AAA Champs
17 Jul	5000m	14:10.96	2	Erfurt, GER	European U23 Champs
22 Jul	5000m	13:48.46	16	London (CP)	London Grand Prix
30 Jul	1500m	3:45.32	1	London (Ha)	BL1
6 Aug	1mi	3:56.49	1	London (CP)	BMC
19 Aug	1500m	3:38.62	7	Zurich, SUI	Weltklasse
21 Aug	2mi (3000m	8:36.73 8:00.9+	8 er)	Sheffield	British Grand Prix
31 Aug	5000m	13:56.81	11	Rovereto, ITA	
3 Sep	1500m	3:50.31	7	Paris, FRA	Décanation
24 Sep	6k Rd	17:23	–	Aldershot (4th leg for N&EB 6th)	Southern Road Relay
16 Oct	10mi	48:59	1	Twickenham	
19 Nov	5k park run	15:06	1	Bushy Park	
26 Nov	CC 10k	29:33	1	Liverpool	Trials
11 Dec	CC 9.84k	27:57	21	Tilburg, NED	European CC
18 Dec	CC 10.68k	32:23	6	Venta de Baños, ESP	

2006

6 Jan	5000m	13:48.19	4	Hobart, AUS	
11 Feb	1mi	3:58.45	3	Wanganui, NZL	
18 Feb	5000m	13:40.79	1	Melbourne, AUS	Victoria Champs
9 Mar	2000m	5:06.34	4	Melbourne, AUS	
20 Mar	5000m	13:40.53	9	Melbourne, AUS	Commonwealth Games
1 Apr	CC 4k	11:27	40	Fukuoka, JPN	World 4k CC
8 Apr	RR	25:27	–	Sutton Park (9th leg for N&EB 1st)	National 12-stage relay
21 May	10k Rd	28:37	2	New York, USA	
28 May	1mi	3:58.36	8	Eugene, USA	Prefontaine Classic
11 Jun	3000m	7:45.25	7	Gateshead	British Grand Prix
24 Jun	1500m	3:39.27	1	Solihull	BMC
29 Jun	3000m	8:27.91	2	Málaga, ESP	European Cup
15 Jul	5000m St	13:49.15	2	Manchester	AAA Champs
22 Jul	5000m	13:09.40	6	Heusden, BEL	KBC Nacht van de Atletiek

28 Jul	1500m	3:39.02	3	London (CP)	London Grand Prix
10 Aug	5000m	13:46.77	3h2	Gothenburg, SWE	European Champs
13 Aug	5000m	13:44.79	2	Gothenburg, SWE	European Champs
20 Aug	3000m	7:51.84	2	Birmingham	GB International
27 Aug	1500m	3:38.02	12	Rieti, ITA	
31 Aug	3000m	7:38.15	3	Zagreb, CRO	
9 Sep	3000m	8:00.60	12	Stuttgart, GER	World Athletics Final
23 Sep	6k Rd	17:14	–	Aldershot (6th leg for N&EB 1st)	Southern Road Relay
30 Sep	1mi Rd	4:05.5	1	Newcastle	Great North
21 Oct	RR	17:02	–	Sutton Coldfield (6th leg for N&EB 1st)	National 6-stage Relay
26 Nov	CC c.7k	19:51	1	Leffrinckoucke, FRA	
10 Dec	CC 9.95k	27:56	1	San Giorgio su Legnano, ITA	European CC
17 Dec	CC	35:31	19	Brussels, BEL	
26 Dec	5k Rd	13:30	1	Stranorlar, IRL	

2007

7 Jan	CC 10.7k	32:22	6	Amorebieta, ESP	
13 Jan	CC 4k	12:21	2	Edinburgh	
11 Feb	3000m	7:50.86i	1	Sheffield	AAA Indoors
17 Feb	1mi (1500m	4:00.46i 3:45.2+ er)	1	Birmingham	Indoor Grand Prix
2 Mar	3000m	7:55.36i	6h1	Birmingham	European Indoor Champs
3 Mar	3000m	8:03.50i	5	Birmingham	European Indoor Champs
24 Mar	CC	37:31	11	Mombasa, KEN	World CC Champs
20 May	10k Rd	28:07	3	Manchester	Great Manchester Run
7 Jul	800m	1:51.27	2	Birmingham	BLP
7 Jul	1500m	3:46.50	1	Birmingham	BLP
15 Jul	3000m	7:42.83	6	Sheffield	British Grand Prix
29 Jul	5000m St	13:40.19	1	Manchester	AAA Champs
3 Aug	2mi (3000m	8:20.47 7:49.8+ er)	2	London (CP)	London Grand Prix
30 Aug	5000m	13:39.13	6h2	Osaka, JPN	IAAF World Champs
2 Sep	5000m	13:47.54	6	Osaka, JPN	World Champs
7 Sep	3000m	7:41.86	5	Zurich, SUI	Weltklasse
14 Sep	5000m	13:07.00	10	Brussels, BEL	Van Damme Memorial
22 Sep	3000m	7:49.89	3	Stuttgart, GER	World Athletics Final

| 23 Sep | 5000m | 13:41.61 | 7 | Stuttgart, GER | World Athletics Final |
| 29 Sep | 3k Rd | 7:56.3 | 1 | Newcastle | Great North |

2008

16 Feb	2mi	8:20.95i	6	Birmingham	Grand Prix
	(3000m	7:46.0i+	2nd	er)	
7 Mar	3000m	8:04.65i	3h1	Valencia, ESP	World Indoor Champs
9 Mar	3000m	7:55.08i	6	Valencia, ESP	World Indoor Champs
6 Apr	5k Rd	13:35	2	Carlsbad, USA	
4 May	10,000m	27:44.54	5	Palo Alto, USA	Cardinal Invitational
	(5000m	13:58.0+	er)		
26 May	10k Rd	28:39	3	London	
4 Jun	1500m	3:42.62	1	Twickenham	
12 Jun	5000m	13:25.01	17	Ostrava, CZE	Golden Spike
21 Jun	5000m	13:44.07	1	Annecy, FRA	European Cup
12 Jul	1500m	3:47.48	2h3	Birmingham	UK Champs
13 Jul	1500m	3:39.66	2	Birmingham	UK Champs
26 Jul	3000m	7:43.26	6	London (CP)	London Grand Prix
29 Jul	3000m	7:39.55	8	Monaco, MON	Herculis
20 Aug	5000m	13:50.95	6h2	Beijing, CHN	Olympic Games
31 Aug	3000m	7:46.39	5	Gateshead	British Grand Prix
5 Sep	5000m	13:08.11	4	Brussels, BEL	Van Damme Memorial
13 Sep	3000m	8:05.97	9	Stuttgart, GER	World Athletics Final
4 Oct	1mi	4:13	1	Newcastle	Great North
23 Nov	10k Rd	29:46A	15	Addis Ababa, ETH	Great Ethiopian Run
30 Nov	CC 9.85k	28:28	4	Leffrinckoucke, FRA	
14 Dec	CC 10k	30:57	2	Brussels, BEL	European CC

2009

31 Jan	3000m	7:40.99i	1	Glasgow	GB International
14 Feb	1500m	3:53.17i	1h2	Sheffield	UK Indoors
15 Feb	1500m	3:40.57i	1	Sheffield	UK Indoors
21 Feb	3000m	7:34.47i	1	Birmingham	Grand Prix
6 Mar	3000m	8:03.26i	3h2	Turin, ITA	European Indoor Champs
7 Mar	3000m	7:40.17i	1	Turin, ITA	European Indoor Champs
25 May	10k Rd	27:50	1	London	
4 Jun	3000m	7:39.02	2	Turin, ITA	Nebiolo Memorial
20 Jun	5000m	13:43.01	1	Leiria, POR	European Team Champs
3 Jul	5000m	13:12.28	11	Oslo, NOR	Bislett Games
	(3000m	7:55.8+	er)		

24 Jul	5000m	13:09.14	1	London (CP)	London Grand Prix
	(3000m	7:53.4+ er)			
28 Jul	1500m	3:33.98	10	Monaco, MON	Herculis
20 Aug	5000m	13:19.94	3h1	Berlin, GER	World Champs
23 Aug	5000m	13:19.69	7	Berlin, GER	World Champs
31 Aug	3000m	7:47.02	9(fell)	Gateshead	British Grand Prix
4 Sep	5000m	13:22.33	13	Brussels, BEL	Van Damme Memorial
19 Sep	1mi Rd	4:02	2	Gateshead Quays	Great North
25 Sep	10mi Rd	46:25	1	Portsmouth	Great South Run
	(10k 28:31+, 15k 43:13+ er)				
17 Oct	RR	16:33	–	Sutton Park	National 6-stage Relay
	(5th leg for N&EB 1st)				
29 Nov	CC 9.85k	28:18	5	Leffrinckoucke, FRA	
13 Dec	CC 9.99k	31:02	2	Dublin, IRL	European CC
31 Dec	10k Rd	28:48.3	3	Bolzano, ITA	

2010

9 Jan	CC 4k	13:28	3	Edinburgh	
13 Mar	CC 12k	34:41	1	Birmingham	UK & CAU CC
21 Mar	5.5k RR	15:46	1	Milton Keynes	Southern 12-stage Relay
	(8th leg for N&EB 1st)				
28 Mar	CC 12k	34:09	20	Bydgoszcz, POL	World CC Champs
31 May	10k Rd	27:44	1	London (St James's Park)	
5 Jun	10,000m	27:28.86	1	Marseille, FRA	European Cup
	(5000m	13:52+ er)			
19 Jun	5000m	13:46.93	1	Bergen, NOR	European Team Champs
10 Jul	5000m	13:05.66	7	Gateshead	British Grand Prix
	(3000m	7:52+ er)			
27 Jul	10,000m	28:24.99	1	Barcelona, ESP	European Champs
29 Jul	5000m	13:38.26	1h2	Barcelona, ESP	European Champs
31 Jul	5000m	13:31.18	1	Barcelona, ESP	European Champs
13 Aug	3000m	7:40.75	2	London (CP)	London Grand Prix
19 Aug	5000m	12:57.94	5	Zurich, SUI	Weltklasse
	(3000m	7:47.3+ er)			
31 Dec	10k Rd	28:32.8	2	Bolzano, ITA	

2011

8 Jan	CC 8k	25:41	1	Edinburgh	
5 Feb	3000m	7:35.81i	2	Boston, USA	
	(2000m	5:04.68i+ er)			
19 Feb	5000m	13:10.60i	1	Birmingham	Grand Prix
	(3000m	7:54.67i+ er)			

4 Mar	3000m	8:02.36i	1h1	Paris (Bercy), FRA	European Indoor Champs
5 Mar	3000m	7:53.00i	1	Paris (Bercy), FRA	European Indoor Champs
20 Mar	Half-mar	60:23	1	New York, USA	
	(10k 29:33+, 15k 43:37+, 20k 57:31+ er)				
30 May	10k Rd	29:15	1	London	
3 Jun	10,000m	26:46.57	1	Eugene, USA	Prefontaine Classic
	(5000m	13:28.5+ er)			
10 Jul	5000m	13:06.14	1	Birmingham	British Grand Prix
	(3000m	8:01.3+	5 er)		
22 Jul	5000m	12:53.11	1	Monaco, MON	Herculis
	(3000m	7:48.6+ er)			
31 Jul	5000m	14:00.72	1	Birmingham	UK Champs
5 Aug	3000m	7:40.15	1	London (CP)	London Grand Prix
	(2000m	5:10.5e+ er)			
28 Aug	10,000m	27:14.07	2	Daegu, KOR	World Champs
	(5000m	13:53.6+ er)			
1 Sep	5000m	13:38.03	2h2	Daegu, KOR	IAAF World Champs
4 Sep	5000m	13:23.36	1	Daegu, KOR	IAAF World Champs
17 Sep	2mi Rd	8:37.72	1	Gateshead	Great North

2012

28 Jan	1500m	3:39.03i	1	Glasgow	GB International
4 Feb	1 mile	3:57.92i	4	Boston, USA	
	(1500m	3:41.90i+ er)			
18 Feb	2mi	8:08.07i	2	Birmingham	
	(3000m	7:37.4i+ er)			
9 Mar	3000m	7:57.59i	2h2	Istanbul, TUR	World Indoor Champs
11 Mar	3000m	7:41.79i	4	Istanbul, TUR	World Indoor Champs
18 May	1500m	3:34.66	1	Eagle Rock, USA	
18 May	5000m	13:12.87	1	Eagle Rock, USA	
27 May	10k Rd	29:21	1	London	
2 Jun	5000m	12:56.98	1	Eugene, USA	
	(3000m	7:50.6+e er)			
22 Jun	1500m	3:47.50	1h1	Birmingham	UK Champs
	(Did not start in the final)				
27 Jun	5000m	13:29.91	1	Helsinki, FIN	European Champs
13 Jul	5000m	13:06.04	1	London (CP)	London Grand Prix
4 Aug	10,000m	27:30.42	1	London (OS)	Olympic Games
8 Aug	5000m	13:26.00	3h1	London (OS)	Olympic Games
11 Aug	5000m	13:41.66	1	London (OS)	Olympic Games

26 Aug	2mi	8:27.24	1	Birmingham	British Grand Prix
	(3000m	7:57.9+ er)			
15 Sep	2mi Rd	8:40	1	Newcastle	Great North

2013

16 Feb	3000m	7:42.00i	1	Birmingham	Grand Prix
24 Feb	Half-mar	60:59	1	New Orleans, USA	Rock 'n' Roll
	(10k 28:39+, 10mi 46:30+ er)				
21 Apr	20k	58:30+	–	London	London Marathon
17 May	5000m	13:15.68	1	Eagle Rock, USA	
	(3000m 8:05.6+ er)				
27 May	10k Rd	29:13	1	London	
1 Jun	5000m	13:05.88	2	Eugene, USA	Prefontaine Classic
22 Jun	5000m	14:10.00	1	Gateshead	European Team Champs
30 Jun	5000m	13:14.24	1	Birmingham	British Grand Prix
19 Jul	1500m	3:28.81	2	Monaco, MON	Herculis
27 Jul	3000m	7:36.85	1	London (OS)	Anniversary Games
10 Aug	10,000m	27:21.71	1	Moscow, RUS	IAAF World Champs
13 Aug	5000m	13:23.93	5h2	Moscow, RUS	IAAF World Champs
16 Aug	5000m	13:26.98	1	Moscow, RUS	IAAF World Champs
15 Sep	Half-mar	60:10	2	South Shields	Great North Run
	(10k 28:59+, 15k 43:02+, 20k 57:19+ er)				

INDEX

An invitation from the publisher

Join us at www.hodder.co.uk, or follow us
on Twitter @hodderbooks to be a part of
our community of people who love the very
best in books and reading.

Whether you want to discover more about a book
or an author, watch trailers and interviews, have the
chance to win early limited editions, or simply browse
our expert readers' selection of the very best books,
we think you'll find what you're looking for.

And if you don't, that's the place to tell us what's missing.

We love what we do, and we'd love you to be a part of it.

www.hodder.co.uk

@hodderbooks

HodderBooks

HodderBooks